the

DRUGS AND ALCOHOL IN THE WORKPLACE

DRUGS AND ALCOHOL IN THE WORKPLACE

A Guide for Managers

Drusilla Campbell and Marilyn Graham

Facts On File Publications
New York, N.Y. ● Oxford, England

DRUGS AND ALCOHOL IN THE WORKPLACE: A Guide for Managers

copyright © 1988 by Drusilla Campbell and Marilyn Graham

Library of Congress Cataloging-in-Publication Data

Campbell, Drusilla.
   Drugs and alcohol in the workplace : a guide for managers /
 Drusilla Campbell and Marilyn Graham.
      p.   cm.
   Includes index.
   ISBN 0-8160-1651-8
   1. Drugs and employment. 2. Alcoholism and employment.
I. Graham, Marilyn. II. Title.
HF5549.5.D7C35 1988
658.3'822--dc19   87-32952
                     CIP

Interior design: Ron Monteleone

Library of Congress Catalog Card Number: 87-32952

ISBN# 0-8160-1651-8

British CIP data available on request

Printed in the United States of America

10 9 8 7 6 5 4 3 2 1

CONTENTS

ACKNOWLEDGMENTS

A book like this is very much a joint effort and would not be possible without the encouragement and advice of many people. A particular debt of thanks is owed to the many members of the alcohol- and drug-treatment community who were so willing to contribute their insights and to the recovering addicts and alcoholics who shared their strength with us in the hope that it would help others to recover. Theirs is the wisdom of experience and, without it, this book would never have been written. Finally, a special thanks to Professor Arthur W. Campbell for his advice on legal matters but, most of all, for his tireless editorial assistance.

—D.C.

Thank you to my husband, Jack, for his love and support, and to my teachers Dr. John Milner, Jack Sumner and Fred Fix. For their contributions and assistance, thank you to Don McClure and Chuck Covey at Starting Point.

—M.G.

FOREWORD

As I read this book, I experienced a growing sense of gratitude for it. At the conclusion, I felt the book had made a statement about drug use in the workplace profoundly unlike any other literature on the subject to date. Writing about drugs in the workplace is difficult, and to produce a work of substance such as this is a worthy accomplishment. This book is not simply another outcry about the billions of dollars lost because of reduced productivity or an aimless question asking why someone doesn't do something about it. Rather it is a unique approach that motivates the reader to do something about drug abuse. The book explains how.

My own involvement in health care spans 27 years and includes both administrative and clinial aspects of care delivery. Our family center has treated more than 11,000 patients since it was founded by John E. Milner, M.D., in 1986. Those of us who work in health care have witnessed substantial changes over the past several years, particularly in the treatment of chemical dependency. We have seen medical interest in the treatment of chemical dependency escalate to very high levels. As people continue to become more enlightened about drug use, we can anticipate even more ingenuity, more creative models of care, and more dedicated support for both treatment and preventive measures. This book would not have been written 10 years ago. No one would have read it.

It will be read today because people are willing to address social problems concerning drug use that not too many years ago would have been left untouched. Businesspersons want to do something, as evidenced by their zeal to learn and to question. Just a few years ago, when our family center would host educational programs for industry, we would attract only a handful of interested management officials, despite weeks of prior public announcements, special invitations, and elaborate mail campaigns. We now host a monthly educational seminar publicized only by word of mouth, and we rarely see less than 60 to 70 company officials, who come not only to learn but to actively participate.

We are a drug-affected society, and we have reluctantly started to admit that alcohol is a drug. As we have witnessed an increasing acceptance of illegal drugs, we have started to realize that drug use includes all forms—illegal, legal, and prescription.

It is frightening to realize that many in our society who would never use an illicit drug are dependent on prescribed medication. It is also frightening to realize that illicit drugs are common in all age groups and social classes. We find grade-school children using and pushing drugs. Cocaine is the common choice of the social elite, and alcohol is in greater demand across all classes than ever before. The most frightening aspect of all this may not be merely the increasing availability of drugs, but our willingness to take them. The market aspects must be considered. Drug supplies increase because they are demanded by our population. And easy access to drugs has led to an increasing phenomenon—the emergence of the polydrug user. Readers should pay special attention to the description of polydrug use in this book.

Polydrug use is a growing problem for society and for those working in drug-abuse treatment facilities. Most clinical models of care are based on precepts that may not account for the polydrug user, and treatment specialists will probably have to develop a very different model for the future. The younger generation of drug users are accustomed to a smorgasbord of available chemicals, and they become increasingly proficient at concocting chemical combinations to produce specific effects. This is also a difficult challenge to addictionologists and researchers attempting to understand the impact of polydrug use on the brain and behavior.

In many ways we are novices when it comes to understanding addiction, even though it ranks by most estimates as the third leading cause of death and impairment. Recent advances in medical technology have not ignored addiction, and in fact there has been more dedicated research in the area of addictionology over the past decade than ever before. But when we recall that as recently as 30 years ago alcoholism, for example, was not considered an illness at all, we can see why, in a relative sense, we are so limited in our knowledge about addiction.

So it is always a pleasure to read a volume such as this that has taken a definable part of the drug issue and so nicely presented the concepts surrounding it. The book is directed at managers in business and industry, yet it will also appeal to a wide range of other individuals, including labor leaders and schoolteachers. It is replete with personal case histories, carefully chosen to give the reader an idea of the range and impact of chemical abuse. It can be read from start to finish, or it can be used as a workbook and consulted only on a specific topic. It is ideal for ready reference. It is practical, well illustrated and easy to read. I am confident this book will find its way into the office of every manager and supervisor who wants to do something about drug abuse in our workplace.

Marvin E. Prigmore
Program Director
Family Center for Alcohol
   and Drug Treatment
Sharp Cabrillo Hospital
San Diego, California

PREFACE

An executive of a large corporation recently referred to drug abuse as "the most serious problem facing American business in the next decade." Although we agree with that statement, we don't think it goes quite far enough. Let us restate it: *Polydrug* abuse is the most serious problem facing American business between now and the end of the century.

In the last few years, arbitration and court cases have made it clear that employers cannot afford to ignore this problem any longer. Apart from the fact that drug and alcohol abuse costs over $100 billion a year, employers are responsible for providing a safe, hazard-free environment for workers. Companies have been held liable for failure to remove an employee whose abuse of chemicals endangers coworkers.

Despite this pressure, in our work with business and industry we have encountered a powerful resistance toward most programs challenging the damage that drugs and alcohol inflict on the workplace. But we believe that to effect any real change, it is essential for employers to get involved. By instituting an aggressive drug and alcohol policy, by training supervisors to document and intervene on behalf of impaired employees, and by providing opportunities for treatment, employers can make a difference not just in business but in the homes and schools and neighborhoods of this country.

Consider the social costs of drug and alcohol abuse: fetal alcohol syndrome is the third leading cause of birth defects; 40 percent of divorces can be attributed to chemical abuse; 5.7 million cases of family violence can be conclusively linked to alcoholism; 50 percent of all fires and the same percentage of deaths from falling result from alcoholism.

Millions of men and women are abusing chemical substances, and most of them are employed somewhere, taking home full salaries for working at two thirds the capacity of healthy workers, enjoying employee benefits while having four times as many accidents, costing society billions of dollars in extravagant health and injury claims.

While most managers acknowledge these grim figures, many have told us that they are reluctant to set up a drug and alcohol abuse program because they feel they don't know enough about the subject to take the first step. We heard this so often that we decided it was time for a book that presents a full and up-to-date picture of chemical abuse as it affects the workplace. Although it is meant to be read from cover to cover, this volume is also intended as a resource. Problems, strategies, solutions—from A to Z—it's all here.

A word about our use of pronouns in this book. Chemical dependency is a disease that affects both men and women, and in parts of the text where we have chosen to use primarily masculine pronouns, no discrimination is intended or should be inferred from this choice.

We hope that when you finish this book you will feel as we do, that employers can take the lead and make a difference in controlling drug abuse. In the next 10 years our government is going to spend several billion dollars to stop the illegal importation of drugs. The kind of program we recommend to business will cost only a fraction of that amount. But, in the end, the whole country will benefit from this program because it aims not just to root out addicts and alcoholics but to change the tolerance our society has toward the use and abuse of chemicals.

What business and industry don't seem to realize is how much clout they have. As someone told us recently: "Parents beseech, teachers teach and preachers preach, but when the boss says, 'Get well or get out,' the addict/alcoholic looks for help."

1

THE PROBLEM

It is natural for men and women to repeat those activities that give them pleasure or alleviate discomfort. If a candid survey of the population were possible, it would reveal that more than 50 percent—and perhaps as much as 80 percent—are obsessively compulsive about some substance or activity: alcohol, drugs, food, sex, gambling, running, spending. Whatever it is, these people depend on it for their psychic comfort. They are addicted.

Some of this addictive behavior is accepted and even admired. For instance, our society respects the addiction to work. When a scion of industry announces that he is a workaholic, he invariably does so with a ring of pride in his voice. Few people would have the temerity to point out that while obsessively involved in "getting there and staying there," this workaholic has sacrificed his and his families' emotional needs. His wife could speak of emotional isolation and loneliness, and his children of the missed birthday parties, piano recitals and soccer games, the promises not kept because of the pressures of business. But at the funeral for a workaholic, the mourners crowd the church and there are no end of testimonials about what a great man he was and how profoundly he will be missed. Compare this to the funeral of a practicing alcoholic. When he dies his family and his few remaining friends heave a collective sigh of relief.

Other forms of addictive behavior are not admired but are accepted as tolerable coping mechanisms. Consider the bumper sticker that reads, "When the going gets tough, the tough go shopping." Although on one level this is only a clever turn of phrase, on another it is a statement about the inability to manage stress without recourse to obsessive behavior. If the bumper sticker read, "When the going gets tough, the tough take drugs," most people would be quick to condemn the sentiment. If this seems a melodramatic view of our credit card society, it should be noted that many self-help groups exist to help "shopaholics" overcome their compulsion to spend.

The message in our society seems to be that addiction in itself is okay. Dependence is acceptable and obsessive compulsive behavior may even be praiseworthy. It is the focus of the addiction that makes all the difference.

What determines an individual's choice of a particular obsessive or compulsive behavior? Why is it that some people are addicted to chocolate, some to work, some to chemicals?

There is no single answer to this question. However, researchers and addictionologists can agree on a variety of contributing factors. In the chapters entitled "Alcohol" and "The Chemical Marketplace," we will examine these factors in detail. For now, it will be helpful to see, in general, how these variables operate across a wide spectrum of addictive behaviors.

Variable #1: Personal History

"I grew up in a wildly disfunctional home. My dad was a mean periodic drunk and my mom cooked and ate all the time. Her kitchen was the only safe place in the house. Before I was five years old, I knew the best way to feel calm and safe was to cut myself a slice of Lady Baltimore cake."

*   *   *

"My father always compared me negatively to my dead older brother. The more sure he was I'd never amount to anything, the harder I worked to prove him wrong and win his love. I ended up a millionaire, and he still compares me to Bennie."

Variable #2: Taboos

"When I was a kid, my folks belonged to a religious group that didn't hold with any kind of worldly pleasure. No dances or movies or plays. Cards were a sin. I wasn't even allowed to play Monopoly. But church socials were feasts. The only thing our religion permitted us to do to excess was eat."

*   *   *

"As a Muslim, I am forbidden by the Koran from touching one drop of spiritous liquor. But I gamble for the thrill of it."

Variable #3: Genetics

"I'm Irish and everyone in my family drinks too much. My mom calls alcoholism the Irish disease."

*   *   *

"I can't drink at all. Neither can two of my aunts. It's like a poison to us. Not one drop or my skin turns hot and feels sort of crawly. My blood pressure skyrockets and I start to sweat all over. I couldn't ever become an alcoholic, but I think I'm addicted to strenuous sports. If I don't run or swim or bike hard four or five times a week, I begin to feel very uncomfortable."

Variable #4: Availability

"There was never any booze in our house, but my dad was a doctor and he kept pills all over the place. I could always get as much speed as I wanted."

*　　*　　*

"Food's the easiest and best cure I can think of for the miseries."

Variable #5: Effectiveness

"Liquor never did it for me. I hated having a hangover, and blackouts were a nightmare. Marijuana was the perfect drug for me because I could stay loaded all the time and hardly anyone knew and it did just what I wanted it to. I smoked dope and I felt fine. I could handle any contingency. I felt confident for the first time in my life."

*　　*　　*

"I liked alcohol and I drank socially. There weren't any drunks in my family that I knew about, although later I heard about an uncle. . . . But when I shot morphine for the first time, it was like being an orphan and finding mother's milk at last. I don't think I was ever really comfortable in my own skin before that moment."

Any addiction, however benign initially, may eventually cause serious problems. But only in the most extreme cases—and then only in small numbers—do addictions to food, work, athletics, and the like cause major problems in our society. It is the wisespread abuse of chemicals that threatens the viability of American life by assaulting every institution, from home to government to industry.

A checkout clerk in a large supermarket reports that 30 percent of her coworkers use cocaine.

A nurse claims that 50 percent of the doctors, nurses, aides, and orderlies she works with use cocaine and pills on the job.

A repair engineer at a nuclear power plant reports that he doesn't know anyone who does not use cocaine or speed at work.

Federal experts estimate that 10 to 23 percent of workers use dangerous drugs on the job. In 1982, alcoholism alone cost U.S. business $77 billion. According to Comprehensive Care Corporation, the nation's largest for-profit HMO, about 44 percent of that sum was in lost and decreased productivity. When the economic costs of drug abuse are combined with those of alcoholism, the price tag to employers and consumers jumps to $100 billion a year.

Though some experts consider these figures too high, and others consider them too low, they still agree on two crucial points: (1) Alcoholism and drug abuse are a disease that is spreading through the American workplace; and (2) no person—employer, worker, or consumer, no matter how sober or drug free—is immune from the ultimate effects of this epidemic.

In this book we take a three-pronged approach to stopping the epidemic of chemical abuse in the workplace.

1. Chapters 1-4 are educational. Their intention is to help managers understand chemical abuse and how it creates problems in the workplace.
2. Chapters 5-8 focus on workplace strategies for identifying impaired employees and breaking through the denial of their disease.
3. Chapters 9-13 discuss treatment and recovery options adaptable to a wide range of workplace sizes and styles.

Let's start by defining some necessary terms.

ALCOHOLISM

Alcoholism is a chronic, progressive and incurable disease characterized by one major symptom: a loss of control over alcohol and other mood-altering chemicals.

Chemical addiction, drug addiction, and drug abuse are all synonyms for what is essentially the disease of "alcoholism." Putting drug addiction together with alcoholism may seem strange at first because in our alcohol-tolerant culture we tend to forget that—like cocaine, marijuana, heroin, Valium, amphetamines and barbiturates—alcohol is a potent drug.

Alcoholism is called a "chronic" disease because once contracted it never goes away. As far as anyone in the treatment and research field can tell, there has never been a case of spontaneously cured alcoholism where the former alcoholic was able to drink recreationally and without problems for the rest of his or her life. It is generally agreed that just as diabetics will always be diabetics, alcoholics will never be "cured" of alcoholism. But they can "recover"—which in the vocabulary of treatment means that so long as they abstain from drinking and using drugs, they have an excellent chance of leading healthy, productive lives.

Alcoholism is a "progressive" disease because it gets worse with the passage of time. In other words, alcoholics develop a reaction to all mood-altering drugs which grows more severe with each passing year until the reaction becomes life-threatening. If the alcoholic continues to drink or use drugs, his "tolerance" (or ability to metabolize the chemical) will at some point decrease markedly, causing serious personality changes and deteriorating health. Moreover, his tolerance will continue to diminish despite abstinence. This is why an alcoholic who abstains from his drug for many years and then relapses always finds his condition worsened. Sometimes the reaction is fatal.

PROBLEM DRINKER

A problem drinker uses alcohol as a coping mechanism. Excessive drinking creates psychological and social difficulties for the problem drinker and others. Family life may be jeopardized, and work may be deleteriously affected. The problem drinker is not an alcoholic, although there is an excellent chance he or she will become one. The problem drinker may or may not have a genetic predisposition to the disease.

A problem drug taker is similarly defined. A person who uses any mind-altering chemical substance repeatedly as a means of enjoying or managing the vicissitudes of life has the potential for a serious addiction problem.

Problem drinkers and problem drug takers create disruptions in the workplace. Like alcoholics and addicts they cause accidents and cost their employers money. The documentation and intervention strategies outlined in this book work equally well for problem drinkers and drug takers as for active alcoholics and addicts.

RECOVERY

Chemical addiction is an incurable and progressive disease for which there is only one guaranteed treatment: abstinence. A recovering addict/alcoholic is one who totally abstains from mood-altering chemicals and has a lifetime program that (a) supports his abstinence and (b) encourages constructive methods of dealing with life problems. The most successful source of such a lifetime program is Alcoholics Anonymous.

POLYDRUG ABUSE

The person whose problem is abuse of alcohol and only alcohol is a disappearing phenomenon on the American scene. Although alcohol or marijuana or cocaine may be the "drug of choice," the polydrug user habitually uses more than one drug. Two decades after the birth of the so-called "drug culture," American alcoholics have adopted the motto of "better living through chemistry" into their lifestyles. Even young abusers are highly sophisticated in the use of other drugs to balance certain effects of alcoholism. A heavy drinker may find that using amphetamines ("speed" or "uppers") helps to overcome a hangover. A heavy coke user may drink alcohol in order to come "down."

INTERVENTION

A workplace intervention (dealt with at length in its own chapter) is the critical point at which the supervisor meets with the impaired person and dramatically demonstrates that his or her job performance is unacceptable. This may also be called constructive confrontation or "creating the crisis." Faced with extensive evidence of unsatisfactory work performance and threatened with loss of livelihood, the properly guided employee will find the courage to face chemical dependency and seek treatment.

DOCUMENTATION

Documentation is the systematic and objective collection of evidence that details the employee's unsatisfactory work performance. It is the manager's first active step toward cleaning up an affected workplace. In the chapter entitled "Documentation" we offer as examples several forms similar to those used by employee-assistance programs. Without documentation, effective intervention is impossible.

RELAPSE

"Relapse" is defined as "returning to a former state." When a recovering individual *relapses*, he returns to the diseased state. In other words, he drinks or uses drugs after a period of not having done so.

Most managers would be surprised at the number of their employees that are impaired. One expert in the area of on-the-job chemical abuse concludes from his experience that as much as 30 percent of the workforce may abuse one or more chemicals. What managers need to know is that every one of these impaired employees costs his employer money. Here's how it happens. According to a congressional committee, impaired workers are absent sixteen times more often than employees without a chemical-abuse problem. They also leave work earlier and take longer coffee breaks. Their afternoon work is frequently inferior to that done in the morning. (For this reason an electronics firm in California instituted a policy forbidding executives to make important decisions after lunch!) Other studies show it takes longer to explain new procedures to impaired employees because they tend to be somewhat rigid in their habits and uncomfortable with changes in familiar work routines. They are also apt to be habitual complainers or troublemakers who become involved in disputes with fellow workers, supervisors and management.

Drug-impaired individuals also add to the cost of doing business by their overuse of medical benefits. If you visit the medical, surgical, pediatric, psychiatric or obstetric-gynecology wards of any hospital in the United States, you will find that 10 to 15 percent of adult patients are being treated for a disease either caused or exacerbated by some form of drug or alcohol abuse. True, medical charts will describe their problems as fracture, burn, concussion, ulcer, liver disease, chronic nosebleed, premenstrual syndrome, obesity, pancreatic disorder, disease of the nervous system, diabetes and so on, but in-depth studies reveal a substantial portion of these ailments stem either directly or indirectly from the abuse of chemicals.

Did you know that the typical drug- or alcohol-abusing employee uses eight times more hospital days than his nonimpaired counterpart? Were you aware that families of drug and alcohol abusers use two to three times as much health-care benefits as the rest of the population? In terms of hospital care and insurance expenses, impaired employees cost business and the consumer almost 20 billion a year.

Impaired employees increase costs in other ways too. For example, they threaten the physical safety of coworkers and the public at large. In a recent year, the National Safety Council reported that 4,920 work fatalities and 987,000 on-the-job injuries were alcohol-related. Impaired employees are three to four times more likely to be involved in accidents at work and four to six times more likely away from the workplace.

For a business how does this translate? In 1984 *U.S. News and World Report* published a story about the abuse of alcohol by railroad employees. Of 45 railroad accidents in the preceding nine years, accidents in which there were a total of $28 million in damage to property and 34 deaths, all were blamed on alcohol. According to American Airlines' corporate medical director, in 1985 a computer operator high on marijuana failed to load an important tape into the computerized reservation system of a major airline. As a result, the computer was down for eight hours at a cost to the company of about $19 million.

Listen to statements by some impaired workers from the state of Washington:

I used to smoke dope during lunch break. Once we raised a frame we were working on and dropped it. That cost the company about 25 man-hours and a couple of guys were nearly hit.

*　　*　　*

My partner lost three fingers in a cut-off saw. We were using dope. Guys would get in a rush when they were using speed and run stuff into their hands. We really screwed up some big orders. It caused a big loss in production.

*　　*　　*

I was a truck driver using dope. My truck was running bad, so I just drained the oil out of it and ran it 'til it blew up. It cost six grand to fix.

Clearly, impaired employees force enormous costs, liabilities, and dangers upon their employers, their coworkers and upon the public at large. But the situation is far from hopeless.

Using the tools in this book, managers can achieve significant increases in workplace productivity, at the same time making dramatic positive turnarounds in the lives of their impaired employees. The unacceptable losses in human and economic resources can be stopped.

Why should business shoulder the burden? First, because the benefit of substantially increased productivity is in its interest; second, because on-the-job documentation coupled with the threat of loss of livelihood gives managers unique leverage over impaired workers; and third, because no other solution appears likely.

Government measures designed to decrease the availability of drugs and alcohol have proved ineffectual, inadequate and often impractical. Despite yearly increases in the budgets of state and federal drug-enforcement agencies, huge quantities of illicit substances continue to flow across our borders every day. In 1985, for example, at least 100 tons of cocaine entered the United States, sufficient to let between 5 and 10 million people use it at least once a month. The cost dropped so low even high-school students could afford it. In the words of one Drug Enforcement Agency official, "It's the marijuana of the '80s. The stuff is falling out of the sky."

Nor has it been possible to stop the illegal entry of other drugs. In a recent year, 2.8 million pounds of marijuana were seized at U.S. border sites, a quantity estimated as only 16 percent of what actually entered the country. The same year 608 pounds of heroin were taken, about 10 percent of what was smuggled into the country.

Government is no more successful at shutting down domestic producers. Home grown, high quality marijuana is a significant agricultural industry in parts of the United States. Custom made "designer drugs"—potent, often deadly chemical compounds—are manufactured in home laboratories in every major city in this country.

But even if government somehow stopped the importation of illegal drugs, eradicated domestic sources of marijuana and shut down the outlaw laboratories, the workplace would still be plagued by impaired employees. Why? From the pervasive abuse of alcohol and prescription drugs.

We are a nation of pilltakers, a culture convinced that there is a chemical cure for every ache and pain. *Harvard Business Review* has reported that within a recent 30-day period, 7 million people abused amphetamines, barbiturates or tranquilizers like Valium or Librium.

Ironically, most of these people began taking prescription drugs for legitimate reasons. They could not sleep or wanted to lose weight; there were problems at home or on the job that made them jumpy or anxious; they suffered from headaches, backaches or depression. For men and women in such pain, prescription medicines began as a blessing. But the blessing became a curse when the patient unwittingly became addicted.

How does this happen? It starts when the prescribing physician neglects to monitor each patient's use and needs. Doctors routinely underestimate the frequency with which their patients increase their own dosage under the logic that two pills should be twice as effective as one.

Patients are not the only force encouraging doctors to over-prescribe. In 1979 the drug-manufacturing industry aimed $5,000 worth of promotion and advertising at each licensed physician in this country to convince him of the efficacy of its products. Confronted with such powerful economic forces and the obvious benefit of so many drugs in easing pain, it would be ludicrous to suggest that the nation's drug problems could be solved by shutting down the pharmaceutical industry.

But even if the abuse of prescription drugs and illegal drugs were to magically stop, the problem of alcohol would still remain.

Of all the drugs our society favors, alcohol has worked itself most deeply into the fiber of our lives. Advertising makes it seem that there cannot be a celebration large or small without alcoholic refreshment. Alcohol is touted in the media and popular wisdom as a remedy for anxiety, sleeplessness, depression and loneliness. After the debacle of Prohibition early in this century, it is unlikely that such control measures will be tried again. Clearly, if every other avenue of abuse were closed to the employee, there would still be alcohol.

Government regulations, commissions, special enforcement teams—nothing has worked against the epidemic of drug and alcohol abuse that has infected American workers.

Until now. Now there is growing evidence that when business leaders take charge and fight the epidemic themselves they are successful. Money and lives can be saved. Let's look at some examples.

General Motors Corporation saves $3,700 per year for each employee enrolled in their employee-assistance program. The total savings for one year was $37 million.

Productivity at **Northrop Corporation** increased 43 percent for the first 100 alcoholics to enter treatment. After three years' sobriety, average savings per rehabilitated employee approached $20,000.

Treatment for personnel of the **Philadelphia Police Department** brought about an average 38-percent reduction in sick days and a 62 percent annual reduction in injured days.

The New York Transit Authority compared before-and-after records of 1,500 alcoholics who had been through treatment. They found savings of over $1 million a year in paid sick leave alone.

One year after alcoholic employees at the **Oldsmobile** plant in Lansing, Michigan received treatment for their disease, lost man-hours declined 49 percent, health care benefits dropped by 29 percent, leaves declined by 56 percent, grievances by 78 percent, disciplinary problems by 63 percent and accidents by an overwhelming 82 percent.

These figures show that treating impaired employees effectively makes economic sense. This book will tell you how to do it regardless of the size or nature of your business. If you already have a program in place, it will give you the tools to evaluate its effectiveness and enable you to make any necessary changes. Through case studies and interviews with experts and by drawing from our own experiences in the treatment field, we have assembled a concise and workable approach to the problem of impaired employees.

In our research and writing we have had the unstinted cooperation of researchers and treatment specialists throughout the country. They have shared with us their most up-to-date materials and testing instruments along with their wealth of experience.

Virtually all you need to know to control chemical abuse in the workplace can be found in this book. One vital ingredient is missing, however, and only you can supply it: the determination to do the job and do it right. Now.

2

MANAGERIAL DENIAL

Denial is a psychological process by which people refuse to admit the existence of something because it is too painful or threatening. It is a mental defense mechanism whose effectiveness depends, in turn, upon the person's refusal to admit that the denial process itself is occurring. To put it most simply, denial is selective inattention.

If people had to acknowledge the true nature and enormity of world problems simultaneously—national debts, nuclear war, terrorism, pollution, hunger, drought, crime, unemployment, disease—few could bear up under the stress. No one person can take responsibility for and solve all these problems. So mental health experts suggest that denial of some problems—namely those over which we have neither power nor responsibility—can be healthy.

But there is nothing healthy about denial of chemical abuse by managers or by their impaired employees. In fact, denial is an integral part of the disease itself. Moreover, when employers and abusers cooperate in the denial process, they unwittingly help the disease to grow. Thus it is crucial for managers to understand how denial operates in the area of chemical abuse.

USER DENIAL

"User denial" is the most commonly documented and written-about form of denial. Virtually without exception, whenever an alcoholic or addict is confronted with the suggestion that he or she is chemically dependent, the first reaction is to deny there is anything seriously wrong. Even if found lying unconscious in a pool of rum, when conscious the alcoholic will insist that there is only "a little problem." Cocaine addicts who spend $500 a week on their habit will swear their drug use is "strictly recreational." While it is true that all addicts and alcoholics experience denial as a symptom of their disease, a recent study indicates that the denial pattern of female addicts and alcoholics may differ from that of their male counterparts.

Sociologist Annette R. Smith, writing in the summer edition of the *Journal of Drug Issues*, reports that while men are apt to be proud of their drinking and to consider occasional drunkenness and belligerent behavior not only normal but highly acceptable, women experience intense shame when they abuse alcohol. Men will deny their alcoholism until they are confronted with the truth in a manner powerful enough to break through years of denial—a loss of family, prestige, money, health, profession.

By contrast, our society is quick to attach disparaging labels to women who drink too much. Perhaps for this reason, women find it more difficult to deny their alcoholism. Among those studied by Ms. Smith, a surprising number reported that they identified their alcohol problem very early. However, when they turned to their families, doctors, ministers or spouses for help and advice, they were told either that they had no problem or that their problem was psychological rather than alcohol-related. The women then used the denial of those around them to avoid confronting their alcoholism. Interestingly enough, even after Ms. Smith's subjects reached treatment, many of their families continued to deny their alcoholism.

MANAGERIAL DENIAL

"Managerial denial" is much less commonly talked about despite the fact that it is partly responsible for the economic woes of thousands of businesses. In this form of denial, managers refuse to admit that an employee is impaired or that impaired employees may be responsible for substantial business losses.

MANAGERIAL NAIVETÉ

Before we take a closer look at managerial denial, let's distinguish between it and managerial ignorance or naiveté. Oftentimes, managers honestly do not know that their workplace is impaired by employees' abuse of chemicals. It simply does not occur to them because in their own social circle drug addiction is not a problem, and a certain level of abuse is so common as to go unnoticed. Perhaps they are out of touch with conditions "on the line" and blame accidents on faulty equipment. And there is always a grabbag of other plausible reasons for their business losses: the economy, the time of year, union hassles, foreign competition, shoplifters—to name some of the most frequently mentioned.

The vignette that follows demonstrates how a single impaired employee may be sufficient to ruin a thriving business when management is ignorant or naive about the prevalence of chemical abuse in the workplace.

> After their quarterly financial report indicated the disappearance of several thousand dollars worth of goods, the owners of an expensive women's speciality store in Phoenix invested in a costly alarm system to prevent shoplifting. The following quarter showed a similar loss despite the alarm system. Security guards were brought in and one-way mirrors installed in the dressing rooms. Nevertheless, the losses continued. When dwindling profits left the owners unable to pay their bills, they began laying off employees. Only then did one of their workers come forward and divulge the facts: for the previous 18 months a senior employee had been stealing from the store to support her cocaine habit. Because she was a women with the power to hire and fire, her subordinates were afraid to accuse her. The owners never suspected an impaired employee could destroy their business from within.

If only managerial naiveté is involved, the solution is easy: replace ignorance with knowledge. Often, however, a manager will resist the truth about his chemically impaired workplace even when it's made clear. Why? Where does this mental blindness get its power over the minds of generally determined and objective businessmen? Usually from the force to two very strong, very natural feelings: protective instincts and hopelessness. Sometimes only one of these factors is operating, but often both are simultaneously involved. First let's examine the denial sparked by protective instincts.

DENIAL BASED ON PROTECTIVE INSTINCTS

Sometimes managers deny the problem in the misguided belief that by so doing they can protect their company. They fear the loss of business, contracts, customers and public image if they admit that their ranks are plagued by chemical abuse.

But the classic example of protective denial occurs where the manager simultaneously denies the existence of a drug-impaired workplace along with his own chemical abuse. (Here managerial denial and user denial are potently combined.)

Let's look at such a manager through the eyes of an employee, Sue. Now a recovering alcoholic in her mid-40s, Sue has not used drugs or alcohol for five years. During the 1970s she was employed in the sales department of a nationally recognized pharmaceutical company, and for several years in succession she won the company's sales awards. Her supervisor, she remembers, was also an alcoholic.

He kept me on, even after I was showing signs of my disease. Although my sales stayed pretty high, they were nothing like they used to be. I was late all the time and went through periods when I missed a lot of work. Then I'd straighten up my act and try to stay clean for a few months—except for speed to keep my energy up. After a while, though, I'd drift back into drinking. My boss never said anything to me, and if I missed a meeting or made a fool of myself in a conference, he'd make excuses for me. Looking back, I can see how we sort of held each other up. I'd cover for him and vice versa. When we were doing weekly reports, we'd stay up all night and sometimes neither of us could speak without slurring our words. It seemed funny then, but now I wonder what ever happened to that guy.

Frequently, protective denial is more subtle than in the example of Sue's boss. The possibility of a drug-impaired workplace may be denied because the very subject of drugs or alcohol brings up painful personal associations, often memories of another's chemical dependency.

Recently, we had an experience that made this form of denial poignantly apparent. We were addressing a group of military men and women on the problems associated with chemical abuse and methods for documenting impairment. During the question-and-answer session that followed, we were aware of one man's extreme hostility toward us and our topic. We let him tell us—in very angry terms, sometimes yelling and stabbing the air with an accusatory finger—that it was no good wasting time getting help for impaired employees, that if they had any "willpower" worth mentioning they would "help themselves" and quit causing trouble for everyone. When he finished his diatribe, we asked him quietly who in his family had been an alcoholic. There was a moment of stunned silence in which the man's expression registered an incredulous blank. "My father," he said as he sat down.

Managerial denial that stems from self-protective instincts is a problem for which there are no simple answers. If you are a manager whose denial is empowered this way, you will not like what you are reading. You may even decide that this book is worthless to you and refuse to consider the matter further. Obviously we cannot force you to do anything. But we do suggest that if the content of these pages disgusts or upsets or irritates you, it may be that some form of managerial denial is influencing your attitude toward the subject of drugs and alcohol in the workplace.

DENIAL BASED ON HOPELESSNESS

The other cmmon trigger for managerial denial is a feeling of hopelessness about the whole subject. Unfortunately mirroring a common misbelief, many managers believe that chemical addiction is a hopeless condition and that nothing can be done to help the employee who suffers from it. Rather than consider positive alternatives, these managers prefer hiding behind a battery of excuses for the worker's condition or justifications that cast the disease as "inevitable." In the vocabulary of treatment specialists, these rationalizations "enable" the impaired employee to continue his pattern of chemical abuse.

How many of these "enabling statements" sound familiar?

"She's got it rough right now. Going through a divorce, supporting a kid."

"If I were married to his wife, I'd drink too."

"I can't lay him off now. He'll be retiring soon."

"He lives for his work. I hate to think what would happen if we let him go."

"Her husband just died. She's alone. No wonder she drinks too much."

"His kid's sick [or his wife's left him]. I don't blame him for wanting to get away from his problems for awhile."

BREAKING THROUGH DENIAL

If managerial denial or ignorance enables a drug-impaired worker and makes excuses for the impaired workplace, what can be done to remedy the situation? The first step is breaking through the wall of denial or ignorance that conceals the subtle signs of drugs on the job.

It was my son made me see it clear. Without him, I doubt I would have thought drugs and alcohol were a problem at the plant.

Gary owns and manages a midsized fruit and vegetable packing plant in California's Imperial Valley. After many financially successful years, he began to lose contracts.

First I thought it was our equipment. My dad operated the plant before me and some of the stuff was left over from his time, but replacing it didn't make a damn bit of difference. We'd gotten this bad rep in the valley and I was at my wit's end how to turn things around.

Over Christmas holidays that year, Gary's son—a college freshmen in San Diego—told his father about the child of family friends who had recently been through drug treatment.

The kid was a heroin addict. I couldn't believe it! I'd known his dad since we were kids together and way back in high school I used to date his mom. I thought heroin addicts were bums like you see on t.v. but this was a nice kid from a nice family.

The boy's story simmered in Gary's mind until the end of the month when his bookkeeper showed him the latest and grimmest financial report. When Gary called us, he didn't really expect to get help, but he was, as he put it, at his wit's end.

You have to understand I didn't want to believe drugs or alcohol were a problem. The plant's like family to me and I've known some of these people all their lives. It hurt to find out there were drugs being sold in my parking lot every day and traded around on the dock. The stuff was coming up out of Mexico and through my place. I started paying close attention to what was going on and I could see why we were losing money. Workers were coming in late, going home early, falling asleep in the locker room. Right in front of me a guy miscalculated with the forklift and dumped a load of tomatoes all over the road. . . . Why didn't I see things like that before? Maybe I just never wanted to.

What follows is an instrument we have used in our seminars to help workers and managers like Gary identify a drug-impaired workplace. Its effectiveness lies in its ability to penetrate both managerial denial and managerial ignorance.

To interpret the questionnaire, look for your "yes" answers to come in clusters of two or three or to create a pattern indicative of wasted employee time, abuse of privileges, etc.

1. Has there been a recent increase in theft?
2. Are there more strangers in and around your building?
3. Do your employees visit their cars at odd times?
4. Do employees go to the rest or locker room often?
5. Are certain employees frequently preoccupied or "in a daze?"
6. Is there an increase in accidents with equipment?
7. Are your workers' compensation claims rising steeply?
8. Are certain employees always too casual about safety measures?
9. Has your product-reject rate risen?
10. Are you receiving more service complaints?
11. Is afternoon work generally inferior to that done in the morning?
12. Has there been a rise in absenteeism—especially on Mondays, Fridays, and during the holiday season?
13. Are the same employees frequently tardy? Absent? Forgetful?
14. Are more grievances being filed?
15. Is there more illness, especially colds and "flu"?
16. Does one group of employees create most of the discipline problems?
17. Are employees taking longer coffee breaks and lunches?

To show in a practical sense how this questionnaire can help, let us return to the Phoenix boutique whose senior employee was addicted to cocaine and stole from the store to support her habit. How might the boutique owners have discovered the cause of their mysterious business losses by using this checklist?

First, goods had disappeared from the store. That was an obvious sign of trouble. But there were undoubtedly other clues to indicate that the workplace was impaired. Probably the cocaine-abusing employee visited the stockrooms and lounge more frequently than seemed necessary; she likely missed work a lot or was late arriving in the morning and after lunch. No doubt she suffered from an endless string of colds and flu throughout the year. These characteristics would make her a less than perfect employee. Still the owners didn't consider firing her because she had been with them from the beginning—or they might have been excessively tolerant and sympathetic because she was a single parent with children to support. Or since she was a first-rate saleswoman with a string of loyal customers, the owners might have unconsciously wanted to overlook her faults.

An examination of store records and interviews with other employees would have uncovered other significant facts. Perhaps long-time customers had complained that her manner had become abrupt and discourteous, or maybe morale problems among less senior employees were sparked by her temperamental behavior. Such an accumulation of evidence clustering around one employee should have been sufficient to alert the owners to the problem. They would then have known the truth, that it was not shoplifters, but rather their own denial or naiveté, coupled with a chemical-abusing employee, that was dragging their business into the red.

Suppose a manager is reluctant to pursue answers to the questionnaire from fear of what they may reveal? What can a manager do with a drug-impaired workplace? The balance of this chapter is designed to counter any lingering managerial denial triggered by hopelessness. A brief history of employee-assistance programs in this country proves that chemical addiction is far from a hopeless disease, and that it is most profitable for business and best for the worker when a manager gets him or her into a treatment program where he or she can get help before it is too late.

One of the pioneering employee alcoholism programs was started by E. I. duPont de Nemours and Company over 40 years ago. In 1942 one of the firm's top managers met William Wilson, the cofounder of Alcoholics Anonymous. He was impressed by the idea that alcoholics could be rehabilitated. With the assistance of Dr. George Gehrman, a program was created that offered treatment as an alternative to termination for employees impaired by alcohol abuse. Similar programs, all based roughly on Alcoholics Anonymous's Twelve Steps to Recovery, were begun at Eastman Kodak, Consolidated Edison and Western Electric. Recovery rates in these early programs were encouraging. Dupont reported two out of three long-term recoveries at a time when the best hospitals had recovery rates of one in five. Today, the examples of success are even more impressive.

In its Marietta, Georgia plant, **Lockheed** enrolls an average of 1,200 employees in outpatient programs while they continue to work. Results of these programs are a 43-percent reduced rate of absence and 21 percent lower medical payments.

Scovill Manufacturing Company estimates that its employee drug and alcohol program saves $185,000 annually.

Kennecott Copper Corporation estimates its "troubled employee" program saves the company $500,000 per year.

The experience of hundreds of companies like these has shown that with treatment an impaired employee can be helped to acknowledge and face the truth of his disease. These companies know that recovering alcoholics and addicts become trusted workers with a strong loyalty to the company that stuck with them in their time of trouble. But impaired employees cannot be helped unless managers take the first step and break through their own denial.

The case of Alan, vice president of a large corporation headquartered in southern California, provides a vivid example of an impaired employee who was helped because his boss, Tom, broke through the barrier of managerial denial. Alan was a practicing alcoholic for 18 years. By his own estimate, he had been out of control for the last five and a half of those years.

But the last six months was when it fell apart. Towards the end, I had everybody covering for me—secretaries, junior partners, even the president of the company. They were willing to do it because those times when I managed to get it together, I was a hell of a worker and worth every penny of my six-digit salary. But after a while, I started doing things that were pretty hard to excuse away. I was absent from work seven days in one month, and when I was at work my temper was so terrible my secretary quit on me after three years. I didn't complete one assignment that whole month.

Alan's direct supervisor was Tom, the president of the company. Tom came to us and asked if we thought Alan was an alcoholic. After listening to a long list of jobs not done, commitments forgotten and workdays lost, we said we thought he might be. When we admitted it was difficult to make an accurate diagnosis without more information, Tom eagerly accepted our uncertainty. He thanked us for our consultation and said he felt better for having talked to us because now he was pretty sure that if Alan had a problem with alcohol, it wasn't really "serious."

A few weeks later, at an important company dinner, Alan got drunk, told off-color jokes in a raucous way and then, to the astonishment of his colleagues and their wives, passed out, his face in the dessert.

Tom called us the next week for information about how to do an intervention on an impaired employee. It took us half an hour to drive out to Tom's office, and by the time we arrived, his managerial denial had again regained control of his good sense. He apologized for making us drive all the way out to see him. He told us he had acted without considering other alternatives. He wanted us to know that Alan was under a lot of stress, that his wife drank too much and made his life miserable, that his kids were terrible. As we talked to him we realized that he was convinced—although he claimed otherwise—that there was no hope his friend and valued employee could ever recover from alcoholism. It came out that Tom had an uncle he was fond of as a child who died of alcoholism under miserable circumstances. He feared the same end for Alan. It took many hours to explain to Tom how crucial it was to confront Alan with the results of his alcoholism.

We helped him to remember the many ways Alan's impairment was damaging the firm. Together we compiled a list of days when Alan came late to work, left early or was totally absent. We encouraged Tom to describe the specifics of Alan's inappropriate behavior at the company dinner and at several meetings where his excessive use of alcohol impaired his normally astute business sense. As the factual proof of Alan's alcoholism grew, it became impossible for Tom to deny it. The actual intervention with Alan himself took only 25 minutes. When we presented Alan with the documentation of his deteriorating job performance, he realized the career he valued was mortally threatened by the disease of alcoholism. Later he told us:

> Once I could admit it, I felt a lot better. My kids had been on my back for months to stop drinking, and I was worried about losing my job. I knew I was out of control, but I needed someone to push me to the edge to make me admit it.

Alan was treated in a 30-day in-patient program. Shortly after he was admitted, his wife also came into the hospital. Today, Alan and his wife have two years of sobriety and are active in Alcoholics Anonymous. He is back at work and, according to Tom, more productive than ever. Since Alan's intervention and successful treatment, Tom has supervised the implementation of an employee-assistance program to help employees whose work performance is impaired by problems they cannot solve alone.

3

THE
CHEMICAL
MARKETPLACE

The choice of drugs available to your employees in the chemical marketplace grows wider every day. Apart from substances that have been around for thousands of years—alcohol, coca, marijuana, opium—modern drug companies constantly develop newer and better ways to override mental and physical pain. Nostrums with names like Valium, Librium, Qualude and Dilaudid have rapidly become part of the culture of chemical abuse.

Additional avenues of chemical abuse have spread through society as garage and basement chemists try to create the perfect "high" with designer drugs that mix and match potent ingredients in new and often extremely dangerous ways. Most of these designer drugs have no legal "identity" and hence pose special problems for law enforcement personnel who can only prosecute for substances that appear on official lists of controlled drugs.

An individual's chemical preference(s) depends upon many factors. For example, among men and women over the age of 45, alcohol is generally the drug of choice. Alcoholism is most common among this population because alcohol is easily available and its use is legal and accepted as "normal" by most segments of society. Nationality also seems to play a part. Most Native North Americans had no fermented beverages prior to the arrival of the Europeans. Today, the incidence of alcoholism is highest—some experts say 50 percent—among this population group. Next in line are

21

the Irish, followed by French, Scandinavians, English and Germans. Although Italians produce and consume prodigious quantities of wine, the frequency of alcoholism is very low among people of that nation. It is even lower for the Semitic races, Africans and Asians.

Among the affluent, those involved in the media, the arts and professional athletics, the popularity of cocaine has been well publicized. In the recent past, before people became better informed about its dangerous and addictive properties, cocaine was perceived as a status drug. A Waterford crystal bowl of cocaine at a party meant that the host was not only wealthy but hip as well.

Marijuana use is high among young people. Unless parents are astute and suspicious, teenagers find it relatively easy to hide use of this drug in the early stages. They enjoy its social effects—plenty of laughter, voluble conversation, a loss of inhibitions. Men and women in creative fields are also attracted to marijuana. A writer who broke a 10-year marijuana habit after extensive treatment told us:

> It was the only thing that worked for me. I hated booze because of the blackouts and the hangovers and all the sloppy stuff. But with dope I never threw up, I never misbehaved in public. I just went about my business in a euphoric haze. Most important, I lost all my inhibitions about writing. When I was stoned, I never lacked for wild, unique ideas. I knew I was a great writer and nothing could stop me. Even rejection and criticism were tolerable.

Although it is temptingly easy to make generalizations such as these about chemical abuse, we caution against relying upon them, for no sooner does a pattern of abuse appear to emerge in a particular age or group or segment of society than we see its opposite. We have known teenagers and middle-class grandmothers strung out on cocaine, trial lawyers habituated to the use of marijuana and children in the throes of alcohol poisoning. The details of chemical preference are, for the moment, still largely a mystery.

There is a great deal of popular misinformation about all the substances in the chemical marketplace. Many unquestioned "facts" of five to 10 years ago have been disproved by recent studies and increasingly sophisticated methods of analysis. The case against marijuana is a good example. If you came of age in the sixties, you might believe that marijuana is a relatively harmless drug, a natural high. You might believe that smoking a joint is less harmful than a few Saturday-night beers. In this case, you would be surprised to know that between 1976 and 1981 this natural, nonaddictive drug accounted for the second largest number of admissions to federally funded drug treatment facilities. You probably do not know that over 50 studies have shown than it is just as dangerous to drive under the influence of marijuana as alcohol. And you might be startled at recent medical evidence linking marijuana abuse with lung cancer, reproductive problems, brain damage and the breakdown of the immune system.

It is not our intention to make drug experts of those reading this book. However, combatting the problem of the impaired workplace requires that managers become at least as knowledgeable as their employees about the history, effects and on-the-job symptomology of chemical abuse. The pages that follow offer background and up-to-date facts about the substances commonly abused by employees, as well as descriptions of the behaviors most frequently associated with their abuse.

ALCOHOL

Judging by the headline stories in current newspapers and magazines, the number-one problem in the American workplace is illegal drugs such as cocaine and marijuana. Most people would be surprised to know that in fact alcoholism is the most costly addiction for business and industry. In 1982, the Office of Technology Assessment estimated the country's economic losses from alcohol abuse at $72 billion to $120 billion. More than any other drug, alcoholism generates absenteeism, excessive medical bills and reduced work and product quality. In the workplace, alcoholic employees are a potent danger to everyone. In 1983, a Senate subcommittee on employment and productivity found that 40 percent of industrial deaths are caused by the use of alcohol. Forty-seven percent of all injuries have the same origin.

The image of the scotch-drinking, martini-swilling American is out of favor in these days of white wine and margaritas; however, the National Institute on Alcohol Abuse and Alcoholism reports that addiction to alcohol is actually on the increase. And while almost everyone can agree on the risks involved in the excessive use of prescription medication, in taking cocaine and marijuana, crack and heroin, there are many conflicting opinions about the use and abuse of alcohol.

To understand alcoholism in our country today, one must understand Western civilization's long and contradictory relationship with the drug.

HISTORICAL PERSPECTIVE ON ALCOHOL

Research indicates that alcohol has been with civilization since earliest recorded history. This is not surprising since the fermentation of sugar occurs spontaneously in nature and one has only to leave a few summer grapes, an apricot or a cantalope on the kitchen counter for a day too long to be reminded of this. The earliest forms of alcohol were not particularly potent. Fermented honey, fruit or grain has a maximum alcoholic content of 15 percent. Nevertheless, as far back as ancient Babylon and the Code of Hamurabi, there is evidence that even this mild brew caused some disruption in

Drug	Trade Name/ Street Slang	Medical Use
Alcohol *(Liquid)*	Various/Booze Grog, Hootch	Home remedy for assorted complains
Amphetamines *(Tablet or capsule)*	Biphetamine, Desoxyn, Dexedrene/ "A"s, "Mollies," "Whites," "Speed," "Hearts"	Treatment of: Hyperkinesis Narcolepsy Weight control
Barbiturates *(Tablet or capsule)*	Phenobarbital, Butisol, Secobarbital, Tuinal/ "redbirds," "downers," "yellows," "barbs," "dolls"	Anesthetic Anticonvulsant Sedative Hypnotic
Benzodiazepines *(Tablet or capsule)*	Dalmane, Valium, Librium/no slang names in general use	Sedative Anticonvulsant Anti-anxiety Hypnotic
Cocaine *(Flakey white crystalline powder, smoked, inhaled, injected)*	"coke" "snow" "nose candy" "White Lady" in rock form: "crack"	Local anesthetic
Marihuana *(Green, leafy, may contain weeds, stems, buds, highly aromatic)*	weed, grass, pot, dope, reefer, Sensi in concentrated form: hashish, "hash" in liquid form: "hash" oil	Under investigation
Narcotics *(Injected, sniffed, smoked, tablet or capsule)*	Morphine, Codeine, Diacetylmorphine, Heroin, Dilaudid, Demerol, Methadone, Talwin, Lomotil, Percodan "horse," "smack," "party pack," "perks"	Various: analgesic, antitussive, antidiarrheal

Symptoms of Abuse		Withdrawal
General	*Workplace*	
Use at times of stress, boredom, blackouts, sneaking drinks, attempts to control or limit consumption, preoccupation with drinking, preference for drinking environment.	Absenteeism, tardiness, inattentive, accident prone, spasmodic work-pace, undependable, excessive drinking at meetings, lunches.	Blood vessels constrict, unstable blood sugar level, mental confusion, hallucinations, fearful behavior.
Agitated, talkative, paranoid, suspicious, heavy perspiration, loss of appetite, excitation, euphoria.	Erratic production, agitation, disregard for rules & regulations, absenteeism, tardiness, interpersonal problems, excessive use of medical benefits.	Apathy, long periods of sleep, irritability, depression, disorientation.
Same behavior as alcohol abuse but more extreme.	Same as above with the addition that employee may appear drunk though abstinent from alcohol.	Anxiety, insomnia, tremors, delerium, convulsions, possible death.
Slurred speech, disorientation, inattention. Drunken behavior without alcohol.	Same as above with the addition that employee performance and moods may vary widely, unpredictably.	Sleep disturbance, anxiety, insomnia, tremors, delerium, convulsions, possible death.
Alertness, excitation, talkative, high energy, quick mood changes, continual sniffles, dry cough, hoarseness, loss of appetite, decreased sex drive.	Mood swings cause problems with other employees, uneven performance, may sell drugs at work or steal from employer. Absenteeism, tardiness.	Irritability, depression, preoccupation with cocaine, apathy.
Various: may be similar to alcohol intoxication; may be manic behavior, talkativeness, hilarity, high energy, may be drowsy, dilated pupils.	Loss of short term memory, slowed responses, sleepiness, difficulty concentrating, erratic production, frequent trips to isolated work areas.	Apathy, fatigue, irritability, depression.
In general: euphoria, drowsiness, apathy, detachment from physical and/or emotional pain, constipation, constriction of pupils.	Unable to think clearly, loss of interest in physical appearance, may sell drugs at work, low motivation. Absenteeism, tardiness, etc.	Watery eyes, runny nose, yawning, loss of appetite, irritability, tremors, panic, chills and sweating, cramps, nausea.

society. In the code we find rules regulating tavern keepers, the use of alcohol and sanctions against its abuse. The ancient Egyptians used alcohol as a recreational drug, but there were also rules mandating who could drink, when and why. Although we might associate opium abuse with imperial China, difficulties with alcohol are of much older origin. Between 1100 B.C. and A.D. 1500, China "went dry" at least 41 times by imperial decree. At one period around 500 B.C. the punishment for public intoxication was decapitation on the spot.

At some time between A.D. 800 and 1000 Crusaders brought back from Arabia the secret of distillation. Hence the word *alcohol*, which comes from an Arabic word meaning "essence." Distillation, a simple process whereby alcoholic content is increased by heating liquid to vaporization and then returning it to a liquid state, produced brandy that was 50 percent alcohol from wine; the heady effects of the discovery, however, were not experienced by the bulk of the population. Distilled liquor was expensive, and so most people remained content with low-potency fermented beer, wine and mead.

And then about 1600, gin was invented. With the discovery that spiritous liquors could be made from virtually any liquid, strong drink became available to the masses. In England, the democratization of drinking brought immense problems because it coincided with the Industrial Revolution, a period of great social upheaval and disconnection when thousands upon thousands of illiterate men and women were forced by economic pressures to abandon their rural homes and enter the cities for employment. Writers of the time describe London as a hell hole of poverty, vice and despair. Crowded together in slums, working in factories under deplorable conditions, hungry, diseased and without any hope of bettering their situation, the people escaped from reality through alcohol—specifically gin, which sold for the equivalent of less than five cents a quart. Historians estimate that in 1750, one third of the London population was alcoholic, while the other two thirds abused alcohol. Public drunkenness was a widespread and tolerated phenomenon. Children were commonly dosed with alcohol and frequently were alcoholic.

Eventually, members of the government and the Church of England recognized the size of the problem and passed laws regulating the distribution and sale of alcoholic beverages. But in a real sense the action came too late, for a cultural attitude, one that accepts the use of alcohol as a means of coping with life's problems, had developed by that time. More than 200 years later, this attitude still colors our own thinking about alcohol.

Colonial America was a hard-drinking society. Although conditions were not as degrading to the human spirit as those in England at the same time, life was still difficult, and both men and women used alcohol because it seemed to make life easier for them. The market for alcohol was excellent, and so it was not uncommon for farmers to convert a large proportion of their crop into alcohol, which could be used for trade or bartering. Furthermore, it was generally held that alcohol was good for the health and strengthening the blood. Most employers encouraged their employees to drink by providing a rum or beer break at some point in the day. In the military of the time, alcohol was considered an absolute necessity. The troops of George Washington at one point threatened not to fight if they did not get their daily ration of grog. And of course there were the social uses of alcohol. Then as now, spiritous liquor was deemed a necessary component of a good party. The household records of John Hancock tell us he served the following to 200 dinner guests in 1792: 300 bottles of wine, plus sufficient sherry, brandy and 136 bowls of alcoholic punch.

In the early part of the 19th century, a movement began to counteract the casual use of alcohol. The first temperance societies did not advocate abstinence, only moderation. The move to make drinking alcohol actually illegal came near the middle of the century. The so-called temperance movement (actually an abstinence movement) taught that alcohol was evil in and of itself and that those who used it were likewise evil. According to the students of American history, the quick success of the movement was the result of the conflict between family- and church-oriented people settling in the Midwest and less stable elements of society—the cowboys, trappers, loggers, gamblers, adventurers and prostitutes.

To understand how public opinion was turned against the use of alcohol, imagine a rural Kansas community in the late 19th century. This is a town that had its beginnings as a wide open and lawless cowtown, but over the years the population has been swelled by farmers, shopkeepers, artisans and their families. There is a well-attended church in the town and a schoolhouse. There are saloons as well, but few of the solid citizens visit these establishments. Imagine how peaceably life goes along in this pocket of rural America . . . until the cattle trains pass through. Suddenly, the town is full of noisy, drunken cowpokes who swagger down the boardwalks reeking of drink and waving their sixguns. Professional gamblers come to town, and prostitutes walk the streets the same as God-fearing women. No wonder townspeople elected legislators who agreed with them that if their towns were to be decent places to run a business and raise a family, something had to be done about alcohol. Ultimately, the power of the temperance movement was felt in the enactment of the Eighteenth Amendment, prohibiting the manufacture and sale of alcoholic beverages within the United States.

CURRENT ATTITUDES TOWARD THE USE OF ALCOHOL

Given our history, today's society is inconsistent and confused about alcohol. Despite the widespread recognition that alcoholism is a disease, many still consider it the sign of a weak or contaminated nature. As recently as 1979, Representative Robert K. Dornan of California voiced what is the opinion of many people when he said, "There is one major cause underlying *alcohol abuse* [authors' emphasis], drug abuse, and many other of the ills that afflict our society; it is an absence of self-discipline."

Our society's confusion over whether alcohol abuse is a disease or a reprehensible failure of the will is aptly demonstrated by the way our laws treat public drunkenness. Most city jails have drunk tanks for alcohol abusers. If this were the normal way we treat men and women suffering from disease, we would not only have drunk tanks but also diabetic tanks for those in insulin shock and epileptic tanks for sufferers from seizures and hay fever tanks for unfortunates who sneeze in the spring.

At the same time that we punish drunkenness by incarceration—as if it were on a par with theft or assault—we encourage drinking. Although 80 percent of all fire deaths, 65 percent of drownings and 70 percent of fatal falls are linked to alcohol use, ads in all forms of media connect sporting events and sporting enthusiasm with drink of one kind or another. In television dramas we are routinely shown men and women who use alcohol for stress relief . . . as did the poor Londoners of 1750.

Many of our courts take a remarkably mild position toward drunk driving, which has been compared to a mental incompetent running amok with a loaded shotgun. In some jurisdictions the punishment is a scolding from the judge and a warning, in others a fine is levied or public service exacted. In still other areas, attendance at a few meetings of Alcoholics Anonymous is required. Much less frequently, a convicted drunk driver is deprived of his driving rights or sentenced to time in jail.

It is clear that our society is very confused when it comes to alcohol. Despite our long acquaintance with fermented and distilled liquors, we still do not know how we really feel about them or about those people who drink them to excess.

PHYSIOLOGICAL EFFECTS OF ALCOHOL IN THE BODY

In recent years, scientists have begun to understand how alcohol affects the body, and through this knowledge they are coming to a better understanding of what alcoholics suffer as a result of their disease.

1. *The Liver*: Twenty percent of alcohol taken enters the blood stream immediately by passing through the stomach walls. The other 80 percent goes from the stomach to the small intestine and thence into the blood. The liver reacts to alcohol as if it is a poison and goes to work immediately to eliminate it from the bloodstream. To do this, an enzyme called ADH attacks the alcohol molecule and converts it into another agent called acetaldehyde, and from that to acetate, which is then converted to carbon dioxide and water, which are eliminated. Normally, the liver accomplishes the conversion of alcohol at a rate of about one half ounce an hour. If large amounts of alcohol remain in the body over a period of time, the liver is overtaxed. It must devote its energy to alcohol oxidation while neglecting other important operations. As a result, toxins accumulate in the blood. The body's cells, tissues and organs are improperly nourished.

2. *Blood Alcohol Level (BAL)*: The concentration of alcohol in the blood is called

the Blood Alcohol Level. Alcohol begins to collect in the blood when a person drinks more alcohol than his liver can efficiently eliminate. The BAL rises and the drinker's behavior, emotions, thoughts and physical ability are affected. BAL is determined by several factors: (1) Body Weight: The heavier the drinker, the more water there is in the body to dilute the alcohol and the lower the BAL. (2) Sex: Because they have less water and more fatty tissue in their bodies, women reach a higher BAL faster than men. During the week before menstruation, alcohol is absorbed more rapidly. (3) Food: BAL rises faster on an empty stomach because the presence of food in the stomach dilutes the alcohol and slows the rate of alcohol absorption into the blood. (4) Mixers: Drinks mixed with carbon dioxide (champagne, cola, quinine, ginger ale, etc.) raise the blood alcohol level quickly. Water and fruit juices slow the process. (5) Concentration: The higher the concentration of alcohol in the drink, the faster the BAL will rise. (6) Temperature: Warm alcohol is taken into the bloodstream more rapidly than cool or cold.

3. *The Cells*: The body's cells are delicately balanced chemical structures that react immediately to the presence of alcohol in the body. The first reaction is a defensive one, but if the alcohol remains in the blood in sufficiently high concentration, the cells adapt and learn to use the alcohol's high energy content as food. The more that alcohol saturates the cells, the more they tolerate it and even require it. Initially, the structure of the cell is strengthened to protect the fragile chemistry within, but eventually, the membranes weaken and, in some cases, are destroyed.

4. *The Brain*: Neurons—cells in the brain—are agitated and disoriented by the presence of alcohol. In this condition, they may fail to make normal connections. Electrical and chemical signals that control cognition, consciousness and virtually all behavior are disrupted. At low doses, the drinker is stimulated and feels happy. He may even, after one or two drinks, experience some improvement in certain kinds of performances—even driving a vehicle. He may be able to express himself with uncommon clarity and flair. After several drinks, however, he begins to show signs of intoxication: slurring of words, confusion, disorientation, poor judgment and impaired motor coordination. A blackout occurs when brain function is so confused that memories are not recorded at all or the recording takes place in such garbled form as to be irretrievable. At the worst extreme, the brain becomes unable to coordinate the organism's life functions. The respiratory system ceases to function; heart beat slows, then stops.

REACTIONS TO ALCOHOL

There is an enormous difference in the way individuals react to alcohol. Imagine a population of 100 individuals chosen at random off any city street across the United

States. Of that number a very small percentage will be unable to tolerate alcohol at all. They will have one drink and find the experience so unpleasant that they will decline alcohol from that time forward. As much as 60 percent of Asians, compared to 5 percent of Europeans, lack the vital liver enzyme that converts acetaldehyde into nontoxic substances. Alcohol makes them feel dizzy, nauseated, and they may experience unpleasant sensations on the surface of their skin.

A second small group of our random population will be unaffected by alcohol. At a party they may accept one drink and hold it all night long without taking more than a sip. At a wedding they will raise their champagne glass to toast the bride and groom and then forget to drink.

A third, and large, group will like alcohol and drink it for pleasure, relaxation and to alter mood. This is the group that goes out after work for a drink and parties on the weekends without apparent ill effects. Faced with a family tragedy, they will probably pull out the scotch or bourbon or gin. If they are tense, they will drink to ease their nerves. If persons from this group are told by their employer that they have been too often absent from work or tardy, if there have been complaints about their job performance or their relationship with their work peers, they will probably be worried enough to seek some kind of help. When they learn that a few too many weeknight parties have been impairing their performance, they will probably alter their social style. They value their jobs and want to keep them. They are willing and able to alter their drinking style to keep their jobs.

Most experts agree that men and women from this third group have the potential to become "problem drinkers" and even, in the extreme, alcoholic. Problem drinkers are those who use alcohol as medication. That is, they drink to change the way they feel. At a stressful time of life, faced with a difficult job, when they are fearful or depressed or lonely or excited, when they wish to celebrate or mourn, these people prescribe a drink for themselves. They use alcohol as a coping mechanism, and while this may work satisfactorily for a time, if their cells adapt to alcohol and become dependent on it, these drinkers have passed from mere problem drinking to the disease of alcoholism.

A small percentage of our random sample of 100—between 10 and 15 percent—will become alcoholic. These drinkers are genetically predisposed to alcoholism. It is this group that most interests research scientists today.

Any reader searching these pages for a definitive statement about the cause of alcohol addiction will be disappointed. The answer to that question remains elusive despite dozens of studies using the most sophisticated research methods. Nevertheless, the existence of some kind of genetic predeterminant—perhaps more than one—appears to be conclusive in the light of scientific findings that demonstrate biological and chemical differences between alcoholics and nonalcoholics.

Boris Tabakoff, a founding member of the Research Society on Alcoholism, told treatment specialists from around the country that studies indicate heredity to be a factor in from 60 to 70 percent of all cases of alcoholism. He told of a study following

80 families over a period of three years that found alcoholism nine times as likely among families where the disease is already present.

Such comparative studies have long been an essential component of alcoholism research. The earliest were done in Scandinavia, where adoption records are available for study. There, researchers discovered that the sons of alcoholics—whether adopted into moderate drinking or totally abstinent families or retained by their natural parents—have a significantly higher incidence of alcoholism than do sons of a non-alcoholic control group. A more recent study done in Iowa confirms that paternal alcoholism is the greatest single predictor of the disease. Among that population, the sons of alcoholics were 25 times as likely to become alcoholics as those without a family history of alcoholism.

The first attempts to link heredity and alcoholism were unsophisticated in comparison to today's minute examinations of the alcoholic's body chemistry. Modern scientists, studying the hormones, blood, brain, liver and other body cells, have found intrinsic metabolic differences supporting the argument that there are genes that influence how alcohol is handled by the body.

Some of the most interesting research connects heredity and the way the body metabolizes alcohol. Dr. Marc Schuckit, a researcher in La Jolla, California, has done studies that show how, in the alcoholic, the breakdown of acetaldehyde into acetate is slower than in the nonalcoholic. Dr. Charles Lieber has discovered a possible cause of this. Within an alcoholic's liver cells, the makeup of the mitochondria, which convert food into usable energy, is abnormal. Schuckit has found that same abnormality among the offspring of alcoholics who are not yet heavy drinkers.

Schuckit and colleagues in New York have also noted a brain wave deficiency among alcoholics. By studying practicing alcoholics and their young sons, Schuckit has discovered that the two groups share this deficiency. This brain wave, known as P300, is normally associated with attention and learning; what role it might play in the development of alcoholism is not yet known. It is but one of several areas of study that may eventually provide a marker for alcoholism and, ultimately perhaps, a way to prevent it.

Heredity does not guarantee that the child of an alcoholic will become an alcoholic him- or herself. No one is predestined to contract the disease, but it is now believed by almost everyone in the field that genetic factors create a strong predisposition that increases the risk of alcoholism. Many believe that not one genetic factor but a multiplicity of genetic factors interact with environmental factors to produce the final level of risk.

THE THREE STAGES OF ALCOHOLISM

However it is that drinkers become alcoholics, the progress of the disease can be divided into three stages that will—allowing for some individualization—apply to all alcoholics with equal validity. If an employer or manager is unaware of the signs and symptoms of the disease, he may be unable to identify an employee as alcoholic until the disease is in its acute phase. Unfortunately, by that time the chances of a successful long-term recovery are dim. Most alcoholics will begin to demonstrate observable workplace symptoms near the middle of the first phase, however. At this early point the intervention process becomes possible and the likelihood of success is great.

Early Stage Drinking

Since our society accepts—and in some cases expects—a certain amount of heavy drinking. it is not easy to spot an alcoholic in the early stage of the disease. Depending on environment, he or she may appear to drink merely to be sociable, and may actually function better after drinking a little. At this stage, the alcoholic can drink as much as he or she likes and rarely has a hangover.

During the early stage of alcoholism, without the drinker being aware, the body adapts to the constant presence of alcohol. Cells alter sufficiently to allow them to continue to function effectively in their poisoned environment. They learn to use alcohol as food and may reject more nutritionally balanced sources. As more alcohol saturates the cells, they come to tolerate and even require it. At this point, when cell chemistry has changed and the body no longer works well without alcohol, a state of *physical* dependence is reached.

Workplace symptoms near the middle of the first stage will be increased frequency of Monday morning absences, late lunches and early departures at the end of the day. At this time, an employee may overreact to real or imagined criticism and use illness as an excuse for inefficiency, errors in judgment and failure to meet deadlines. In general, a manager can be alerted to possible trouble by a deterioration in an employee's level of performance, which, although slight, will be pervasive.

Middle Stage Drinking

In the middle stage, the chronic drinker requires a steady flow of alcohol to keep from suffering acute distress. Cells, the basic units of the body, can no longer function without it. Although the drinker may deny being addicted to alcohol, the persistent craving proves the denial wrong. So long as just the right amount is drunk—no more than the cells can process—the drinker is all right. Too much alcohol and drunkenness results. Too little and the body craves relief.

What happens when the drinker ingests no alcohol or tries to stop drinking altogether at this middle stage of his disease? Immediately, blood-sugar level plummets. The chemical balance in the brain changes. Hormone levels rise and fall unpredictably. Blood vessels constrict. Brain cell function becomes wild. The dry alcoholic is confused, discoordinated, unable to focus thoughts. Little wonder he or she rarely stops drinking for long when it is known alcohol will immediately end all suffering. Ironically, at this stage the drug is both the "cause" and the "cure" of the disease.

Despite discomfort, some alcoholics do stop drinking at this stage . . . for a time. These so-called periodic drinkers are able to withstand the discomfort of withdrawal (often with the help of prescription medicine like Valium) when it is the only way to silence a complaining spouse or threatening employer. Because the periods of active alcoholism alternate with those of abstinence, many people—particularly managers— are unwilling to call these drinkers alcoholics. There persists in our society the image of the alcoholic as a hopeless drunk lost in the gutters of skid row when in fact only 2 percent of alcoholics fit this description. Periodics are just as much alcoholics as those individuals who drink themselves steadily, daily, into the grave. The only difference is that periodics take a little longer to reach the same end and are less likely to be identified by their employers. This makes them very costly to the workplace.

There are many workplace symptoms at the middle stage of the disease since, at its most extreme, the employee is probably functioning at only about 50 percent efficiency. Absenteeism and punctuality become major issues, although the alcoholic will excuse his or her behavior with a variety of stories. At this stage, nothing is ever the alcoholic's fault, including the time he or she gets to work or leaves in the afternoon. The alcoholic's behavior becomes so untrustworthy that no one can ignore it, and coworkers may cover for the drinker's failure to pull his or her own weight. Responsibilities are shirked at the same time as accomplishments and importance are exaggerated. The alcoholic avoids associates and is difficult to get along with. Work pace is spasmodic. Injuries are sustained both on and off the job. In extreme cases, alcohol may be brought to work in a thermos of coffee or juice. The alcoholic drinks at lunch.

There may or may not be noticeable physical symptoms of alcoholism. Hands may shake. Eyes may be bloodshot and the area surrounding them puffed and swollen. There may be a persistent cough, weight loss, headaches and chronic gastritis.

Late Stage Drinking

By the late stage of alcoholism, the alcoholic is obsessed with drinking; it has come to mean more than anything else in life. Extreme agitation, hallucinations and physical pain occur when the drug is withdrawn. The system becomes totally infused with alcohol. He or she may suffer heart disease, liver ailments, impaired vision, hypertension, severe weight loss, periodontal disease and other problems, convulsive disorders, pancreatitis and acute chronic gastritis. Clearly, in the late stage of the disease, the drinker has passed from tolerance to general deterioration and systemic breakdown. The cells have reached the limit of their adaptability and are now so thoroughly poisoned and weakened that they no longer function properly. Abstinence is virtually impossible at this point without constant medical supervision for, despite the fact that the alcohol is killing the drinker, it is the only medicine that will eliminate the pain suffered when forced to go without a drink.

An alcoholic who reaches this stage and is still employed has probably had a checkered work history involving many job changes and positions of decreasing responsibility. He or she is often absent and frequently takes time off without forewarning—sometimes several days in succession. He or she may fail to return to work after lunch and may often miss appointments. Medical benefits will be used excessively. Domestic problems are likely to interfere with job responsibilities. He or she cannot be trusted and is known to lie habitually. Money problems are commonplace and it is not unusual for wages to be garnished to pay child support, alimony or other debts.

Few people who reach this final stage ever find their way into permanent recovery. One way or another, sooner or later, the alcohol they love and need and fear will kill them.

The two vignettes that follow tell stories of very different people with widely different drinking styles. Bill was a steady drinker, Joanne a periodic drinker. Despite their differences, both individuals' disease progressed through the early and middle stages before help was sought.

Bill was a self-employed architect whose workstyle and drinking pattern were compatible. A "social drinker," he never even kept a bottle at home because he did not enjoy drinking alone. As a boy he had been something of a loner, shy and lacking in self-confidence. In college he learned that with a few drinks in his system, in the convivial atmosphere of a cocktail lounge or club, he became relaxed and gregarious.

The first stage of Bill's alcoholism lasted many years, until he lost his wife and children through divorce and went to live alone in a new town. At that point, finding himself in a community of strangers for the first time in 20 years, his self-confidence and self-esteem dropped to their nadir. Fairly rapidly, he began to drink more than his metabolism could handle and his alcoholism slipped into the second stage.

I'd start in the morning early, with a cup of coffee and a little drink at the club. There were a bunch of us who showed up there between 6 and 7 A.M. There were some characters, I can tell you. I got so I looked forward to hearing about their shenanigans every morning. Anyway, after an hour or so, I'd cross the street to my office and work awhile. Then around about mid-morning, I'd drop back in at the club for another cup of coffee.

And another drink. Over a period of 10 years, Bill made countless trips to the club for breakfast, lunch and coffee breaks. In the course of time he lost his reputation as a talented professional and his practice dwindled to nothing. He hocked heirlooms and valuables to pay his debts, and was involved in two drunk-driving incidents before a judge finally sent him to the country farm. Nevertheless, it was hard to convince Bill that he was an alcoholic because he never drank at home and he never drank alone. Like so many people, he identified alcoholism with cheap wine and lives spent in alleys and flophouses. His persistent belief that because he did not fit this image he could not be alcoholic was the barrier than kept him from accepting help when it was offered by Alcoholics Anonymous.

Joanne is an attractive women in her mid-40s who has been sober for several years. Before seeking treatment, she was a practicing alcoholic for 17 years. During her drinking days she was employed as a salesperson for a nationally known company.

I was a periodic drinker. Right up until the end, I could stop anytime I knew I had to. Once, when I was trying to keep my marriage together, I stopped for almost a year. It was no pleasure going on the wagon, but I could always do it when I had to. Of course, I used this to convince myself I wasn't an alcoholic. When I was drinking I always managed to cover my mistakes with a smile or fast talking. I had a fabulous sales record and so I knew my boss would overlook a lot just to keep me on. I always looked good and I never passed out on the job or did anything gross like that. When I had a hangover, I used to stay in bed until mid-afternoon, then get dressed up, grab my Gucci briefcase, and charge into the office an hour before quitting time. Everyone thought I was a real go-getter out on calls all day.

Joanne's drinking continued in this on-and-off manner for many years before she found she could no longer keep up the pretense of being a "go-getter." She needed a drink in the morning to steady her nerves, and she began to plan her day around those times when it would be possible to take a drink. As her absenteeism, tardiness and forgotten appointments increased, her sales diminished. She carried a flask of vodka in the glove compartment of her company car. Eventually, but not until she had cost her employer thousands of dollars in medical benefits and lost accounts, she was confronted with her unacceptable work behavior.

As the stories of Bill and Joanne show, it is not always easy to identify an alcoholic. However, if there is one place where this form of impairment can be spotted early, it is in the work environment. Bill's alcoholism went unnoticed largely because he worked alone. If he had been employed as an architect in a firm with an employee assistance program, he would have been forced to confront his disease in terms impossible to deny: missed deadlines, excessive absences and coffee breaks, overlong lunch hours and forgotten appointments.

If Joanne's employer had broken through his own managerial denial, he would have been able to confront her with her unsatisfactory work performance long before she began to lose money for his company. As she admits, the signs were all there, but because she was an excellent saleswomen who never stopped looking good and because her drinking style was periodic, her employer remained blind to an impaired-employee problem for years.

COCAINE

Cocaine—whose nicknames include "nose candy," "coke," "snow," "dust," and "flake"—has been a part of Western culture for thousands of years. When the Spanish conquered the Incan empire in the 16th century, they found cocaine, in a form called *coca*, used throughout Incan society. A Spanish administrator of the time concluded, "If there were no coca, there would be no Peru." Despite this hyperbole, there is historical evidence that the success of the Incan lords in ruling their huge kingdom was due in part to the controlled distribution of coca leaves. Coca placated the hungry, strengthened the weary and made the unhappy forget their sorrows. Coca leaves acquired a sacred importance to the royal Incas as well, becoming an essential element in wedding and initiation ceremonies. At funerals, mummified corpses sometimes had coca leaves placed in their mouths, and bags of the plant were put in their tombs to ease the trip to the next world.

The Spanish conquerors forbad the religious and ceremonial use of coca, but its use among the Indian peasants was allowed to continue—perhaps because it kept them docile and subservient to their Spanish masters as it had for the Incan lords before them. In 1787, a Jesuit priest suggested that coca be used as a common substitute for tea and tobacco. Although this did not happen, after the Peruvian wars of independence the coca leaf became part of the country's official coat of arms.

By the mid-19th century, cocaine was well known and favorably received by the medical community in the United States. It was touted in medical journals as a cure for addictions to morphine, opium and alcohol, and highly recommended for the treatment of timidity, fatigue, nervousness, colds, catarrh, stomach problems and depression. One eminent physician called it "the best remedy against worry." By century's end it had become a common surgical anesthetic.

Among the general population cocaine was accepted as an all-purpose panacea. Singers used coca preparations to soothe their voices, and athletes believed it improved their performances. Sarah Bernhardt, Jules Vern, Emile Zola, and a czar of Russia are all on record as having praised cocaine. A chemical entrepreneur named Angelo Mariani combined wine with coca leaves and marketed the concoction as the "wine of athletes." His mixture of pure coca leaves without the wine was believed to have prolonged the life of Ulysses Grant long enough for him to finish his memoirs.

To this day, the name of one of the world's most popular soft drinks bears testament to the historical use of cocaine. Though today's manufacturers of Coca-Cola would probably just as soon forget it, the facts are that between 1886 and 1906, Coca-Cola was marketed as a powerful tonic made with cocaine.

In the 20th century, cases of cocaine abuse and addiction began to appear with more frequency. Despite the fact that the highest abuse category was the white medical profession (whose members had plentiful access to the drug in pure form), cocaine abuse was widely regarded as another "black problem." White racism spurred popular campaigns to outlaw cocaine. Popular exaggerations abounded of the prodigious effects cocaine produced in black men and women; evidence suggests some employers provided it to black workers engaged in heavy labor in an effort to work them to exhaustion.

Gradually, medical, governmental and finally public opinion turned against the drug. In 1906 the Pure Food and Drug Act forbad the interstate shipment of food and soda water containing the drug and put restrictions on the importation of coca leaves. In 1914 Congress passed the Harrison Narcotic Act that made it illegal to possess the drug except by prescription. After this, broad recreational use of cocaine diminished, although it remained available to the criminal element of society, to the entertainment world and to the very rich.

In the 1960s the popular use of cocaine began rising again. As if the historical clock had been set back 100 years, cocaine was praised for its positive effects on the mind and body. In the 1980s cocaine abuse reached epidemic proportions—despite conclusive medical evidence of its dangers. It has become the drug of choice for millions of young, upwardly mobile Americans.

From a recent sampling of 500 callers to the Cocaine Hotline (800-COCAINE) the following statistics emerge. Most cocaine users are white and between 20 and 40 years old. One out of every three users is a woman, and only 15 percent are from racial minorities. The average cocaine user has completed 14 years of school and earns a salary of $25,000 a year—with one in seven earning $50,000 or more. Of this group of conventionally "successful" people, almost half admitted to stealing from employers, families or friends to support their cocaine habit. Forty-two percent had wiped out all their assets in the pursuit of cocaine.

Nor do experts predict a decline in cocaine abuse in this affluent population. In 1985, Joseph Pursch, the Medical Director for CompCare (the world's largest commercial program for drug-and-alcohol rehabilitation), told a reporter for *Fortune* magazine, "We've seen a 100 percent increase in the number of high-level executives coming to us for treatment compared with five years ago. I'm sure that a year or two from now, it'll be another 100 percent or more. Drugs have taken the business world by storm."

There are countless stories of the way cocaine has ruined the lives of successful men and women. The vignette that follows—the story of Vince—differs from many of these only in that it has a happy ending.

When Vince became a partner in a large legal firm with offices in several American and European cities, he was given shares in the firm and a salary that made him a rich man. At just over 40 years of age, he knew he had "arrived" at last and could begin to enjoy the good life. Now when he talks about himself as he was, his ruggedly handsome face wears the rueful smile of a man who has seen it all and lived to tell the tale.

I had a beautiful wife and a baby son who was going to win the Heismann Trophy someday. I drove a BMW and Linda had a Mercedes. Our house was featured in architectural magazines. I mean, it was all there, everything was in place for the American Dream come true.

But instead of being able to relax with his accomplishments, Vince discovered the pressure to prove his worth was even greater at this level of the company.

I told myself they never would have made me a partner if they didn't have confidence in my ability to produce. But I guess I never believed all those pep talks. I was running scared from day one. I worked all the time. I even dreamed work. And when I wasn't in the office or working at home, I was out of town drumming up business. I hardly ever saw Linda or the boy. And when I did get home, I was too exhausted to enjoy either one of them.

One night when Vince was out of town, an acquaintance offered him cocaine. He found it raised his spirits and gave him the extra energy he needed. Vince began using cocaine for those off hours when he really wanted something to lift him out of exhaustion.

My marriage really improved for a while. Linda and I started calling coke our "marriage counselor." Sex was great again and I felt like I could work and party forever.

Vince moved from weekend, to workday, to around-the-clock use. One morning, two years after snorting his first line of cocaine, he woke up in the detox ward of an urban hospital where they told him that if he did not enter a rehabilitation program, cocaine would probably kill him. He didn't believe the doctors. He was convinced he could stop using cocaine on his own. For a time his "white knuckle" abstinence worked.

Then I guess I forgot about the hospital or maybe what the doctors said didn't matter anymore compared to the temptation to snort a few lines. I don't know why I did it. I don't even care. What happened happened. Linda left me. I sold my condo and my car. I rode the bus so I could spend every penny I had on drugs. The only people I knew were druggies like myself so my life seemed normal. I could find excuses for everything I did.

One day three of Vince's partners confronted him with a list of grievances the firm had compiled over a period of months. He had missed 17 days' work, all but one being a Monday or Friday. He had been late filing papers seven times and had forgotten three important client appointments. His secretary complained because his dictation was incoherent and he constantly asked her to rearrange his schedule so that he could leave the office early or come in late. Without once mentioning cocaine or addiction, the partners told Vince he would have to get help for his problem or lose his job.

The meeting humiliated Vince; he was totally demoralized and confided that he "might have a little problem with cocaine." He expected to be fired on the spot. Instead, his partners were supportive. They told him that if he would enter a treatment program that had a proven record of success with drug and alcohol abusers, he would be welcome to return to his job afterward.

> Treatment was the hardest thing I ever had to do and a dozen times I went to phone someone to come get me out. But I knew if I did that, I'd lose my job and be out on the streets. When I thought about that, treatment only seemed like the second worst thing in the world so I stuck it out long enough to get a real understanding of what was happening to me. When I realized I had a disease, I was so grateful. I could deal with a disease.

Today Vince has been cocaine-free for three years. He is a trusted and valued member of the same law firm that urged him into treatment. He spends eight to 10 hours a week as a volunteer counselor for recovering addicts at a local halfway house and recently married a woman he met at a meeting of Cocaine Anonymous.

When Vince was a young man in high school and college, when he was busy winning awards and an appointment to the law review of a prestigious law school, no one could have guessed he would become a drug addict. Like so many other men and women who have succumbed to the lure of cocaine, he was attractive, charming, energetic and intellectually gifted. And yet near the end he might have given it all away for another line of cocaine. Why? What is the appeal of cocaine to men and women like Vince?

There seem to be four main explanations for the powerfully addictive force of the drug. First, the debilitating coke "low" that follows heavy use of the drug encourages users to take more cocaine to get rid of the bad feeling. This new "high" is, of course, followed by that predictably miserable "low," triggering the cycle again.

A second explanation is in the nature of the drug "high" itself. Cocaine provides independent-minded, risk-taking, high-achieving individuals like Vince with a feeling of power and confidence that is particularly appealing to men and women in competitive, stressful professions. This would explain why cocaine is so prevalent among professional athletes, who know their team and millions of fans depend on them to win a game or a title. These men must put their egos and their careers on the line every time they pitch a ball or go out for a pass. Cocaine can provide the illusion of power to make such stressful work tolerable.

A third reason why this chemical is so habit forming is that most people underestimate its power and believe the thoroughly disproved myth that cocaine is nonaddictive. Until his life began to fall apart, Vince had never failed at anything that counted for him. He was one of life's winners and he knew it. From the start, he believed he could manage his use of cocaine just as he had managed his education, career and marriage.

There is a fourth explanation for cocaine's affect. Increasing evidence indicates that cocaine actually changes brain chemistry; in effect it "rewires" the user's personality. A laboratory animal given free access to heroin will limit itself to amounts that don't debilitate the body. But given the choice between food and water and cocaine, the same animal will choose cocaine to the exclusion of those things necessary for survival.

Dr. Martin S. Gold, one of those who has studied cocaine abuse most closely, explains the animal's behavior this way. "Cocaine appears to act, in part, by subverting the 'natural reward' brain pathways and thus confuses the animal just like the person as to what is biologically and organismically important and what is trivial or dangerous." Put another way, healthy nonaddictive men and women are neurologically programmed to seek certain basic goals: food, water, shelter, friendship, sex. Brains of cocaine addicts appear to be reprogrammed so that getting and using cocaine becomes more important than these survival objectives.

Changes in brain functions and behavior are only part of the whole picture of the effect of cocaine on an individual. It is extremely damaging to the body as well. It substantially stresses the heart, making it beat too fast or irregularly. It may cause angina, shortness of breath and high blood pressure; it destroys membranes in the throat and nose. Heavy users become painfully sensitive to strong light. When combined with alcohol, it may cause seizures and death. New studies show that heavy use can destroy 60 percent of the brain cells related to motor skills, leading to a condition similar to Parkinson's disease.

Despite these dangers, cocaine is an increasingly popular drug in the workplace because of its effects and the fact that—unlike marijuana and alcohol—it is an easy drug to use at work.

Cocaine abuse has many physical symptoms. Some may be excused as the effects of a persistent cold or flu bug: loss of energy, sore throat, headaches, hoarseness, sinus problems, nausea, vomiting, sniffles or itchy nose. Other symptoms are less easily explained, however. Nose bleeds are common, and serious cocaine addicts may require plastic or nasal repair surgery. Heavy users habitually lick their lips or grind their teeth. Heart palpitations, difficult breathing, seizures, convulsions or loss of consciousness may occur.

What are the job-related symptoms of cocaine abuse in the workplace? An employee's personality may change. Before becoming addicted, he or she is apt to be one of the most highly motivated, creative and energetic people on your payroll. Even after addiction the impaired worker will still go through periods of outstanding work performance. Alternating with these, however, will be radical mood swings that make him or her difficult to work with and impossible to correct or make suggestions to. At one moment he or she is jolly and hardworking; the next, short tempered and abusive. Periods of decreased confidence alternate with periods of hyperactivity and grandiosity.

When addiction becomes extreme, the addicted worker loses interest in personal appearance and hygiene. Job performance suffers. Competitiveness decreases. Like the alcoholic, the cocaine addict does not return phone calls, is frequently absent or late and disappears from the office without explanation. Appointments are missed and unwise decisions are made. Vince told a story from the middle period of his addiction.

> I was in a plea-bargaining situation and I remember I went along with the DA just so I could get out of his office and into the john for a toot. I know now that if I'd really been with it, I could have gotten our client the good deal he deserved. I just couldn't be bothered.

Increased cocaine abuse drives employees into financial difficulties that may cause them to embezzle from their employer. (Remember last chapter's vignette of the women's boutique?) Or it may lead workers to support their own habit by selling drugs to others—spending more time dealing to coworkers than doing the job you pay them for.

CRACK

Crack is a cheap and deadly form of cocaine, most popular with men between the ages of 20 and 35. Known in the West as "rock," it takes only a few weeks to become addicted to this drug. Crack is made by heating ordinary cocaine in a solution of baking soda and water. This mixture is then dried and broken into tiny chunks. The pellets are generally smoked in a glass pipe; however, they can also be powdered and put in marijuana cigarettes. Users get an immediate and intense rush from their first "hit." It is followed quickly by a crash so demoralizing that the user can only focus on the next hit to get him up again.

Observable symptoms of crack abuse are chronic sore throat and hoarseness. Breathing may be labored and there is likely to be a loss of apetite. Whatever damage cocaine does to the heart, lungs and nervous system, crack does faster. In a matter of a few months a man addicted to crack cocaine may become physically ruined, incapable of normal feelings and suicidally depressed. Crack is frequently fatal.

MARIJUANA

Marijuana—known variously as "weed," "sensi," "maryjane," "pot," "grass," "dope"—has been available in the chemical marketplace for decades. Until the mid-

20th century its use was largely limited to entertainers, minorities and others on the fringes of middle-class society. In the turbulent 1960s, however, smoking dope became a popular pastime for educated and rebellious young people from all classes of society. Many people believed then—and still do—that marijuana is a natural "high," a harmless, untainted substance straight from Mother Nature's garden.

However, the seemingly simple substance called marijuana is in reality a combination of 421 known chemical compounds—which when smoked break down into over 2,000 chemicals. This makes marijuana the most chemically complex of all illegal drugs. Sixty-one of these chemicals are unique to the marijuana plant (or *Cannabis sativa*) and are called "cannabinoids." To understand how marijuana impacts the body, we must examine the effects of these special chemicals.

Cannabinoids are *lipophilic*, meaning "fat-loving." They seek out and seep into fatty cell parts, including those in the brain—which is one third fat. Eventually, the body discharges these chemicals through the bloodstream, but only very slowly. For instance, it takes about a month for the body to become clear of all the chemicals in a single marijuana cigarette or "joint." If one of your employees smokes more than one joint a month, he is never really drug free.

Scientists have only begun researching the special effects of each of the marijuana plant's 61 cannabinoids. Of the six for which there are current studies, THC, an hallucinogenic or mind-altering substance, has received the most attention because it is THC that causes the marijuana "high."

In the 1960s, when marijuana moved into the nation's colleges, high-rise and suburban communities, the amount of THC in the marijuana found in the United States was relatively slight—less than half of 1 percent. Today, when pot is big business, growers have learned to cultivate a plant that has as much as 6 percent THC. The most expensive pot may have more than 10 percent. Hashish is the resin from the marijuana plant and contains even more THC than marijuana. Hash oil, a highly concentrated extract of hashish, may be as much as 20 percent THC. To illustrate the advances in marijuana horticulture, a drug counselor we interviewed said that if farmers could grow vegetables as successfully as people have learned to grow pot, today's tomatoes would weigh 100 pounds.

In recent years, medical research has compiled hard medical data linking marijuana to many diseases. There is data connecting it to damage to the reproductive and endocrine systems; other studies show that marijuana stresses the heart by increasing its rate between 50 and 100 percent as well as causing a significant rise in blood pressure.

Many studies prove marijuana's damage to the lungs is greater than that caused by ordinary tobacco. The cancer-causing chemicals benzanthracene and benzopyrene are present in pot smoke in quantities 50 to 70 times greater than in tobacco smoke. In one study when human and animal lung cell cultures were exposed to both these lethal fumes, the marijuana smoke caused cancerous lesions to form substantially more rapidly than did the tobacco smoke.

While it is true that employees impaired by marijuana demonstrate their impairment—absenteeism, tardiness, extreme moodswings, erratic behavior, lost opportunities, forgotten commitments—in ways that are similar to an alcoholic or cocaine abuser, dealing with them in the workplace and in treatment has shown us that they have some attributes that are peculiarly their own.

The marijuana abuser is frequently difficult to get along with. He may be paranoid or dreamy and half asleep, forgetful, silly, or self-consciously profound. He may treat you as if you do not exist at all or buttonhole you to chatter endlessly about his view of the world. If he is a student, he loses interest in his books. If he is an athlete, he is too tired to work out.

Because marijuana causes the pupils of the eyes to dilate, an employee who abuses the drug may wear dark glasses at inappropriate times—at an indoor meeting, for example—and will be resentful if you ask him to remove them. He often talks a lot and, though what he says does not make much sense to you, to him it seems perfectly clear or even profound. He might come up with wonderfully creative but impractical ideas. His sense of humor may seem bizarre. He laughs at something which, to you and others, is complete nonsense. At the greatest extreme of abuse, the emotions of the marijuana-impaired employee may seem abnormally flat, as if his brain has been turned off. He musters interest in only the most routine matters.

It is in the workplace performance that the marijuana abuser's impairment is most clearly demonstrated. In addition to frequent tardiness, absences, forgotten appointments and deadlines, he is likely to visit his car at lunchtime and on breaks and to be sleepy on the line or at his desk. You may come upon him, staring into space while your memo marked URGENT lies unnoticed before him. He has a hard time completing a simple project because he makes it much more complicated than it needs to be.

It is often extremely difficult for marijuana-impaired employees to learn a new task or procedure because one of the physiological changes that marijuana has caused in their body is the loss of short-term memory. Their memory may be so impaired that they lose track of a conversation in mid-sentence. They will have difficulty remembering names and directions, and even familiar routines become a problem for them.

Marijuana is not physically addictive in the same sense as alcohol or heroin. In withdrawal the addict does not suffer seizures or aching bones, hallucinations or nausea. Because of the way cannabinoids are stored in body fat and discharged slowly, the pot addict is saved from physical suffering during withdrawal. However, marijuana is highly addictive psychologically. When the drug is taken from an addict he may suffer little or no physical distress, but his emotional suffering—anxiety, insomnia, disorientation, exhaustion, depression—will be acute.

Behind the wheel of a moving vehicle, the marijuana addict is a danger to everyone.

The following vignette about Lannie demonstrates how chronic marijuana abuse affected the driver of a school bus for a large public school system.

> I drove a school bus while I was in college and it was just incredibly boring. Plus, a lot of the kids were monsters. I always smoked a joint before my morning route and in the afternoon too. A lot of times I never would have gone to work at all if I couldn't have smoked a little dope first.

Lannie is a clean-cut athletic man in his late 20s. He is studying to be a dentist now but five years ago he signed himself into a 30 day in-patient treatment center for his addiction to marijuana. While high on marijuana, he had an experience that, he says, changed his life.

> It was around the middle of my route and I had maybe 25 kids on the bus. I came to an intersection that had a yield sign on my street and I did like I was supposed to, I slowed down and looked both ways. I saw there was a car a block, maybe a block and a half, away coming down the hill toward the intersection. I should have waited until he got by, but instead, I drove halfway into the intersection. Then I stopped. I don't know why, but all of a sudden, I forgot what I was doing. I knew that car was coming, I knew I had to get out of its way, but I couldn't figure out how to do it. I'd been driving since I was fifteen years old and suddenly it all went out of my head. I sat there in that school bus full of kids and just stared dead ahead. My mind was a total blank.

Several things happened at that point. The schoolchildren began yelling. The driver of the oncoming vehicle slammed on his brakes and his horn at the same time. Finally Lannie figured out that by putting his foot on the accelerator he could move the bus out of the intersection.

> I didn't stop smoking dope right away after that, but the memory of those brakes screeching and the kids yelling stayed with me. Eventually, I know that was what made it possible for me to stop denying that I had a problem with marijuana and get help for myself.

PRESCRIPTION MEDICATION

During the last 20 years, the widespread abuse of prescription medicines has received extensive media attention. Although the medical and pharmacological professions attempt to see that these dangerous drugs are not misprescribed, it is estimated that a million people are addicted to them in one form or another. In the workplace, the employee impaired by abuse of prescription drugs is—like the alcoholic and the cocaine and marijuana abuser—a costly and often dangerous liability.

AMPHETAMINES

The group of drugs called amphetamines goes by various street or slang names, of which only a few are "speed," "hearts," "uppers," "Mollies," "bennies," "dexies," "copilots" and "whites." They were first prescribed in the 1920s and were dispensed to soldiers in World War II to stave off fatigue. Today, most individuals innocently begin their abuse of amphetamines because "speed" keeps them awake to finish a project by deadline or because they believe it helps them appear alert at a meeting following a cross-country airplane trip. Or a doctor might prescribe the drug because his patient wants to lose weight. Certainly amphetamines do induce wakefulness and decrease interest in food, but there are other biological effects as well. Users of amphetamines experience an increased heart and pulse rate, high blood-pressure and heavy perspiration. In cases of extreme abuse the user's temperature is elevated and he is apt to have hallucinations or convulsions.

For a time, an employee who abuses amphetamines may seem to be a real "go-getter," the sort of nonstop worker supervisors know they can trust to get the job done even if it takes all night to do it. However, the negative symptoms are there as well. The heavy user is also likely to be jumpy, nervous, extremely talkative and, possibly, paranoid. Periods of peak performance will alternate with periods of ineffectiveness. Jumpiness and nervousness or agitation make it hard for this employee to stay in one place for long. He is often away from his workstation, talking to other employees, making frequent trips to the rest room. He may also show disregard for company rules and regulations, look for and use shortcuts in procedures and safety precautions. Eventually, he may earn the reputation of a malcontent or trouble maker.

Sherry began using amphetamines when she was in high school.

I went to a private school that had stringent academic standards and being the only child of high-achieving parents, I was expected to be at the top of my class. No excuses tolerated. Unfortunately, I was also expected to be active in school sports and government and, of course, I took the usual piano and dancing lessons. And on top of everything else, I had to be pretty and popular. My dad was a doctor, and he knew I was working hard at school so every exam period, he'd let me have some pills to keep me going. As far as I know, he never told me he was doling out amphetamines and that they were addictive. He just seemed to assume I'd take them once or twice a year and forget all about them between times. But that wasn't the way it worked, of course. He kept a drawer full of drug samples in the kitchen and I just used to help myself. I must have had a buzz on most of the time from about the age of 15, but no one seemed to notice. I kept getting good grades and winning awards and dating the captain of the football team and everyone was happy.

Sherry's on and off use of amphetamines continued through college and her years at a prestigious business school, where she earned her MBA with highest honors. After graduation, she took a plum job with an international construction company.

For a while, everything was great. The job kept me traveling and the perks were the kind I dreamed about in school. By that time, I knew the pills were dangerous so I went through periods of abstinence. But I always came back to them when the heat was on. After a while, I realized I was trapped in a pattern of speeding to get the work done, to stay awake after long flights, to get myself going in the morning. And then drinking when I had to calm down. More and more, I realized I was abusing pills and alcohol, but nobody every said I drank too much because there's always a lot of drinking in the construction business. I was good at my work, but unless I had to be nice to get the job done, I was a bitch to be around—always in a bad mood, snapping at everyone, constantly complaining unless things were done just the way I expected. I went through three administrative assistants in one year. I knew I had to stop drinking and get rid of my pill habit, but for a long time I was too scared to try. You see, I'd created this house of cards and called it my life. I was petrified what would happen when I didn't have my pills or the booze to support it. Finally, some things happened that made me realize I couldn't trust myself anymore. I was missing appointments, lying to cover up, making some very bad deals. But maybe I wouldn't have done anything to help myself if I hadn't gone home for a visit and one morning my dad caught me with my hand in the goody drawer and insisted I check myself into the hospital.

It took Sherry more than a year to become comfortable without amphetamines and alcohol. After the physical symptoms of her addiction disappeared, it was necessary for her to overhaul every aspect of her life. Today, she is a valued member of a smaller, much less prestigious firm. Her salary is less than half what it was in the days when she crossed the International Dateline as casually as most people cross the city limits. She travels rarely and uses no mind altering chemicals at all.

I'm afraid to put anything in my system now for fear I might use it to help me be something or someone I'm not. I'm 35 years old and just finding out who I am and what I really want in life. I just don't have any more time to fool around, trying to please my folks or a demanding boss or whomever. You know, I've just begun to realize that the real me, the honest-to-God Sherry, never wanted that MBA anymore than she wanted to learn classical ballet. But I thought I had to do those things or I wouldn't be loved or liked or paid a good salary. Now I'm trying to find out what it is I expect from myself and to heck with everybody else.

BARBITURATES

In the jargon of the chemical marketplace, barbiturates are known familiarly as "dolls," "barbs," "yellows," "downers," and "redbirds." Many people first learned of their abuse in the Jacqueline Susann novel, *Valley of the Dolls*. Although fiction, the book realistically described the experience of three women who maintained high-energy careers during the day through the use of amphetamines and could only get relaxation by taking larger and larger doses of barbiturates at night.

In the early stages of barbiturate abuse the physiological symptoms are likely to be slurred speech, a slowed heartbeat and pulse rate, and behavior similar to that of one under the influence of alcohol. An overdose of barbiturates causes shallow respiration, clammy skin, dilated pupils, a weak and rapid pulse. In the worst cases it can bring on coma and death. Because barbiturates accumulate in the body, withdrawal is a long and extremely painful process.

Barbiturate abusers show disregard for company rules and regulations, but are probably too depressed and noncommunicative to be called troublemakers. You may suspect that they are drunk, but there will be no smell of alcohol to confirm your guess that their poor production and many mistakes stem from this form of abuse.

Joanne told her doctor a story he might have heard before but it was sad enough to overcome his reluctance to prescribe barbiturates for sleep. Her husband was an alcoholic who abused her both physically and verbally. She was the main support for the family, which included two teenage children, both of whom were in and out of trouble at school. It was imperative that she get her sleep at night, but she was tormented by sleeplessness, waves of anxiety and frightening panic attacks. She was terrified that if this continued she would lose her job. The doctor wrote a prescription and told Joanne that she needed psychological help.

Barbiturates did more than help Joanne sleep. They blurred the outlines of her troubled world and made it possible for her to tolerate the abuse of her husband. Even her fears for her sons dimmed in the barbiturate fog in which she increasingly engulfed herself. She moved through her workdays in a calm haze, performing tasks routinely. When her doctor refused to fill any more prescriptions for her, she found other sources for her drug of choice.

During the last months of her life, Joanne lost what little interest she had in her appearance. She stopped taking care of the house and at mealtimes her family was left to its own resources. She was criticized by her employer for being slow and sleepy on the job. Assignments were never completed on time and frequently her employer found mistakes. Joanne roused herself enough to promise that she would improve her performance, but it never happened. She became more depressed and unable to cope with even mundane, day-to-day affairs. In June she was given her termination papers, and the following weekend she took an overdose of barbiturates and was found dead in her bed. Because Joanne left no suicide note, law enforcement officials determined that her death was accidental.

BENZODIAZEPINES

The most commonly abused benzodiazepine is Valium, which was first prescribed for anxiety in the early 60s. In all, there are 36 benzodiazepines available, however. The most familiar names are Librium, Tranxene, Dalmane, Serax, Ativan, and Xanax. For many years, it was believed that benzodiazepines were harmless in the low-dose, or therapeutic, range. Now, however, it is known that this drug has a prolonged half-life in the body, and even low dosages may, over a period of time, create a drug-dependent state. Withdrawal from benzodiazepines involves a gradual reduction of doseage to minimize the pain and acute psychic distress involved. Characteristics of withdrawal are irritability, anxiety, panic, tremors and palpitations, profuse perspiration, and in some cases seizures and convulsions. Getting a good night's sleep becomes an obsession with most recovering benzodiazepine addicts, and we have talked to individuals who did not sleep more than four hours a night for the first two years of their recovery.

More women than men become addicted to this drug because it is more likely to be prescribed for them than for men. Dr. Robert MacFarland of Sharp Cabrillo Hospital in San Diego tells why. "Benzodiazepines are generally prescribed for anxiety disorders. A woman who feels jumpy, moody, can't sleep—she'll tell her doctor this—and if he can't find anything physically wrong with her he may prescribe a benzodiazepine. What she needs is counseling, of course, but the doctor hasn't got time to find out what's really happening in her life. And the patient goes away happy. The drug really does make her feel better so she's satisfied with the level of care she's receiving. By contrast, men come to see the doctor when they break their finger or want a mole removed. They rarely share their feelings so they don't get the same prescription."

Benzodiazepines produce complicated and potentially dangerous side effects. For one thing, patients sometimes have a paradoxical reaction to the drug. Although they take the medication for its calming effect, it may actually induce irritability, excitation and rage. It can also produce drowsiness, fatigue and slowed responses, making it difficult to drive a car or operate machinery. Even walking can become a challenge. Althought the drug is prescribed frequently for insomnia, it may worsen a sleep disorder. Finally, when combined with alcohol or barbiturates, benzodiazepine creates what is called a synergistic effect that intensifies the drug reaction and increases the risk of fatal overdose. Put another way, when two drinks are taken with two benzodiazepine tablets, the total, in effect, is six drug doses, not four.

In the workplace, the physical symptoms of this form of drug addiction are difficult to spot. In the early stage of addiction, an employee may appear to be competent and calmly in control of every situation. But over a period of years, as the chemical substances accumulate in the body, cracks will begin to appear in the perfect exterior. Instead of being tranquil, the employee is apt to become irritable, forgetful, frequently anxious and paranoid, sometimes disoriented. Work performance will deteriorate and eventually it will become difficult to perform even minor tasks.

At the time of her addiction, Marlene was employed as a social worker by a large urban county in the Midwest.

My job was to investigate child-abuse cases and to do the job day in and day out, I had to be able to turn it off at night. I learned really early that there had to be an uncrossable line between my home life and work life. That was a cardinal rule for me.

Then my husband had a heart attack and was forced into semiretirement. He was only 36 years old. Suddenly, I was the big wage earner. I started getting stress headaches and couldn't sleep nights. I was on edge every minute, worrying how the family would get by. I just couldn't take the pressure, I guess. And one day when I went to the doctor about a sunspot on my leg, I started to cry and couldn't stop. He was wonderfully sympathetic. I remember he said anyone in my position would be feeling bad. He prescribed some Valium. That was in the early 1970s.

For a long time, the pills were great. I mean, they made me feel like I could manage the world if I had to. Nothing, but *nothing*, got to me. I developed this reputation in the departmnt for being Lady Cool, unflappable. They gave me the cases no one else could face—the baby murderers, the kids abandoned in dumpsters—and it got so it was a matter of pride with me that I never complained.

In 1979, Marlene made the first of what would be many visits to psychiatrists. She told them she was agitated and depressed, and they told her that was perfectly natural for a woman with a stressful home and work situation. All but one of the psychiatrists listened to her litany of troubles and then prescribed more benzodiazepine. Only one doctor told her she was addicted to the medication and refused to treat her unless she gave up her prescriptions.

I told him I'd rather die and I meant it. See, instead of getting better now, life was getting so much worse. I needed my pills more than ever. Everything took me longer to accomplish. The simplest little form would drive me crazy and I'd have to make three, four copies before I'd get it right. And testifying in court was next to impossible. That was a big part of my job and I'd got so bad I just panicked thinking what some lawyer might ask me. I told every kind of lie to keep from going to court.

The words of the doctor who refused to treat her stayed in Marlene's mind despite the damage drugs were doing; they nagged her constantly.

In my work, I'd seen what drugs could do. Three quarters of my cases involved drugs of some kind. But I was scared to give up my pills. And I'd heard about withdrawal from benzodiazepine. I knew it was bad and I'd probably have to go in the hospital to do it. There didn't seem to be any way to make the whole thing easy so I preferred not to think about it.

Finally, one of the county lawyers with whom Marlene had frequent dealings confronted her when he saw her taking pills before a court appearance. Marlene did not bother to deny her problem.

I was just too worn down to fight it anymore. I told him not to bother reporting me. I said I'd do it myself.

NARCOTICS

Narcotics are opium derivatives that act on the central nervous system to create a variety of sensations from euphoria to a coma-like state. The most common narcotics are morphine, codeine and heroin, drugs that have been used by medical practitioners since the 19th century. Narcotics are most frequently taken intravenously, although some people ingest them by sniffing or smoking. The reactions are various. Many people experience a sense of detachment from the environment while others report a rush of euphoria and a sense of immense well-being. At the extreme, the reaction is drowsiness, apathy and a slowing of physical activity.

There are several common misconceptions about narcotics. For example, most people believe that heroin is *always* addictive. The experience of soldiers in Vietnam proved this to be untrue, however. There, the social use of heroin was quite common. Instead of getting drunk, men got high on a very pure grade of heroin out of Southeast Asia. A doctor who worked with this population told us, "All but about 15 percent of those men had no trouble kicking the habit once they got home."

Another misconception about heroin addicts is that they are "on the nod," too lost in their opium dream to rouse themselves to do a day's work. The opposite is often true. The doctor who worked with Vietnam veterans told us he had seen many heroin addicts who were fully employed. "The ones who come into the hospital are mostly blue-collar workers who start off using the stuff socially. I don't know why, but there seems to be a concentration in certain kinds of jobs. We see a lot of roofers and sheet metalers, machinists."

The most dramatic story of a narcotic addict who continued to work while his addiction was in full bloom came to us from a doctor named Ray.

> I guess you'd say I was the product of a normal middle-class family. My parents were moderate social drinkers. As far as I know, my brother and sister have never had any problems with addiction. I never really did any drinking until I was in college. Then I was in a fraternity and once, in a drinking blackout, I did something that offended an entire sorority and resulted in their refusing to have anything to do with our house from that time on. Well, that scared me because I didn't like to think of myself being so out of control.

Ray became a controlled drinker. It was his rule throughout college to drink only two drinks a weekend, and he stuck to that rule. As a matter of fact, his attitude toward his heavy-drinking fraternity brothers became quite condescending. He did not realize that his obsessively controlled drinking was more an indication of early alcoholism than were their spirited high-jinks.

> I got into the medical school I wanted and I did very well. That was in the 60s and everyone was doing drugs of some kind or another. I tried most of them—pot, LSD,

mushrooms—and they never did much for me. I stuck to my two-drink rule and studied hard and it all paid off. I graduated with honors and got one of the best internships on the West Coast. I was going to be a great brain surgeon.

Everything was proceeding according to Ray's lifetime plan until the day that reality caught up to him. Several things happened about the same time. His girlfriend left him. He wrecked his new sportscar. Worst of all, he realized that he didn't like doctors and he didn't want to practice medicine.

It came over me all at once and I was miserable. I'd never felt so bad before. I'd wanted to be a doctor since I was eight years old and I'd devoted my whole life to realizing that dream. Now, all at once, I was 28 years old and I hated it.

At about this time, Ray was an intern working where the patients suffered a great deal of pain. One day he drew 10 milligrams of morphine to administer to a suffering man. He gave him 5—all that was required—and watched in fascination as the patient's pain evaporated. Almost immediately the patient was calm, smiling, apparently content.

By that time, I'd given plenty of morphine, but I never was so struck as I was that day. The way the drug took away the pain was almost like magic. I decided that I needed to know how it worked. I told myself it was "good medicine" to do some experimenting. I even convinced myself that somewhere back in med school a prof had told me no doctor should prescribe something he's not willing to try himself. Anyway, I took the leftover 5 milligrams home instead of disposing of it and that night I injected myself.

It was amazing. It was like "Eureka! I've found it!" The whole world made sense to me. You could say the universe fell into place. It was okay to be in medicine even though it was a crappy field and everyone in it was an asshole. The whole world was okay.

The morphine didn't make me sick. It didn't interfere with any of my abilities either. That was what was peculiar. See, I was doing this very scientifically. I was checking myself for pain thresholds and testing myself as far as motor coordination. And it didn't affect anything. Well, obviously it did. It affected my judgment, but who knows about things like that? When your judgment's gone, how do you judge?

Within a month, Ray was taking something every day. He could not understand this sudden development in his life. He told himself that he was under stress. Every weekend he tried to stop using. And every weekend he got flu-like symptoms that made him so uncomfortable that when Monday—and work—rolled around, he had to take more of his drug to manage his hospital work. At no time did he consider that he was addicted to morphine and that the mysteriously recurring flu-like symptoms were withdrawal pains. In medical school he had been taught a little about alcoholism and nothing at all about drug addiction. Months passed.

It became a challenge to get what I needed. I'd heard stories about nurses not giving full doses and I was very proud about not doing that. I thought that was terrible and I swore I'd never do it. Of course, if I'd had to I would have. I think I would have killed my mother to get what I needed. But for me it was easy. I switched to a synthetic called Talwin which was easily available in hospitals in those days. At the nurses' station there was always a cart full of ampules and I'd just grab a handful. Swear to God, it was that easy.

As time went on, Ray tried several times to get help. He saw psychiatrists who told him he was under stress. He was hospitalized in programs where they told him he was under stress. At one facility he was told he would have to remain in the psychiatric ward for 30 days. He was given weekend passes to go into town and afterwards his urine was tested to make sure he'd stayed "clean." During this time, Ray bought clean urine from an alcoholic who was on the ward with him and passed it off as his own. The scam worked until the technician testing Ray's urine found traces of thorazine, the drug doctors were administering to the alcoholic. During all this time, no one told Ray that he was an addict. Did his colleagues know or guess?

Yes, I've had a couple of them say since that they knew but didn't think it was their place to say anything. This whole business of doctors and responsibility is very complicated. For one thing, doctors are suit conscious. No doubt some of them thought if they accused me of being an addict and it turned out not to be true, I could turn around and sue them for defamation of character. And there's always a reticence about questioning another doctor's expertise. Doctors depend on each other, and they support each other by remaining noncritical. It's a form of denial too. When I used to scrub they could see the needle tracks on my arm. Some even asked me where they came from and I told them my cat scratched me. They were glad to believe me.

I've seen the same thing with nurses. They can come to work drunk with a bottle in their purse and someone'll enable them with an excuse. Her husband beats her. She's under a lot of pressure. The time that doesn't happen is when a nurse is diverting drugs for her own use—stealing from the hospital and mistreating the patients. Then everyone jumps on her at once.

When I was a resident, I was operating all the time. I did everything from minor to major surgery like craniotomies where I operated on the brain tissue itself. Most of these turned out really well, thank God. On long cases, I'd go into withdrawal in the OR. I'd start yawning and my eyes would water. My nose ran and I'd be sneezing. Sometimes my mask would be soaked before I finished. My bones ached like crazy too and I'd speed way up and start closing as fast as I could. Once I actually stopped in the middle, went out and shot up in the men's room, came back and finished the surgery. I told everyone I had colitis.

The chief of neurosurgery finally confronted Ray. He had been leaving syringes around and a nurse had reported him. The chief suggested Ray get psychiatric help.

After that Ray worked at a variety of medical odd jobs: a plasma lab, a medical clinic where most of the practitioners were improperly licensed or impaired in some way. He hated his life and despised what he had become, but he still could not acknowledge that he was an addict.

I developed an allergy to Talwin and if I didn't get it in the vein right, my whole arm swelled and got red and itching. The skin ulcerated and there was more and more tissue destruction. I knew I had to stop and I kept telling myself I was going to stop. Every hit was the last one. I'd tell myself when I shot up that this was the last time so it didn't matter if it ulcerated again. The tissue on my arm was rotting and gangrenous. I took massive quantities of cortazone to counteract the allergic effect but after a few years that stopped working. And I had all kinds of side effects from the cortazone. I gained about 50 or 60 pounds and my legs swelled up. I got ulcers. I was so depressed I took antidepressents, which meant I couldn't drive. The combination of the Talwin and the antidepressent made me goofy.

Eventually, Ray made a serious attempt at suicide. He was found in his apartment by the woman he would eventually marry. Paramedics rushed him to the hospital, where he lay in a coma for four days. But even this was not enough to make him stop injecting drugs.

Ray's life became a pattern of withdrawal. He might go without narcotics for a few days—once he managed six weeks—but he always returned to them. It may be impossible for anyone who has not experienced what this man did to appreciate the depths of his despair, the utter blackness of his denial. He still would not say the word "addict" and apply it to himself.

Finally, he was forced to face the truth. His medical license was threatened.

I was in private practice then and the Federal Drug Enforcement Agency caught up with me. They'd been investigating one of the pharmacies that supplied me and when they looked at the records it seemed like my needs were excessive. That's why I was investigated. They didn't threaten me or anything. At least not directly. They just said they didn't know if I had a problem with drugs or not but that if I thought I did I should call up this particular guy who headed up a diversion committee for physicians and who might be able to help me get my life straight. That's when I got scared. I realized I might lose my license and I wouldn't be able to practice medicine anymore. But instead of thinking how to be honest with this man, I started right off figuring how I could con him.

My plan was not to use for a week before the interview and then say that I used to have a problem but that was in the past. Only I couldn't stop myself from using and it ended up that 15 minutes before my appointment with the man who held my professional fate in his hands, I ducked into the bathroom and shot up. So I went to the interview loaded. Eventually, I had to meet with the whole diversion committee. There was one guy on it who was a recovering Talwin addict and he saw right through me. They told me I had to go to the hospital, but I hid out for about two weeks until they caught up with me. This time, I went into a hospital treatment center where they really knew about addiction. I found out I was an addict, and after the shock wore off, I was relieved. I finally knew what was wrong with me.

That was six years ago.

DESIGNER DRUGS

Designer drugs are usually analogs of controlled drugs, slightly different but having many of the same properties. They are generally manufactured in small outlaw laboratories and often they are technically legal—temporarily—under provisions of the federal Controlled Substance Act because their molecular structure differs slightly from that of the controlled drug. Thousands of people possess the expertise to create these analogs. The ingredients are often cheap and readily available, the forumlas so simple they can be mixed by unqualified "biker" or "bucket" chemists. The design mistakes of these so-called chemists can be disastrous. An analog of the painkiller meperidine (Demerol) was found to contain a deadly neurotoxin when 400 drug abusers were suddenly struck by a syndrome similar to Parkinson's disease.

These powerful drugs need only be used in minute quantities. It has been said that with the contents of less than a full shopping bag, the entire addict population of a large city could be stoned for years. When such small amounts are involved, it is relatively easy for chemists working in illicit laboratories to go unnoticed by authorities.

Hundreds of deaths are attributed to designer drugs, and experts agree that many more deaths and toxic reactions go undiagnosed because these drugs are most commonly used by heroin addicts who overdose because they fail to respect the potency of even a fraction of a teaspoon of the analogs. Use of analogs may be spreading. From Atlanta there was a report of teenagers smoking a substance they called "juice": an analog mixed with cocaine. In urban areas a "casual" drug user may purchase cocaine and heroin cut with a designer analog.

One such category of analogs is based on the synthetic anesthetic fentanyl, which is used in hospitals. Fentanyl and its designer cousins pack a punch. In doses no larger than the head of a pin, they are described as being 100 times as strong as morphine and 20 to 40 times as strong as heroin. A group of analogs best described as cousins once removed from fentanyl are 2,000 to 6,000 times stronger than morphine. Dr. Will Spiegelman, an addiction specialist at Stanford University Hospital, says, "It can take years to become addicted to alcohol, months for cocaine and one shot for fentanyl."

The danger inherent in designer analogs is immense because a virtual clone can now be created for any abuseable substance. And totally new compounds—like Ecstasy, a derivative of an amphetamine and an hallucinogen—can be introduced to a population apparently willing to try anything that promises a new, more thrilling "high."

When Frank became a doctor there was no question what his medical specialty would be.

I always liked drugs. I grew up in a semirich artsy suburb in the 60s. When I was in high school, my parents were very hip. They smoked dope, did mushrooms, dropped acid. The whole thing. They never made much effort to hide what they were doing from us kids. I grew up knowing as soon as I could, I'd do drugs too.

I chose anesthesiology because the money is great. I mostly wouldn't have to get up in the middle of the night or do any heavy duty diagnostic stuff. I'd get to watch the surgery and be part of the team but I'd never have to put my own hands on someone's liver or heart or whatever. And it kind of turned me on to think of giving people drugs.

Frank married a nurse who also enjoyed using drugs, and for three years after his residence in a large urban medical center, they alternated work with play that included heavy drinking, marijuana and cocaine.

Somewhere along the way, I got hooked on cocaine, and so did Judy, my wife. We were both so buzzed all the time that we had to find some way to get down. Plus, there was other stuff going on. I look back now and I see how we were living was insane. We never rested. We acted like the world was some kind of playpen. We were in debt for expensive cars and a house at the lake. Both our families were hassling us. My older brother, who was also a doctor, just stopped having anything to do with me, and that was hard to take. And then, sometime while all this was going on, one of my buddies suggested Judy and I try morphine. The next thing I knew I was diverting the stuff from the hospital pharmacy and writing fake prescriptions. I couldn't believe I was doing it, but I did it anyway.

Before long, Frank and Judy became paranoid and suspected that at any moment hospital authorities would discover they were stealing drugs.

The crazy thing is we never thought of stopping. Instead, I can remember we went out to dinner and we had a very long serious talk about how we were going to obtain drugs away from the hospital. If someone had been watching us, they would have thought we were discussing the pros and cons of buying a new house. We were very logical about it. Judy did some inquiring. I talked to a couple of guys I knew and we ended up with the name of someone—a chemist who used to be with the DEA but had gone into business for himself. He ran a legitimate laboratory as well as making a fentanyl analog for his friends.

Judy told us:

Everything got bad from then on. Before we went outside the hospital, Frank and I could easily rationalize our drug use one way or another. What people don't understand is that denial comes easily to people in the medical profession. Actually, if you ask me, it's a necessary ingredient. We learn real early to deny our feelings. We're exhausted most of the time, but we tell ourselves we aren't. Our hearts ache for some patients, but we tell ourselves we don't feel anything. Someone dies and we want to grieve, but we brush it off. We say things like "death is part of life" and just keep on going. Plus, it's easy to deny you have a problem when you know you're still doing a good job. That's another thing most people don't understand. Drugs like fentanyl aren't like booze. My dad used to drink, and when he was loaded he was a sloppy fall-down drunk. For Frank and me, it was way different than that. I did my job and I did it well. It wasn't like Frank ever was out of control in the OR. He knew just how much dope to take to keep him out of withdrawal and still able to focus on the gauges. It may be hard to believe, but even after our friendly neighborhood chemist got shut down and Frank and I were buying on the street, we continued to believe we had professional integrity.

There is no telling how long Judy and Frank might have continued in this way before being found out. Intervention for them came from a family member: Frank's brother Lenny:

I knew what was going on for a long time. Maybe I should have stepped in earlier. All I know for sure is that it was the hardest thing I ever had to do. I loved my little brother, and I knew when I confronted him, he might never forgive me. But I also knew he was killing himself. He couldn't see it, of course, but it was perfectly plain something was wrong—wrong with both of them. Judy used to be this cute little ticket and Frank loved clothes. He dressed like something out of *Gentlemen's Quarterly*. There at the end, they were slobs. Half the time it looked like Frank had drooled down his lapels. I was ashamed to be seen with him. And his shirt collars were so dirty he looked like the before part of a TV ad. And you couldn't talk to them. They were bad tempered and didn't know how to have fun anymore. It was virtually impossible to have a conversation that amounted to more than a half dozen sentences.

Lenny told Frank and Judy that if they did not go into a drug-treatment program voluntarily, he would report them to the hospital authorities. At first Frank and Judy were furious. They left Lenny's house swearing they would never return.

But I couldn't ignore what Lenny said. I knew him, and I knew if he once threatened to do something, he never backed down. I thought about quitting my job before there could be an investigation, but if I tried to work somewhere else, Lenny'd mess that up for me too. I'll tell you, it was the strangest feeling. I wanted to quit using and I wanted to use. I wanted to quit my job and yet I knew that all my self-respect was tied up in being a doctor. Whatever I felt, I felt the opposite, which meant I was virtually immobilized. Judy was the same. We just took our syringes to bed with us and zoned out for two days. We never answered the phone or ate anything. Finally Judy called Lenny and told him that if he wanted us to go into a hospital, he'd have to take charge.

That was 16 months ago. Today Frank and Judy are heavily involved in addiction programs that involve the medical community. Judy lectures on alcoholism and addiction at two schools of nursing, and Frank has "gone public" with his story, hoping that by doing so more doctors and nurses will be able to confront their own addictions.

Because I'm a doctor, people tend to listen to me, so I also go out to schools and clubs and whatall, wherever someone'll give me a chance to say my piece. I talk about designer drugs and the menace I think they are. Not just to me and other doctors, but to kids who're looking for a new way to get a kick. Kids, who think they're immortal and that it never hurts to experiment a little. I talk to a lot of kids in school and I tell them this stuff kills.

POLYDRUG ABUSE

With all the chemicals available in the marketplace, polydrug use is becoming the norm. Cocaine abusers swallow pills to get themselves out of the terrible low that follows heavy cocaine use. Alcoholics pop pills to sustain them through a workday during which it will be impossible to take a drink. Pot smokers use "speed" to bring theselves out of a marijuana stupor. Amphetamine users—"speed freaks"—take tranquilizers or barbiturates to slow themselves down enough to get a night's sleep. Whatever drug your employee is using, there is another available that will intensify or ameliorate its effect.

Mixing drugs and alcohol is particularly dangerous. The most recent research indicates that in the body, alcohol and drugs that depress the central nervous system are metabolized by the same liver enzyme. When drugs and alcohol are taken in combination, the liver can work only on one substance at a time. Invariably, priority is given to alcohol. The other chemical must wait to be eliminated by the body's natural processes. And while they are waiting, their tranquilizing effects increase. If enough of the drug is taken, a toxic reaction similar to a coma may result. To further complicate the situation, in the body of an alcoholic—even at an early stage of the disease—the cells have been chemically altered. The result is that the alcoholic does not experience a drug's effect in the same way that a moderate or nondrinker does. Instead, he is able to tolerate drugs affecting the central nervous system because his system is already tolerant to alcohol. This phenomenon is called *cross-tolerance*. With repeated exposure to sedative or tranquilizing drugs, the alcoholic will develop an addiction to them more quickly than a person whose cell chemistry has not been altered by alcohol.

The vignette that follows tells what happened to Bob, a polydrug abuser we met when he entered a treatment facility.

I always believed drugs and stuff were like toys to help you get through life and have a good time. I smoked weed and drank beer when I was in high school and after I got out I went to work for a big construction firm and I still drank and smoked. All the guys did and if I'd not done that kind of stuff, they woulda thought I was weird.

Bob is 6-feet-3-inches tall and weighs just over 200 pounds. He has a broad smile and a hearty booming laugh. He looks like a man who enjoys working and playing out-of-doors.

After a few years, I started making good money so I could afford a little coke. Like two or three times a month. There was this guy came by the site and some of us'd buy from him on our break. But crystal was cheaper so we did a lot of that, which was great except for the morning after. I'd take speed to move the old bones, see? I liked 'ludes too. Sex was great with 'ludes. And a couple of times a guy I knew gave me some pills he got from a doctor, stuff called Dilaudid, that he said was good as heroin. I never tried heroin—I snorted it a few times but that doesn't count, right? I never wanted to mess with needles like an addict.

Eventually, Bob's polydrug use got him in trouble. One day at the construction site, he lost his footing and fell two stories to the rocky ground. He was hospitalized for two months and during that time he was persuaded to get treatment for chemical abuse.

It has not been the purpose of this chapter to make you an expert on the symptomology of drug and alcohol abuse. Nor did we intend that you should go through your workplace crying "Addict!" or "Alcoholic!" whenever an employee appears agitated or depressed or comes late to work. Rather, the purpose of these pages has been to familiarize you with the commonly abused chemicals and the behaviors that most often indicate that an employee is impaired by them. In our work, we have learned that managers and supervisors feel more confident in their ability to help impaired employees when they are well informed about the chemical marketplace.

As we have seen, drug use may intially appear to enhance employee performance. In creative fields, cocaine and marijuana may be regarded as enabling the creative process. In the beginning, benzodiazepine seems like a boon because it permits an employee in a stressful position to tolerate emotional strain at levels that would normally make him ill. The use of stimulant drugs like amphetamines extends the hours an employee is capable of working and boosts his or her energy to a level necessary to fill those extra hours. Even alcohol may seem like a beneficial social and business lubricant when used in moderation. In time, however, abuse of any chemical will poison even the most resiliant system. In an employee, this damage will manifest itself in deteriorating work performance.

An employee may abuse chemicals for a long time before the damage shows. But once the point of damage is reached, his downward slide is usually swift and steep. Passengers on a roller coaster rarely crash when they reach bottom. In that world of carnival unreality, the ups and downs and excited squeals continue until the ride ends and the passengers disembark, ready for their next adventure. The real world of chemical addiction is very different. In the crash that is inevitable for all drug and alcohol abusers, health and families are destroyed. Jobs are lost. Self-esteem vanishes.

But the chemically addicted person who gets help in combatting the disease has a chance to lead a happy and fruitful life. The roller coaster ride ends not in death but in sobriety. By being aware of the signs of workplace and employee impairment, by understanding the facts about the chemical marketplace and by being willing to intervene on employees whose performance is unsatisfactory, a manager or supervisor can literally save lives and at the same time increase business or industrial efficiency and productivity.

Most employers believe they have only two alternatives when confronted by an employee's deteriorating job performance: toleration or termination. This naive point of view wastes both lives and money. No employer needs to tolerate shoddy work performance. No employee needs to be fired as the result of suffering from a disease he or she has no power to control.

Intervention and treatment are the life-saving, money-saving alternative.

4

THE
FIRST
STEP

Step one in the corporate assault on drug and alcohol abuse is the creation of a comprehensive statement of the organization's policy. Included in this policy statement should be an explanation of all relevant procedures (see chapters "Documentation" and "Intervention") and a description of the program your company offers troubled employees (see "Establishing an Employee Assistance Program"). We divide the writing and implementing of the policy statement under three headings:

1. *Conviction*: You will have to convince important people in your organization that the policy and program are necessary.
2. *Consensus*: A team of writers representing all levels of the company will have to agree on the contents of the policy.
3. *Commitment*: You and your team will have to obtain a commitment to the principles of the policy from the entire workforce.

CONVICTION

Before you do anything else, you must convince your top-level managers that a policy and program are really necessary. This groundwork is crucial, for without their wholehearted support any drug and alcohol program is certain to fail. On-line supervisors must know that the steps they take to enforce company policy are endorsed throughout all levels of management and that in the event of employee complaints or administrative entanglements, management will support their efforts to keep the workplace clean.

You can expect to meet widespread resistance at this point. Denial will come in the guise of fiscal impossibility, personnel problems, naiveté and hopelessness. However, the material contained in this book will prepare you to meet arguments like these with persuasive facts and figures.

- We don't have a drug or alcohol problem in our organization.
- Our employees are too intelligent (sensitive, aware) to get involved with drugs.
- The supervisors will never be able to handle the responsibility.
- The unions will never cooperate.
- We don't have the staff to manage a program.
- There will be too much paperwork.
- We can't afford it.

How you go about convincing your people depends on the size of your company, its power structure and the intensity of the managerial denial you encounter. Persuasion may take as little as a few hours working one-on-one with key managers—those known to have influence among their colleagues—in order to release the power of peer pressure throughout your workplace. A more elaborate method involves convincing small groups of managers through in-house seminars conducted by an expert from a local drug and alcohol or employee assistance program.

In some cases, these two approaches can be combined effectively. For example, when the top management of a large wood-products corporation in the Northwest realized that impaired employees were costing the company millions of dollars and causing many accidents, the American Society of Safety Engineers (ASSE) was brought in to convince the rest of management of the need for a comprehensive drug and alcohol program. The ASSE developed a video presentation aimed specifically at the timber-products industry. The ASSE found that it was necessary to convince only a few top people of the need for a program. These few quickly spread the word, and through peer pressure the idea was sold.

If your people remain stubbornly reluctant, remind them it can be very expensive not to have a policy. In the most recent employee-grievance procedures and wrongful-discharge suits, arbitrators have repeatedly found in favor of employees and *against* the employer who does not have a clear and well publicized policy on drugs and alcohol. In the words of one Occupational Program Consultant, "If you don't have a policy or treatment alternative, arbitrators say you *do* have a policy and that is to *not* have one."

More directly stated, the trend in recent decisions is to obligate employers to agressively offer some variety of treatment in lieu of termination for impaired performance. An employer is not constrained to tolerate impaired performance indefinitely, but summary dismissal without ample warning can be financially risky. A popular marine park in California found this out to their regret.

An employee was accused of smoking marijuana while at work and fired on the spot. The employee sued and the case went to arbitration. Because he had been dismissed without warning and because the marine park made no effort to provide a rehabilitation program for its impaired employees, the parent company was ordered to award the employee $1 million.

CONSENSUS

The core of any drug and alcohol program is a clearly agreed upon statement of company policy regarding the use of drugs and alcohol by employees. Although this may seem obvious, surprisingly many companies have drug policies that are so outdated they fail to address the nature and scope of today's problems. Many more companies have no written policy at all.

Your drug and alcohol policy should be the product of a team of workers selected from every major department of your business. Such broad-based employee input will ensure that your policy is both realistic and relevant to problems actually encountered in the workplace. Labor representatives or junior employees must be included in the writing process as well as managers and supervisors. Typically, conflicts with labor center not on whether to have a policy and program but on how it should be administered. By taking pains to include influential leaders of this faction as early as possible in the planning process, you will have the advantage of their considerable power working for, and not against, your policy and program. The American Society of Safety Engineers (with wide experience in formulating policies for various businesses) recommends the team have more non-management and hourly representatives than top-level decision makers. Don't forget to include men and women from the departments of personnel, security, safety and medicine. A working group of 10 to 15 individuals is considered ideal.

It may be possible for your team to formulate a policy on its own; however, many companies find that hiring an experienced facilitator helps the group reach consensus more quickly. If you wish this kind of help, we recommend you contact the Association of Labor-Management Administrators and Consultants on Alcoholism. This organization, known by its acronym ALMACA, specializes in matching up occupational-program consultants and employers. ALMACA will provide you with the names and addresses of their members in your area.

ALMACA
1800 N. Kent St., Suite 907
Arlington, Virginia 22209
(703) 522-6272

Writing a policy without the assistance of a facilitator will challenge your skills as a moderator and mediator, but the experience can be a valuable one if it creates a shared sense of concern among members of the team. If yours is an organization with 100 or fewer employees, it can be an especially fruitful experience. The questions, topics, guidelines and policies on the following pages are aimed to assist you and your group in reaching the consensus necessary for a meaningful policy on drugs and alcohol in the workplace.

One of the first things that will become apparent is that team members almost always underestimate the complexity of the task ahead of them. To surmount this psychological hurdle, to reveal the team's biases, strengths and weaknesses, and to discover the function of drugs and alcohol in your organization, we recommend you begin the writing process with a structured discussion. In such a discussion there are no right or wrong answers. The aim is gathering information that will make the actual writing process easier. The following questions are suggested as a starting point. They will probably prompt others appropriate to your particular work environment. (You will need to remind your team that alcohol is a drug.)

- What constitutes drug abuse?
- Is there such a thing as recreational drug use?
- Are caffeine and nicotine drugs to be concerned with?
- What drugs are acceptable in the workplace? Why? Under what conditions? Are there exceptions?
- Are there drugs that some employees may use on their days or times off that affect job performance and job safety? Does the employer have the right to develop policies that affect employees' private time?
- Are there places on the worksite where drug use is acceptable? What about executive drug use?
- Is drug use among employees' families a concern? Can it affect productivity? How?
- Are drug tests and searches justifiable? What are the options other than tests and searches? How can employee rights and employer concerns about drug abuse be reconciled?
- How should an employee be warned that his job performance is unsatisfactory? How can help be made available to employees?
- Is prevention education effective? Can prevention education programs be made mandatory?

It has been our experience that many employers have never seen or worked with a comprehensive drug and alcohol policy. For this reason, we have included three samples of policies in this chapter to provide guidance and to serve as a checklist of considerations for your team.

Sample #1 is based on the policy of a large utility company and is notable for its brevity, punitive tone and failure to include alcohol abuse.

1. The illegal use, sale, or posession of narcotics, drugs, or controlled substances while on the job or on company property is a dischargeable offense. Any illegal substances will be turned over to the appropriate law-enforcement agency and may result in criminal prosecution.

2. Off-the-job illegal drug use which could adversely affect an employee's job performance or which could jeopardize the safety of other employees, the public, or company equipment is proper cause for administrative or disciplinary action up to, and including, termination of employment.

3. Employees who are arrested for off-the-job drug activity may be considered to be in violation of this policy. In deciding what action to take, management will take into consideration the nature of the charges, the employees' present job assignment, the employee's record with the company, and other factors relative to the impact of the employee's arrest upon the conduct of company business.

4. Some of the drugs that are illegal under federal, state and local laws include, among others, marijuana, heroin, hashish, cocaine, hallucinogens, and depressants and stimulants not prescribed for current personal treatment by an accredited physician.

5. Employees undergoing prescribed medical treatment with a controlled substance should report this treatment to their supervisor or the company medical department. The use of controlled substances as part of a prescribed medical treatment program is naturally not grounds for disciplinary action, although it is important for the company to know such use is occuring.

Sample #2 is also based on an actual policy currently in use. It employs the "carrot and the stick" principle. Employees are required to sign that they have read and understood the document at the time of hiring. They are presumed to know that if they have a problem and ask for help before their job performance is negatively impacted, their problem (whatever it is) will be treated with respect and concern. Failure to request help will result in the stick—dismissal. What is missing from this policy is any mention of the use of alcohol for business purposes.

1. This is a statement of the company's concern about alcohol and drug abuse as it affects job performance and the work environment and as it undermines the public's confidence in the company. It is clearly stated that the company will take disciplinary action against employees who use, distribute or possess controlled substances on or off the job and who violate company alcohol regulations.

2. Employees must report for work ready to work and in fit condition. Being under the influence of any drug (including alcohol) is prohibited.

3. Chemical abuse is recognized as a disease and the company provides help opportunities, although the responsiblity for seeking help rests with the employee. If the employee seeks help on his own then his job security, confidentiality and promotional opportunities are protected.

4.   Employees who use or distribute drugs on the job are subject to discharge and legal action.

5.   If an employee is arrested off the job for use of the illicit drugs, the company will consider the nature of the charges, his record with the company, present job assignment and other relevant factors before taking action.

6.   If an employee is under treatment with a drug that could alter his ability to to his job, it is his responsibility to inform his supervisor and accept job reassignment.

7.   Employees are requested to sign the policy statement.

Sample #3 comes from a multinational firm employing many thousands of men and women. Despite the size of the company, the policy has points you will find helpful in the creation of your own policy. This document is notable for the care with which it defines the specific occasions when various forms of alcohol are considered appropriate.

SUBJECT: Drugs

The use, distribution, sale or possession of any drugs or other controlled substances for nonmedical reasons, on company premises or in any company work environment (including parking areas) is prohibited. Disciplinary action, including possible dismissal, will be taken in cases where violations occur. (Possession alone, depending upon the circumstances, may or may not result in dismissal.) Employees who are not under the influence of any such nonmedical drugs are prohibited from company premises or any other company work environment.

This company position is the same whether narcotics, marijuana, sedatives or stimulants are involved.

Managers are responsible for communicating to every employee that, regardless of trends toward more lenient local laws regarding marijuana violations, the company position applies to all drugs or other controlled substances, including marijuana.

SUBJECT: Liquor Policy

The following are principles of the liquor policy:

Alcoholic beverages are not served on company premises.

Alcoholic beverages are not served as part of any business meeting held by the company to conduct its internal affairs.

Light alcoholic beverages such as wine or beer may be served at company-sponsored social functions at outside facilities. Management must consider whether serving wine or beer is appropriate to the particular event and, if so, insure that the service is managed with good judgment.

No alcoholic beverages should be served at any company function where children are in attendance.

Social club activities, held off-premises and paid for on a personal basis, are not affected by the liquor policy.

SUBJECT: Drug Abusers and Problem Drinkers
Medical Aspects of Drug Abuse

Information about the signs and symptoms of excessive use of alcohol or taking of drugs subject to abuse may be obtained by managers through consultation with company medical departments.

The principal knowledge required of a company manager is sensitivity to the behavior of his or her employees. Work performance is the key issue. Changes in performance and in behavioral characteristics may indicate the onset of a wide range of emotional and physical problems. At times such changes can be a manifestation of problem drinking or drug abuse. In either event the resources of the company medical department should be enlisted.

Cases referred to the medical department will be carefully evaluated. The abuse of alcohol and drugs must be regarded as a symptom of a complex underlying health problem. After diagnostic evaluation, the medical staff, often in conjunction with the individual's family physician, will recommend specific treatment programs. In most instances the program will include abstinence from the substance involved. The program will utilize both company and community resources for anyone diagnosed as a drug or alcohol abuser. Hospital and medical expenses incurred under the program in approved institutions and by physicians or other eligible practitioners will be covered under the company medical plan benefits. Under the program, employees are prohibited from taking any unscheduled vacation and must in advance clear all absences through the medical department or local medical consultant. Periodically, the medical department will interview the employee and may conduct physical examinations and laboratory analyses.

Employees who are placed on a rehabilitation program because of performance or behavior problems attributable to drug or alcohol abuse are subject to dismissal for failure to correct such problems.

Management Education
The best way for all managers to become familiar with the identification and handling of drug abuse and problem drinking is to include education on the subject in management development classes.

All company Medical Departments are in a position to provide professional instruction on this subject.

SUBJECT: Drug Abusers and Problem Drinkers
Although the company has a relatively low incidence of alcohol and drug-abuse problems, it is imperative that all managers clearly understand our position on all such forms of abuse. That position is the same whether alcohol, narcotics, marijuana, sedatives or stimulants are involved. Managers are responsible for communicating to every employee that, regardless of trends toward more lenient local laws regarding marijuana violations, the company's position applies to all drugs or other controlled substances, including marijuana.

Simply stated, the use, distribution, sale or possession of any drugs or other controlled substances for nonmedical reasons, on company premises or in any company work environment (including parking areas) is prohibited. Disciplinary action, including possible dismissal, will be taken in cases where violations occur. (Possession alone, depending upon the circumstances, may or may not result in dismissal.) Employees who are under the influence of any such nonmedical drugs are prohibited from company premises or any other company work environments.

At the same time, the company recognizes the health implications of alcohol and drug abuse. Company medical departments are prepared to evaluate and assist employees in programs of rehabilitation. In every instance of suspected employee alcohol or drug abuse, managers will consult with their local or area medical department and, where appropriate, Personnel and Legal.

Definition of a Drug Abuser

An alcohol or drug abuser is defined by the company as an individual whose use of such substances for nonmedical reasons adversely affects satisfactory job performance or interferes with normal social adjustments at work. This becomes both a company medical and a management problem. All company medical departments have detailed instructions regarding the identification and treatment of employees with such problems.

Use, Sale or Possession of Drugs

Incidents involving use, possession, sale, or distribution of illicit drugs may require the company to notify appropriate authorities. Such action will be taken only after review with the responsible personnel, medical, legal and security staff in the company.

Arrest or Indictment in Connection with Drugs

Employees who are arrested for a charge related to illegal use, sale or possession of drugs or alcohol are subject to the applicable practices concerning arrest and conviction.

If after arrest or indictment on a drug or alcohol charge a decision is made to continue the employee at work, the manager will send the individual to a company medical department for evaluation under the company's program for drug abusers and problem drinkers. Should the medical department confirm a diagnosis of addiction or abuse, participation in the program will be a condition of continued employment. Arrangement will be made by area medical directors for local medical consultation in locations not served by medical departments. In all instances the employee will be urged to consult with an attorney before reaching a decision with respect to participation in the program. However, failure to participate, whether with or without legal counsel, will result in dismissal.

Any manager who suspects such a problem case should discuss the situation immediately with the appropiate local medical department or physician. This is important not only so that such cases can be referred at the earliest possible moment, but also so that managers who may not be sufficiently experienced to evaluate such cases properly will not draw inaccurate conclusions.

Recognizing the highly individual nature of these problems, the diagnosis and handling of each individual case should be closely coordinated between management and the physician.

Applicants with a History of Drug Abuse

Applicants having a past history of a serious drinking problem or of drug abuse and who have demonstrated an ability to remain free of use or under medically acceptable control may be considered for employment.

Bearing in mind the previous discussion and the sample policies, the following list of guidelines can be used to fine-focus the team's attention on the items to cover in your organization's policy.

- What is prohibited? When and where? What about employee banquets, recognition dinners, executive dining rooms, etc.?
- Off duty involvement with drug or alcohol abuse will result in what? How will such cases be reviewed? What will be the factors considered?
- Drug screening: Who? When required? When optional? Follow-up screenings?
- When, under what circumstances, will an employee be searched? Can a car be searched? A locker?
- How will your policy handle those caught selling or distributing?
- How will unsatisfactory work be documented?
- How will an employee be warned that his work is unsatisfactory?
- What channels are available to help the troubled employee?
- What about job protection for an employee who gets treatment?
- What about confidentiality?
- What about prescription medication?
- Who is responsible for informing the employee of the policy?

When a draft version of your business' drug policy has been agreed upon by team members, copies of it should be posted throughout the workplace.

The wording of this early draft policy and any accompanying memoranda is important and will affect the way your employees react to the policy itself. Whenever you speak or write about the policy and the program that will accompany it, people will be listening with a critical ear. And it's virtually certain that much of the response will be negative—at least in the beginning. At first, a drug and alcohol policy may seem threatening to some employees. To others it may seem like an intrusion into their private life. A few will regard it as just another management weapon. But attitudes are not cast in cement, and people frequently change their minds. Make sure that all your memos are designed to win friends for the policy and program.

BE STRAIGHTFORWARD

We recommend that you state the problem clearly so that everyone will understand that the health of the company is put at risk by the handful of employees who abuse chemicals. Some managers are reluctant to be candid for fear their company image will be tarnished by even the mention of the problems created by drugs and alcohol in the workplace. They choose to speak guardedly. Their memos are vague and easily misinterpreted. Invariably, the drug and alcohol policies at such companies are ineffective because it is clear that management does not really wish to acknowledge the problem, so why fine the employees?

BE POSITIVE

A good drug and alcohol policy sets clear and understandable limits on employee behavior. It is not a punitive document aimed at searching out malefactors. It does not attach negative labels to any group. Memoranda that accompany copies of the policy should also be positive in tone.

ENCOURAGE DISCUSSION

In all memoranda, we recommend that you encourage discussion among employees and specifically solicit their input. Let them know that you want their suggestions about how to make the policy most effective. Many experts believe that one reason drugs and alcohol are a problem in today's workplace is the secrecy in which we have traditionally shrouded the subject. A vital first step to overcoming this corporate denial is encouraging employees to talk about the problem. And if at this stage you discover your workplace is more seriously impaired than you thought—so much the better. You will be able to face the problem squarely if you know its full extent.

COMMITMENT

No matter how carefully your team works to write a drug and alcohol policy that is fair, no matter how seriously they solicit employee opinion, it will still be necessary to "sell" the policy to the workforce at large in order to gain widespread commitment to its principles. Your company's drug and alcohol policy needs the enthusiastic commitment of all those men and women who do an honest day's work month after month, year after year, and form the backbone of American business and industry. Their support is crucial for the success of your policy and program.

The best salespeople will be the members of the policy-drafting team. Their own commitment as well as their recently enhanced education are likely to convince many doubters of the policy's necessity and worth. In some work environments, a button-wearing program has influenced peer opinion in favor of the firm's drug policy. Workers who would never voice their personal convictions aloud are often willing to wear buttons that make strong statements against workplace drugs and alcohol when they see a team member proudly displaying one on a lapel. Tee shirts, stickers and bumperstickers can be similarly utilized.

Your policy may also be boosted by articles in company newsletters or memos. These should explain why it is important for your company to have a drug and alcohol policy. Be frank and factual about the problems drug and alcohol abuse are causing in the workplace. If drugs and alcohol threaten the company's financial stability—say so! Help employees understand why keeping a drug-free workplace is a cooperative effort.

We know of several companies that include in their in-house publications anonymous letters written directly to drug-and-alcohol-abusing employees. The letters inform these employees that their impairment works against fellow employees, jeopardizes everyone's job, and that it will not be supported or covered up anymore. Specific information is included on how troubled employees may get help without threatening their job security. Nevertheless, the letters also make clear that continued violation of the company's policy will result in dismissal.

Increasingly, companies are choosing to involve workers' families in the effort to widen the range of opinion against drug and alcohol abuse. To this end, you may include copies of your company's policy, brochures, letters and articles, buttons and bumper stickers in payroll envelopes, or inside direct mailings to workers' homes. Booths, banners, posters and attention-grabbing displays at company picnics, work fairs and open houses will also help to spread the word that your business has a clear policy against drug and alcohol abuse and that fighting abuse in the workplace is a cooperative effort in which the whole family can become involved.

Finally, remember that a drug and alcohol policy is not a punitive document. Its most effective use is twofold. First, it brings the subject of drug and alcohol abuse into the open and focuses attention on a pervasive problem that is commonly denied, ignored or tolerated. Your employees can no longer claim as their defense ignorance of the company's standards. Second, the policy provides the basis for your company's program to help troubled employees. Just as these workers cannot claim ignorance, the supervisor is now absolutely required to take action to improve work standards. The drug and alcohol policy provides the rationale under which supervisors can be trained to document unsatisfactory job performance and conduct workplace intervention.

5

TRAINING SUPERVISORS AND VOLUNTEERS

Working in the field of alcoholism and drug addiction, we are often struck by what a contradictory creature the human animal is. One might assume that supervisors would be enthusiastic about doing their part in the workplace campaign against drug and alcohol abuse when there is clinical evidence of the damage done by drugs and alcohol, when every newspaper and magazine carries stories about drug-prevention measures, when national heroes are literally dying from chemical abuse. Yet, in our experience, the opposite is true.

Few supervisors are eager to become involved. They offer many excuses—paperwork, ignorance, lack of time—but what it comes down to is the peculiar fact that for any number of reasons, the subject of drugs and alcohol is difficult for most people to handle. Yet, to make your company drug and alcohol program a success, these reluctant supervisors are the very people you must depend upon. The question of how to enlist their support and overcome their reluctance has been the subject of much study by occupational behaviorists. Their best findings make up the bulk of this chapter.

Whether you choose to implement the drug and alcohol program yourself or to enlist the help of an employee-assistance program, supervisors wil require training and preparation for their responsibilities. The purpose of all supervisory training is to educate and motivate.

EDUCATE

Despite a superficial knowledge garnered from the media, employees are largely ignorant about drugs and alcohol, particularly how they affect the workplace. One of the first goals of supervisory training is the presentation of some hard facts. Going into a training program, most workers assume drugs and alcohol cause problems at *other* worksites. To enlist their support, it will be necessary to overcome this mistaken assumption. Confide in them. Tell them that last year the company lost X number of dollars due to excessive absenteeism. Talk about the kinds of accidents that put every worker at risk, the rising cost of insurance benefits and any other information you have to prove there is a problem at your company.

Although your supervisors will not be asked to hunt down addicts and alcoholics, they will need some basic education about drugs and alcohol. Like most people who read the paper and watch TV news, they probably think they know plenty already. Actually what they have is a great many half-truths and downright misinformation. How many, for example, know that marijuana abuse may cause a breakdown of the body's immune system? Do they know that a glass of beer has just as much alcohol as a martini? How many realize that alcohol is this country's most commonly and dangerously abused drug?

In most communities you will have no difficulty finding sources of reliable information about chemical addiction. Some cities and counties have opened special offices intended to answer questions and educate the public on the subject. To determine if yours is one of these, just call the information number for all county and city offices. In the phone book under both "drugs" and "alcohol" will be dozens of numbers to call. Hospitals and treatment centers are also excellent resources.

We know of a small company in Southern California that employs fewer than 100 men and women, the majority single people under 30 years of age. The owner suspected that many of his company's problems—an extremely high rate of absenteeism, dips in productivity at certain times and on certain days, increased complaints about product quality—might be caused by employees impaired by drug use. The company was too small to make an elaborate drug and alcohol program feasible, but the owner decided he could create a small program based on education.

He called the director of a nearby hospital-treatment program and discussed his needs. Two weeks later, a speaker from the treatment program—a well-informed young woman who was herself a recovering alcoholic with many years of sobriety—began a series of seminars aimed at educating every employee in the company on the facts of drug and alcohol use and misuse, signs of abuse in the family and workplace and treatment alternatives.

Although a live presentation is an excellent way to educate employees and correct misinformation, there is a growing body of written and taped material relating to all aspects of chemical abuse. One of the best sources for books, pamphlets, brochures and audio/video tapes is the highly reputable Hazelden Foundation, Box 176, Center City, Minnesota, 55012. Within the continental United States, the toll-free number for one of Hazelden's Educational Outreach Specialists is 800-328-9000. In Minnesota and outside the continental states, the number is 612-257-4010. Although information is available from many other sources as well, Hazelden materials are an excellent place to begin sorting the truth from the myths surrounding chemical abuse.

Your supervisors must be conversant with details of the company drug and alcohol policy and program. No one should be left with any doubt about the extent of labor and management commitment. Obviously, if your supervisors think you are only giving lip service to the problem, they will follow your lead. If they believe organized labor disapproves of the policy and program, they may subvert any efforts you make.

Initially, supervisors are going to think they are being trained to "bird dog" addicts and alcoholics. Many times throughout the training, the trainer will repeat that when it comes time to work with individual employees, the supervisor's only concern is patterns of deteriorating job performance like those described in the next chapter. If they go looking for alcoholics and addicts—sniffing breath and suspecting every runny nose—they are likely to miss all the other signs of lives falling to pieces. In fact, there is some evidence that looking for addicts and alcoholics instead of focusing on job performance actually leads to fewer referrals. A trainer can correct the areas in which employees operate under false information.

One common mistake has to do with the results of an intervention procedure. Some supervisors hold to the view that an intervention will "ruin" an employee's career. The trainer can set them straight about this by pointing out that the company policy is nonpunitive and that an intervention is intended to *save* the employee's career and even his life. The trainer can make sure they understand that there is no use waiting for a problem to disappear of its own accord. Problems don't go away when they're ignored: marriages get worse; finances get further in the red; alcoholics go from sick to very sick to dead.

One of the most frequently expressed objections of supervisors concerns the need to document unsatisfactory work performance. They sometimes act as if they are being abused when asked to do what they are uniquely qualified to do: supervise employee performance. The real problem relates to their own performance, however. Although they are not generally aware of it, supervisors fear they will make mistakes on documents and that those errors will come back to haunt them. The trainer can modify this negativism by showing supervisors that the forms are easy and quick to use. Hands-on experience documenting the workplace behavior of fictitious employees goes a long way toward relieving supervisors' anxieties.

MOTIVATE

Education and modifying supervisors' erroneous beliefs provide valuable motivation for supervisory cooperation in the program. But there is more you can do to fire their enthusiasm. Let your people know you will be judging their ability to supervise by the way they use the program. Make sure they understand that in your eyes, there is a correlation between a healthy work environment and supervisors who document employee performance, manage work evaluations confidently and have an active concern for the well-being of those who work under their supervision.

We recommend that two trainings be held for supervisors. The first and most basic of these will educate and motivate with the aim of immediate program implementation. The second training is a troubleshooting session in which specific supervisory problems are discussed and the reactive problems of supervisors are addressed.

BASIC TRAINING
FOR SUPERVISORS

Planning and conducting training sessions is a skill in which many people specialize. To determine who will lead yours, we suggest you look first to your own pool of employees. If someone on your staff specializes in giving trainings on such things as employee health, safety, insurance and the like, his office is the natural place for you to begin your search for a trainer. Another starting point is with a business colleague who has organized similar supervisory trainings at his worksite. Barring these alternatives, we suggest you call the treatment facilities in your area and explain your need. Most have an industrial outreach or community outreach specialist whose job it is to conduct training sessions. Shop around for the one who most suits your needs. The cost should be minimal, perhaps nothing at all.

The training should not be held until your program is ready to go. Ideally, your trained supervisors will leave the conference room with all the appropriate forms and booklets, prepared to begin documenting job performance immediately.

Obviously, a trainer must be an expert in the field of chemical addiction. But more than this, a good trainer is a sensitive judge of situation and character, able to present the subject in a nonthreatening manner. It is definitely not the job for a self-righteous amateur armed with myths and half-truths. Such a person can do more harm than good, as happened when a large metropolitan high school, unable to use a qualified trainer, enlisted a health-education teacher to train a group of peer counselors in the dangers of marijuana. Afterwards, the students told us that the teacher/trainer knew less about marijuana than they did. Her outdated facts and melodramatic style of speaking undermined the credibility of the school's efforts to inform students about the risks involved in even so-called recreational drug use.

Where and when a training is held will vary according to management's commitment to the issue. Experience has shown that voluntary trainings held after work or on weekends will not be well attended. Attempts to cover the material by means of a brochure or a five-minute talk between shifts do little more than waste time and money. In our experience, those managers who have chosen to include the training session in the supervisors' workday have received benefits that ultimately made up for cost in off-the-job man hours. When a supervisor is pulled from his regular work station and told to spend two hours listening and asking questions about chemical addiction, a clear message goes out to every employee: the management of this company is serious about keep drugs and alcohol out of the workplace.

No more than 25 supervisors should make up a training group, and the session should last a minimum of two hours. Actually, two hours is scarcely enough; but an experienced trainer guided by a carefully specific plan can cover a good deal of material in two hours. The drawback to short training sessions is that they are largely in the lecture format. Experience has shown that training that encourages supervisory participation has the greatest long-term effectiveness.

Although you will probably not be doing the training yourself, we believe that employee programs work best when management fully understands the procedures and their rationale. Therefore, both you and the trainer will want to be clear about the specific behavioral goals you have. We recommend you make a list that looks something like this.

At the end of the first training, supervisors will:
1. be able to communicate job performance expectations to each other and to those they supervise;
2. be able to detect patterns of impaired job performance;
3. be able to use all documents with confidence;
4. be able to go through the intervention process with confidence;
5. be able to explain the company's drug and alcohol program;
6. be able to answer questions regarding the program.

Each training, whether it lasts two hours or two days, should be divided into five sections.

SECTION ONE: MOTIVATION

This is the motivational phase, during which employees are educated not only about drugs and alcohol in the workplace but about all the personal issues that may affect job performance. The trainer may solicit supervisory input as to what such issues are: divorce, children, finances, health, etc.

In this section the trainer emphasizes the positive goals of documentation and job intervention. He makes it clear how the employee is helped, how the workplace is made to function more efficiently and profitably, and how the supervisor's position is enhanced.

SECTION TWO: PERFORMANCE EVALUATION

At this point, supervisors need help identifying the criteria for a job performance evaluation. This may be the first time in their careers that they have been asked to specify acceptable and unacceptable levels of performance. Some jobs carry with them a list of specific factors that constitute poor, fair, good and excellent job performance. Others depend on the supervisor's specialized knowledge of the job. However your workplace is organized, this discussion can be a valuable and effective focusing tool that will enable supervisors to observe and evaluate employees more fairly and effectively.

The following hypothetical discussion, while extremely simplified, will give you an idea how trainers handle this difficult aspect of training.

Trainer:	Fred, what kind of employees do you supervise?
Fred:	Draftsmen.
Trainer:	Let's start with draftsmen then. What characteristics describe a good draftsman? How would you describe his performance?
Fred:	He makes accurate measurements. He uses his drawing equipment correctly. His printing and numbers are easy to read. His drawings are clean. . . .
Trainer (to the whole group):	What can the rest of you contribute?
Tom:	He gets to work on time.
Fred:	He meets deadlines.
Jim:	He stays at his drawing board except for breaks.
Tom:	He doesn't leave early.
Trainer:	Can you put that in positive terms, Tom?
Tom:	He works a full day.

This is the kind of discussion supervisors warm to. At first they may be slow to contribute but once they get the idea of what is expected, they can usually give a detailed description of acceptable job performance. While the supervisors talk, the trainer jots down the descriptive items in a list.

Trainer:	Now that we have a good idea what makes a good draftsman, let's figure out the characteristics of unacceptable work performance. Fred, can you get us started on this list?
Fred:	He talks when he should be drawing and he drinks with the contractors at lunch.

Jim: Makes mistakes in his calculations.
Tom: Comes in late and leaves early.
Fred: Loses his equipment.

The aim of this section is consensus. Although certain generalized statements can be made describing all good employees (e.g., they come to work on time and don't take unnecessary sick days; they get along with other workers and have good safety records), workers in particular jobs will demonstrate particular characteristics of excellence and inadequacy. At the end, the supervisors will be able to agree upon what those characteristics are.

SECTION THREE: DOCUMENTATION

When they understand what is meant by acceptable and unacceptable job performance, the supervisors can be shown how to use the documentary forms. At this time, the trainer will caution them about the absolute necessity for confidentiality. It is also appropriate to clarify the procedural format at this time.

Experience has proved that unless supervisors are forewarned and repeatedly reminded, they will have difficulty getting down to the actual documentation. They will find numerous excuses—too much to do, forgetfulness, etc. Closer to the truth is the fact that most supervisors go through a period of denial—like everyone else connected with the disease of chemical addiction. Prepare your supervisors for this. Give them some background on denial, and help them understand how they are likely to behave with an impaired employee if they don't take care of the situation by documentation and intervention.

Studies of supervisory behavior show that they first try to ignore the problem. Sometimes they do a little more work themselves or try some reassignments. They often make excuses for the impaired employee to avoid examining him and his problem directly.

Next they are likely to try talking with the individual, giving a little advice and a Dutch uncle's offer of help. It is surprising how many supervisors report having loaned impaired employees money.

Third will come the pleading and/or threatening stage: straighten up, or else.

Finally, acting out of frustration, guilt, anger or hurt (and frequently a combination of all four), the supervisor takes disciplinary action. Action that fails more often than not because it is rarely supported by adequate documentation.

In the upcoming chapters on documentation and intervention, we present a format that allows for three warnings of increasing severity before a supervisor must take disciplinary action. Later in the book, we talk about Last Chance Agreements. If you decide to follow our format and include the Last Chance Agreement or if you prefer to create an agreement of your own, you will want your supervisors to understand each step.

SECTION FOUR: ASSISTANCE

How employees are helped by your program depends on the choices you make after reading this book. Many employers prefer not to involve themselves directly in the helping aspect. For them a contracted employee-assistance program is perfect. But perfection may be expensive depending on your locale and the number of employees in your organization. Probably the least expensive assistance program provides each supervisor with a supply of booklets listing the community health resources available to employees. Entries include a range of drug and alcohol treatment centers, agencies providing family, child, marriage and financial counseling, self-help groups like AA, the mental health association, and so on. The booklet also describes what insurance coverage is provided for employees. Supervisors are instructed to make these booklets available to employees at all times but most especially on the occasion of an unsatisfactory job-performance evaluation.

Any number of program variations are possible between this example and the extensive in-house operations run by many large companies. Whether you prefer a structured program or one with many options and choices left up to the employee, the chapter entitled "Establishing an Employee Assistance Program" provides step-by-step procedures to put a program into operation.

Regardless of how employees are offered help in your company, during the fourth segment of the training the trainer will familiarize supervisors with the agencies, treatment facilities and self-help organizations locally available. At this point in the session, most trainers encounter a supervisory bias against social service agencies. The opinion often expressed is that they are run by ineffectual do-gooders and waste taxpayers' money. Obviously, supervisors who feel this way can do more harm than good. Their objections need to be addressed and modified.

This is also the time to talk about insurance. Supervisors need to know, in general, what their company policy will cover. Is it medical alone or is treatment for mental health problems included? Is payment in full or a percentage of the bill? Make sure they know where to send employees for answers to the questions they can't answer themselves.

SECTION FIVE: QUESTIONS AND ANSWERS

This is the time for an open exchange of ideas.

A few of your supervisors will have no questions, no complaints. They will understand and manage the documentation and intervention process with no trouble. Many more will have trouble at least initially, and for them you need to make some kind of help available. There should be one person on your staff who can advise and reassure troubled supervisors when they encounter a particularly trying employee or when, as is often the case, they wonder about the standards they have set for job performance. Many supervisors experience high stress levels during the first year of a drug and alcohol program. They are gratified and relieved when management acknowledges this by providing them with an advisor to take care of the small problems before they grow large and threaten the whole program.

TRAINING TECHNIQUES

If the trainer has time, he is well advised to involve supervisors in the training process. There are many techniques for doing this, a few of which are described below.

- Overhead transparencies or slides can draw the audience's attention to specific facts, statistics, flow charts.
- Buzz sessions work well during Section Two of the training. Rather than the trainer working at a blackboard with the whole group and laboriously going through several different job descriptions, divide the supervisors into small groups. Let each group reach a consensus for the characteristics of excellence and inadequacy for one or two jobs. At the end each chooses a spokesman who presents the information to the whole group. In this way, a large number of people can cover quite a lot of material quickly.
- Movies are available to clarify each segment of the training. THE INTERNATIONAL INDEX TO MULTI-MEDIA INFORMATION is a listing of films, slides and tapes covering almost every subject. Included are many titles relevant to supervisory training. The INDEX is available through most libraries.
- A video camera used in connection with role playing can help a supervisor to understand his strengths and weaknesses when confronting an employee. But the first video session is rarely successful. Usually people are much too embarrassed by the sight of themselves on the screen to learn anything from the experience. The video camera works best with small groups in long training programs when it is possible to film everyone at least twice.
- Role playing is an excellent way for supervisors to overcome their fear of the job performance interview. Three people are chosen for each scenario. The trainer sets the scene.

For example:

Mo Smith is a draftsman with five years experience. During the last two months you have documented his coming late to work X times, leaving early X times, taking long lunch hours X times. On two different occasions he has lost expensive pieces of drafting equipment. His drawings were smudged and dirty on X occasions. He made calculation errors on X plans.

The scene to be role played is one of constructive confrontation between a supervisor and the employee, Mo Smith. While it is going on, the third participant acts as the critical observer, checking off items on two lists.

Supervisor's Effective Intervention Techniques:
- Tells employee how and when his/her performance is impaired
- Discusses only job performance, is not distracted
- Makes sure the employee understands criticism
- Makes sure employee understands that this is a time limited warning
- Details available help: EAP, medical benefits, etc.
- Solicits employee commitment to correct problem

Supervisor's Ineffective Intervention Techniques:
- Is distracted by employee's discussion of personal problems
- Presents inadequate documentation of impaired performance
- Tries to tell the employee what his/her problem is
- Tries to give advice
- Lectures the employee
- Threatens the employee

After each role playing, let the person acting the supervisory role evaluate his own performance first. Then discuss the observer's checklist. Each person should have the opportunity to assume each role.

The trainer will probably encounter aversion to this training technique. He will be told what he already knows: if supervisors wanted to be actors they wouldn't be supervisors. But it has been our experience that role playing touches some deep chord in all of us—perhaps a childhood memory or the wish to escape the limitations of ourselves if only for a few moments—and almost everyone can enjoy and learn from it.

FOLLOWUP TRAINING FOR SUPERVISORS

Wade supervises the night shift at a popular 24-hour restaurant—one of hundreds in a nationwide chain. According to his company's drug and alcohol policy, it is his responsibility to document impaired job performance and conduct interventions in the form of performance reviews. Wade has been through a company training program and had no trouble with the procedure until a new cook came to work the night shift. He was a big, tough-talking man who routinely punched-in late and took frequent breaks to go sit in his car. His orders came up overcooked and messy. The kitchen was not kept clean and everyone who worked with him complained of his bullying manner. Although Wade kept some records documenting this behavior, he found it impossible to confront the cook in a job performance review. Weeks passed and Wade began taking tranquilizers to cope with feelings of inadequacy and self-loathing. The job he once enjoyed became a burden to him.

Susan manages a radio station connected to a large university that has a drug and alcohol policy requiring documentation and intervention. As part of her duties, she supervises two dozen talented specialists: engineers, producers, and on-air-personalities. One of these, Jackson, was a disc jockey for an all-night jazz program. Jackson did his own engineering and so worked most of the night alone. Although he had a large and loyal following, some listeners began to complain that broadcast quality was inferior. Jackson left the turntable unattended. Records that got stuck stayed stuck. His programming was repetitous. His hourly news headlines were garbled and unprofessional. Some of Jackson's humor was inappropriate to the public airways. Susan knew she should confront Jackson with the documentation of his impaired job performance, but she was reluctant to do so. He was known to have a ferocious temper, which she feared arousing. Susan is an excellent manager and normally has no trouble dealing with both men and women. Her inability to deal with Jackson made her begin to doubt her fitness for the job.

The stories of Wade and Susan demonstrate that able and well-trained supervisors may have trouble implementing their company's drug and alcohol policy when it calls for a confrontation over job performance. Although Wade and Susan did eventually overcome their difficulties, the change did not occur magically or overnight. Each took part in supervisory training that helped them understand the reasons for their discomfort.

The followup training should be conducted six weeks to three months after the first session. It can be conducted by the same trainer, held in the same room; even the same people participate. For this training it will not be easy to define specific behavioral goals. In general, what the trainer will want is to:

- answer employee questions about the program and procedures;
- further educate where necessary;
- further modify attitudes;
- overcome supervisory reluctance to intervene.

It is this last item that can make the big difference in the way a program works. Susan and Wade were well informed about the workings of their programs and they were familiar with the documents and procedures. Nevertheless, they were virtually paralyzed when it came to intervening on behalf of the cook and Jackson.

Anger, guilt, feelings of inadequacy and fear—these are the four painful emotions an impaired employee can arouse in a supervisor. It is quite normal for them to react to these powerful and unpleasant feelings by avoiding the employee who causes them. Under these circumstances, an intervention is the last thing they want to do. Wade took tranquilizers and came to work late so as to minimize contact with the man who made him feel weak and inadequate. Susan went looking for another job because fear of Jackson's temper made her doubt her ability to function as a professional.

Wade and Susan were helped by a training session that emphasized the *feelings* associated with the documentation and intervention process. Encouraged by the training facilitator to share openly with other supervisors, they came to appreciate that having feelings of anger, guilt, inadequacy and fear did not make them failures at their jobs. As a matter of fact, they found themselves in good company. However, the real help came when they understood how their feelings were *reactive*, triggered by the behavior of the employee.

Special training techniques have been devised to uncover and lessen the negative power of supervisors' reactive feelings. The trainer asks supervisors to list the general characteristics of an impaired employee. These are written in a list on a chalkboard or overhead transparency. Then they are asked what feelings these characteristics arouse in them. Replies such as "I get angry" or "I feel guilty" are encouraged and written on a parallel list. Finally, supervisors are asked to describe what they do when they expereince the behaviors listed in the second column. Answers in the third list range from "Nothing" to "I went home early" to "I kicked the dog."

What is the purpose of all this listing? It encourages supervisors to talk about what is bothering them, to discover the common threads in all their reactions, to sympathize with one another and—in the best trainings—to understand that in some ways their behavior has been similar to that of the impaired employee. They, too, have denied a problem rather than deal with it. They, too, have been concealing their problem from the world. When this similarity between themselves and their nemesis is revealed, there is generally a lot of laughter. Feelings of guilt, anger and fear begin to dissipate.

"I never got over my fear of Jackson," Susan told us many months later. "And when I finally did the intervention, he got angry just as I knew he would. But I pulled it off anyway and I think that's because I really had myself scoped out. I knew what was going on in my mind and the training taught me to pay attention to those internal messages and respect them. After that I never had any feeling things would get out of control."

EVALUATION OF SUPERVISORY TRAINING SESSIONS

When your program is established and appears to be running smoothly, it is time to solicit your supervisors' reactions and comments about the way they were trained. You will want to know which sections of the training program were most helpful and which were the least. Ask questions regarding the techniques used, the time alloted to the sessions, and the specific subjects covered. Leave an empty place on the form and request comments. A sample form is included in the chapter titled "Establishing an Employee Assistance Program."

TRAINING VOLUNTEERS

Depending on the kind of program you decide to have, you may wish to include employee volunteers in the fight against chemical abuse. How and by whom you company's volunteers are trained will vary from program to program. Often the same person who educates and trains supervisors to document impaired performance can prepare a core of volunteers in the workplace. In programs around the country, these volunteers go by many names—referral agents, key employees, peer counselors. But in general, their job description is the same.

The volunteer is a good listener, a person who relates well to his coworkers at all levels and has a good work record. Volunteers may come from the rank and file of employees, from special offices like personnel and medical, from your organization's population of recovering addicts and alcoholics. One company we know started its program with a single volunteer—a vice president who came out of treatment for alcoholism convinced that no one should have to suffer from such a terrible disease. The vice president abandoned his anonymity and made it clear to the entire workforce that he was there to answer questions about drug and alcohol abuse. He told us, "What no one ever talks about is how lonely life is for a drunk. You just know you're the only person suffering this way and you're so tied up with guilt and denial and fear of being found out. . . . I wanted the guys I worked with to know they didn't have to be lonely if they didn't want to. My door was open."

Volunteer employees do no documentation or job intervention, but they can be one of the most powerful, positive influences in the workplace. The trained volunteer works right alongside the troubled employee and acts as a bridge between that employee and whatever program management provides for assistance. If the volunteer thinks the coworker has a problem with drugs, he or she can come right out and say so directly—a practice strictly forbidden to supervisors—providing the conversation is kept private and confidential. The volunteer is an information resource, a sympathetic, confidential listener with an opportunity to help troubled coworkers before their problems grow serious enough to interfere with their work and home lives.

The Sacramento Unified School District has an extensive and successful program for people they call volunteer referral agents. A 16-hour training makes sure volunteers understand precisely the strengths and limitations of their role. They are given firsthand information about community agencies and services they can feel comfortable about recommending to troubled employees who confide in them. They learn some basic interviewing, listening and communicating skills and are given a packet of resource materials that is periodically updated at followup sessions.

The Los Angeles Police Department trains volunteers called peer counselors. These men and women receive intensive three day training in personal crisis identification, suicide assessment, active listening, drug and alcohol abuse referral and general personal crisis issues. In one recent month, 49 counselors made contact with 143 employees or family members.

Supervisors and volunteers work toward the same goal. But never as a team. It is not the volunteer's job to carry information to the supervisor, nor does the supervisor ask the volunteer to act on his behalf. If the volunteer is perceived as being a representative of management, employees will feel angry and threatened by a loss of confidentiality.

Confidentiality is a key word, one that must be repeated again and again. If anything can kill a program to help troubled employees, it is too much talk. Supervisors and volunteers must understand that theirs are positions of trust and responsibility.

6

DOCUMENTATION

Documentation is objective evidence of an employee's impaired job performance. It serves various important purposes, the first of which is to break through the denial barriers erected by users of alcohol and drugs.

In Chapter 2 we talked at length about managerial denial and the various means by which it can be thwarted. User denial is even more difficult to penetrate because it is an essential component of the disease of chemical addiction. Denial is the way addicts and alcoholics rationalize their continued abuse of chemicals. Denial can develop to a point that the chemically addicted person truly is unable to see that chemical abuse is destroying his life.

The form denial takes is as individual as the men and women possessed by it. A woman working in a high-powered job may deny the severity of her problem by convincing herself that chemicals are necessary to her success. A policeman may deny the damage drugs are doing to his life by telling himself he works in a hostile world and could not continue to do the job without drugs as a buffer between himself and reality. The man raised by rigidly religious parents may believe that his addiction is a terrible weakness or moral stigma over which he has no control and must constantly work to conceal by denying its very existence. The heavy beer drinker may insist he only drinks recreationally. The woman convicted of drunk driving denies responsiblity for a rear-end collision by blaming the driver in front of her.

Examples of denial are endless. In our work we have known addicts and alcoholics with denial systems so strong they sacrifice homes and families before parting company with their drug of choice. Others we have known blamed everything from poltergeists to witchcraft before acknowledging the trouble drugs and alcohol brought to their lives.

Breaking through user denial is probably the most difficult aspect of drug and alcohol treatment. However, wide experience in the field has shown that intervention in the user's workplace is the most effective way to accomplish it. Supported by careful documentation, workplace intervention generates a feeling of crisis for the user. Faced with the chance he may lose his livelihood, the employee may finally take responsibility for his impaired performance.

Documentation serves a second purpose. If an employee's denial system holds firm through even a well-orchestrated intervention and his job performance continues to be unsatisfactory, some disciplinary action must occur. Suspended, demoted, or fired employees have been known to file lawsuits against their employers, demanding reinstatement. However, if the employer can precisely document the worker's impairment and point to reasonable, good-faith intervention efforts and offers of help, it is unlikely that he will have anything to fear from such a court action.

Documentation consists of evidence that falls under one or the other of two labels: "direct" or "indirect."

DRUG TESTING

This form of direct documentation is gaining in use and acceptance. Drug tests gather direct evidence of drug use. It is estimated that by the end of the decade, 80 percent of companies will use some form of testing to protect themselves against drug-abusing employees.

We have been told that testing employees for drug use makes good sense because it is quick, easy, and "tests don't lie." Well-intentioned reformers and technological entrepreneurs advocate this approach for all types of employees—from those who handle nuclear weapons to those who throw baseballs. Although it is true that the tests are quickly given and results generally easy to obtain (certainly the process is much quicker than documentation and intervention), there are many logistical and legal problems associated with the tests at all phases. Furthermore, without national standards to guide employers to the best laboratories, the uninformed businessperson is vulnerable to the hazards of an unregulated, fast-growing marketplace. Nevertheless, there are jobs in which public safety is an overriding concern and urinalysis may be an appropriate way to deal with the drug problem. For employees who deal with dangerous substances and equipment, for pilots, bus drivers, and railroad employees, for those whose work demands a high degree of public trust, testing may be recommended.

If you believe that drug testing is suitable for your workplace, there are a number of points to consider.

1. When will the tests be administered? Randomly, for cause, or as part of pre-employment screening?
2. What are the legal considerations of testing?
3. How will testing affect labor relations?
4. What method of testing will be used? Blood? Urine? Hair?
5. Who will be tested?
6. How is a testing laboratory chosen?
7. Where will the testing take place?
8. How much will the testing cost?

Let us examine each of these questions in detail.

WHEN WILL THE TESTS BE ADMINISTERED?

Randomly

The first point for any employer to consider is the potentially demoralizing effect random tests have on the workforce. Employees complain about working in "a police state." They believe their privacy is being invaded, their rights away from work abridged. However, if it is believed that the safety, productivity, or economics of the company are being adversely effected by employees who abuse chemicals, then the scales may tip in favor of such testing. If this is your choice, you need to consult your company attorneys and become informed as to the legal and labor issues involved. *All employees must be informed that random testing is a condition of employment.*

For Cause

In general, courts and arbitrators are more likely to favor employers who test for cause than those who act arbitrarily. In 1986, a New York court blocked application of a Brooklyn Union Gas Company drug-testing program when the union requested that arbitrators be brought in. The court agreed and noted in its decision that "to arbitrarily test without any reason whatsoever . . . is an impingement on the right of the individual." The court went on to state that where "good cause" was shown, it would take no exception to testing.

Preemployment Screening

From a legal standpoint, this seems the safest point at which to test for drugs. Unlike employees, job applicants cannot seek relief under the terms of collective bargaining agreements. Nevertheless, implementation of a preemployment screening program must meet the same test for accuracy, fairness and confidentiality as does any other program.

WHAT ARE THE LEGAL CONSIDERATIONS OF TESTING?

Constitutional Concerns

Private employers are generally not bound by constitutional or Fourth-Amendment restrictions on searches and seizures. This means that private companies enjoy considerable latitude in their efforts to dig out the roots of chemical abuse in the workplace. However, in some instances the line between private and public companies becomes difficult to discern. If your company operations are subject to government regulation or if you receive a large proportion of your financing from the government, you should be aware that some constitutional limitations may apply to your right to randomly test your employees for chemicals.

Discrimination Against the Handicapped

Federal law clearly states that a *practicing* alcoholic or addict is not considered handicapped. However, it is demonstrated in case law that a *recovering* alcoholic or addict is. Accordingly, in 1978, a district court found that, based on the federal Vocational Rehabilitation Act, for the city of Philadelphia to deny employment to applicants with a history of drug abuse amounted to discrimination against handicapped persons.

As a rule, state laws distinguish between abusing addicts and alcoholics and those considered to be in recovery. Taking this one step further, California law specifically forbids discrimination against employees who enter alcohol rehabilitation programs.

How does this relate to drug testing in the workplace? First, it underscores the importance of testing all employees or applicants without prejudice. Second, it reminds employers that they may not hold an employee's *former* drug or alcohol abuse against him. Finally, it protects employers against those practicing addicts and alcoholics who claim drug testing discriminates against the "handicapped." It clearly does not.

Defamation

A frequent theme of this book is the absolute necessity for confidentiality when dealing with all aspects of employee drug and alcohol abuse. Failure to follow the highest standards in this regard can result in expensive damages against employers. For example, a case involving a discharged railroad employee who was wrongly accused of having methadone in his system resulted in $200,000 in damages being awarded the employee. As the case of Houston Belt and Terminal Railway showed, the courts are likely to find that even an apparently harmless intraoffice document may be sufficient for a finding that entitles an employee to financial compensation because his character has been defamed. But regardless of the outcome of a suit for defamation, the procedure is always expensive. An employer can avoid costly litigation by exercising discretion and confidentiality in all matters relating to an employee whose fitness for work is in question.

Tort Principles

Employees of private companies may bring claims against their employer based on tort law applying to invasion of privacy. Invasion of privacy is defined as the intentional intrusion—physically or otherwise—upon the solitude or seclusion of another or his or her private affairs or concerns. A person found guilty of doing this is subject to liability to the other for invasion of privacy if the court finds the intrusion would be highly offensive to a reasonable person.

Although there is not as yet case law on this issue in connection with drugs in the workplace, experts agree that employers should institute drug testing only when a case can be made for the legitimate necessity of the procedure. When it can be shown that employees who abuse chemicals are adversely affecting productivity, workplace morale and harmony, causing accidents or violating security, employers are more likely to prevail in a court proceeding.

Employment Discrimination

The courts have upheld the right of employers to refuse employment to job applicants testing positive on a drug test that is part of the company's standard work application process. However, the precedent will hold only when the tests are administered with care and fairness across the board to all applicants or to all applicants for a particular position.

The manager of a large drug-testing laboratory told us that of the preemployment screens his firm does for a variety of employers, 15 percent come up positive. We asked an EAP director if this number seemed high. "Not at this stage," he told us. "Testing applicants is still pretty new. There are still a lot of applicants who don't know they're going to be asked to give a urine sample. In time, after it's more routine, drug users will mostly stay away from companies that test. Sites will probably get a rep for being clean or dirty."

Wrongful Discharge

Over the last few years, there have been increasing exceptions to the inviolability of the employment-at-will doctrine that permits employers to fire workers for any reason—or for no reason. The as-yet-undecided case of Ms. Luck, a female employee who refused to submit to a random urinalysis for drugs, may determine whether an employer has the right to fire noncompliant employees or whether under some conditions this is deemed wrongful discharge.

In the case of *Luck* v. *Southern Pacific Transportation Co.*, the plaintiff claims she was wrongfully discharged in violation of public policy. Her complaint cites state constitutional provisions regarding privacy and freedom from self-incrimination and alleges that the company violated statutory provisions prohibiting employers from making arbitrary, unrelated and unreliable tests a condition of employment. Finally, the employee has furnished the court with excellent job performance records that appear to prove her capacity to work was never in question.

Whether the court ultimately finds in favor of Luck or Southern Pacific Transportation Company, management can learn a lot from Luck's allegations. The facts of the case read like a cautionary tale for employers. According to the complaint, the employee (and almost 500 of her coworkers) was given no prior notice that drug tests were to be given. Assuming this to be true, it appears to support her claim that the tests were arbitrary. She alleges that following her refusal to be tested, she was questioned about "her personal beliefs, her attitude toward her person, her bodily functions, and her right to privacy." Again assuming the truth of her allegations, this mode of invasive questioning is clearly outside the perimeters allowed employers.

What can an employer do to avoid becoming involved in drawn-out and costly cases such as this? The best protection is to be open and straightforward, making it clear to all employees that drug testing is part of company policy and the employer has just cause to terminate employees who fail to submit to tests. New employees can be required to sign a document stating they understand and agree to this policy as a condition of employment.

HOW WILL TESTING AFFECT LABOR RELATIONS?

When management operates under a collective bargaining agreement, drug testing must be contemplated in the light of upholding of the principle that management's duty to bargain with labor is a continuing one. Thus, a decision by an employer to begin testing without including labor in the decision-making process may be legally unsupportable. In considering the viability of testing in a union shop, the key questions management should ask itself are these: Does the testing affect the working condition of the employee and is the policy reasonable and equitable?

Potomac Electric Power Company would have been well advised to ask these questions before it announced that an employee's failure to submit to urine and blood tests or his obstructing the search of his locker, lunch box or person would constitute just cause for immediate dismissal. Local 1900 of the International Brotherhood of Electrical Workers took the utility to court, where the judge found that management's policy was "draconian" and constituted "invasions of privacy which are almost unheard of in a free society. . . ."

When drug-related disputes between management and labor have resulted in arbitration rather than court action, certain general principles have been applied in the decision-making process. If an employer elects to implement drug testing, his policies and procedures should be measured against the following four principles of arbitration.

Specificity

Arbitrators often consider the specific wording and terms of a company drug and alcohol policy as well as its collective-bargaining agreement when making their decision. In a rather extreme example, one arbitrator held that a precisely worded policy prohibiting the taking of any drug while at work should be extended to include the taking of prescription medication. Thus the employer was able to discipline an employee who took Valium for which he had a doctor's legitimate prescription. At the other extreme—but being equally as specific—arbitrators have failed to uphold termination of an employee for possession of drugs when provisions against possession were not precisely articulated in company policy.

Possession

In cases of an employee found in possession of drugs (either in or out of his system), arbitrators generally take a hard line in favor of management. This is particularly the case when possession constitutes a risk to the public, as it did in the case of a Washington, D.C. bus driver who had drugs in her system at the time she was involved in a bus accident.

Place of Use

Even off-duty use of drugs can be cause for termination if an employee is apprehended selling drugs or possessing "hard" drugs such as heroin. An employee of Martin-Marietta Aerospace lost his job when he was found guilty of selling cocaine to an undercover agent. The termination was appealed to arbitration and upheld although the employee pointed out that his behavior occurred away from work and that while at work his performance was satisfactory. Interestingly, one of the arbitrator's considerations was the risk to the employer that this employee might sell drugs on the job and cause problems throughout the workplace.

Justifiability

Arbitrators frequently examine incidents in the light of "reasonable cause." Was the employer justified in testing a particular employee at a given time? Employees at a Kraft Inc. plant were observed congregating in an isolated part of the company warehouse. An arbitrator found that since the odor of marijuana was detected, management had reasonable cause to believe the employees were using drugs.

In general, if your company operates under a collective-bargaining agreement, you will be wise to include labor representatives as you begin to establish a company drug-testing policy. Although you may encounter problems initially, these will be minor compared to those likely to occur if you try to thrust a policy on unwilling employees without consultation.

WHAT METHODS OF TESTING WILL BE USED?

Urinalysis

Because it is considered the least intrusive test for chemicals, urinalysis is the screen most frequently used. According to Dennis Sumwalt, Assistant Sales Manager for American Clinical Laboratories and a licensed toxicologist, urine screens have another advantage as well. Proof of chemicals remains in the urine for longer than in the blood. "If an employee regularly snorts a little cocaine before work, evidence of the drug is gone from the blood in three to four hours, five at the most. But levels of it can be found in the urine for the next two to five days depending on certain variables." Sumwalt gave the following as general time frames within which an employee might produce a positive urine screen.

DRUG	TIME FRAME
Amphetamines	2-7 days
Barbiturates	2-3 days
(except Phenobarbital)	
Benzodiazepines	up to 7 days
Cocaine	2-5 days
Marijuana	15 days
Narcotics	2-3 days

The time frame will be affected by a number of variables.

1. Amount of drug taken
2. Individual metabolic rate
3. Frequency of drug use
4. pH of the urine
5. Fluid intake
6. Concentration of urine sample
7. Mode of ingestion
8. Type of urine screen used

Blood Testing

Blood tests have two primary drawbacks that you as an employer should consider: the short time that evidence of drug use stays in the blood system, and the tests' intrusive nature. But there is an occasion when a blood test can be particularly useful: when you are testing an employee "for cause." A hypothetical situation will make this clear.

Suppose that you own a small air-freight company operating between several midsized cities. You see that one of your pilots is behaving peculiarly at the time he checks in for a flight. His speech is slurred, he laughs and jokes inappropriately, his voice is loud. Although you cannot smell alcohol on his breath, you and others note that he is acting drunk. You ask him to report to an occupational health center for a blood test.

Why a blood test? Why not a urine screen?

If your pilot has just taken a drug—within the last hour, for example—it will not show in his urine unless he is a regular user. If this is the first drug he has taken in the last two weeks and only a urine screen is administered, it is likely to come up clean despite the fact your pilot is obviously unfit for work.

A blood test will also determine if your employee has been drinking. Since alcohol evaporates quickly in the urine, urine screens are not satisfactory when testing for alcohol.

Hair Analysis

Not so long ago, a national news magazine ran a short article about the perfect drug test. It would be totally nonintrusive and absolutely uncheatable. An employee would merely be asked to remove a strand of his hair for analysis.

Although the article made it seem like hair analysis was the technology of the future, it has been used in poisoning cases for many years and is considered to be highly reliable in that context. As a means of testing for drugs in the workplace, however, one EAP official told us, "it's flakey!" The chief problem associated with this method relates to the time frame. Traces of drugs can be found in the hair long after ingestion. An individual who snorted cocaine once, six months previous, might come up with a positive test although he has not used it since.

WHO WILL BE TESTED?

The answer to this question may prove vital to the success of your drug-testing program. Will you test only "for cause" or do you prefer to risk the ire of the courts and arbitrators as well as the morale of your workplace by instituting a system of random tests? You may decide that testing job applicants is the least problematical.

Whomever you elect to test, keep in mind these guidelines.

1. Treat all job applicants fairly. You will be asking for legal trouble if you single out for testing only job applicants of a particular sex, race or nationality or only those who have long hair, beards or wear leather jackets. It is wise to test all applicants for a particular position.

2. Inform your employees if you will be testing randomly. Let them know why you

have chosen this method and attempt to win their support rather than encouraging an adversarial relationship. If you will be testing "for cause," make clear the reasons for your decision. You may wish to have new employees sign a document indicating that they know random or "for cause" tests are a condition of employment.

3. Treat all tests confidentially. An official of a consortium-style employee-assistance program told us the story of a workplace where confidentiality was not a concern. An employee who submitted a positive drug test and was put on probation became the butt of jokes when his coworkers heard about it. Several days running, urine-sample bottles were left at his workstation with the note: "for drugs or pee, whichever you prefer." The employee filed a grievance that resulted in a costly overhaul of the company's drug-testing program.

HOW IS A TESTING LABORATORY CHOSEN?

According to speakers at the 10th annual Arnold O. Beckman Conference on "Drug Abuse in the Workplace," the technology for testing urine for drugs of abuse is so reliable that it can be performed with virtually no false positives. Unfortunately, not all laboratories use the most reliable technology or properly trained technicians. Although legislation that would allow only state-certified laboratories to do drug testing is being considered in California, Maine, Maryland and Oregon, there are no federal regulations to determine the qualifications of a laboratory claiming to have expertise in drug testing. Employers may find themselves at the mercy of careless or poorly equipped laboratories employing scarcely trained technicians unless they follow certain guidelines when choosing their lab.

Guidelines for Choosing a Testing Laboratory

To determine what labs are located in your area, consult the Yellow Pages of your phone book, a local drug treatment center, or an occupational health center or industrial medical clinic. The National Institute on Drug Abuse (NIDA) has opened a hotline to assist employers. The number is 800-843-4971.

When speaking over the telephone with a laboratory manager or sales representative, ask what kind of urine screen they do. If they do not answer, "Emit" or "RIA" or GC/MS we recommend you try another number on your list. These are the names of the most sophisticated and reliable screening procedures. Other testing methods are not dependable for the results to hold up in court.

Once you have found laboratories using the most accurate technology, pay each facility a visit and spend time talking to the sales representative. An EAP representative told us, "Employers shouldn't be afraid to ask questions, but a lot of them are. Because drug testing is a scientific field, most businessmen don't expect to understand the answers so they never ask the questions. The result is that a lot of third-rate laboratories are making money off tests that aren't very good."

(2) Ask the sales representative about lab compliance with the NIDA voluntary accreditation standards. These cover requirements for confirmation of positive tests, inspections, chain of custody, personnel and quality-assurance procedures that labs should follow.

(3) Ask about the credentials of the lab employees. Some labs hire high-school students to run their screens. According to Richard Hawks of NIDA, the laboratory director must have "documented scientific qualifications equivalent to that of a person certified by the American Board of Forensic Toxicology or the American Board of Clinical Chemistry in Toxicological Chemistry." If the wording is vague, Hawks says it is because NIDA wishes to keep the standards from becoming too restrictive. For further information on certification, call the American Board of Forensic Toxicology (301-333-3299) or the American Board of Clinical Chemistry (606-233-5654).

(4) Ask the laboratory representative to take you, step-by-step, through the lab's testing procedures. The example of American Clinical Laboratory's testing procedure for urine screens will provide you with a standard of comparison.

"The first thing to remember," Ellen Edwards of ACL told us, "is that the lab is the *disinterested* party. It shouldn't have anything to do with the actual collection of urine. That should be done by medical personnel at some kind of medical facility chosen by the employer."

At the medical facility, however, certain practices are required in order to assure the integrity of the specimen and the confidentiality of the person giving it.

- The employee himself chooses a collection bottle from a quantity of bottles supplied by the medical facility
- The toilet cubicle has a single door
- Bluing agent is added to the water in the commode
- The employee giving the sample wears only a hospital gown; preferably sarong-style around the waist. Although some employees or job applicants may object to this, the rationale behind it is quite valid. The goal is to insure the integrity of the sample. We heard of a job applicant who taped a condom full of clean urine under his arm where it was hidden by the sleeves of his hospital gown. Once in the privacy of the toilet cubicle, he put the warm (from the heat of his body) urine in the sample bottle.
- An employee of the medical facility stands outside the cubicle and checks to make sure the sample in the collection bottle is warm.
- The employee or applicant watches as the sample is transferred from the collection bottle to a bottle furnished by the laboratory. The cap is taped shut with a tamperproof sheild encoded with identification. The employee or applicant signs a chain of custody form, asserting that the sample is his. A photo identification is taped to the top of the form.

• The sample is assigned a number; only the medical facility keeps the portion of the form that correlates picture, name and number. In this way, confidentiality is assured.

• A lab courier checks the tamperproof seal and signs on the chain of custody form (on which there is only a number and not the name of the employee or applicant) that he has received a specimen of good integrity. The specimen is then placed in a locked box in his car and taken to the lab.

   It is important to underscore the necessity for keeping a chain of custody form. In the event that the employee or applicant argues that the sample tested was not actually his, the lab will have to produce documents showing the name and official function of every person who came in contact with the specimen.

   In the laboratory, the integrity of the sample and the anonymity of the donor continue to be of primary concern.

• When the specimen enters the lab, the container is examined for anomalies. If there is any imperfection in the seal or if the numbers on the seal appear to have been altered, the sample is discarded and another requested.

• The chain of custody continues to be tracked as the specimen moves through the laboratory. The sample is placed in a secure location, the key of which is in the possession of a designated person at all times. The chain of custody form is filed.

• An internal chain of custody is initiated by the supervisor of the team that will do the analysis. All who handle the sample must be named on this second custody form. At the termination of the testing, the internal chain of custody is attached to the one already filed. In the case of a positive screen, the original sample is kept in a locked refrigerator while further confirming tests are run.

   It is essential that all positive screens be confirmed by a second testing procedure. False positives *do* occur. According to Dr. William H. Anderson of Harvard and Tufts universities, quoted in the *Wall Street Journal*, "In the case of drug testing, 90 percent accuracy would be considered unusually good." If you intend to use the results of the test to take action against an employee, *courts require confirming proof*.

• Negatives are discarded within two weeks. Confirmed positives are kept in a locked forensic freezer for 90 days, after which time they are discarded. If the employer requests, they are kept for additional time.

   The procedures of American Clinical Laboratories are excellent. Not all laboratories are as careful, however, and the results of their carelessness can be costly. Flawed lab procedures were held accountable in the case of a San Diego Gas and Electric employee who was fired over a false positive reading on a test for marijuana. SDG&E settled the case out of court, and the woman was given her job back when it was discovered the unnamed lab had not confirmed the findings.

(5) Finally, ask the laboratory spokesperson how much the drug screening will cost—per employee. If the price is as low as $10 or $15, we believe you should question the reliability of the laboratory. The technology involved in the most reliable testing procedures is not cheap. A single piece of equipment may cost as much as $100,000 and well-trained and qualified technicians command high salaries. It is impossible to cite a price that will apply to tests done nationwide since cost will vary from region to region. However, ACL, which is located in a sophisticated and competitive market, tells prospective contractors that every negative specimen will cost less than $35. A confirming test will cost an additional $30. Added to these prices will be those charged by the medical laboratory where the specimen was collected.

Direct documentation of an employee's possession or use of drugs can also be obtained by searching employees' persons, cars and lockers and by the use of drug-sensitive dogs. These methods are discussed in the chapter entitled "Primary Prevention." Regardless of the testing or surveillance procedures you are considering, we believe you should take into account the following points.

1. *Reliable* direct evidence is never easy to obtain. Unless employers use the utmost care at all phases of the operation, they risk litigation which wil be costly—regardless of the outcome.
2. Even when personnel at all levels are screened, gathering direct evidence is likely to widen the division between labor and management and create antagonism that heightens stress in the workplace and negatively affects the quantity and quality of production.
3. Consider the expense. Random tests, testing every job applicant, even testing for cause is expensive. And in the event that the tests result in litigation, you and your lawyers may be involved in court procedings for months, even years.
4. Finally, and we think most compellingly, direct-evidence procedures have no necessary connection to the successful treatment and rehabilitation of drug-impaired employees.

The authors favor documentation by means of *indirect* evidence for the majority of workplaces. Despite our labeling this type "indirect," such evidence is both reliable and difficult to abuse. It requires no technology, no testing, no secret agents and no trained animals. Many segments of organized labor already support its use. Most important, it is a dramatically effective way to implement a program for rehabilitating impaired employees instead of terminating them.

Documentation through indirect evidence is based on a simple premise that has been verified through countless studies: chemical abuse creates clearly identifiable patterns of impaired job performance.

To initiate this approach, two groups of employees are given special training to sensitize them to patterns of negative change in an employee's job performance and relationships at work. The role of each employee group is explained below.

SUPERVISORS

These are the people in the best position to evaluate an employee's job performance. In essence, their documentation role has them do that for which they are already specially qualified: keep accurate records of their employees' job performance and conduct performance-evaluation interviews.

Your supervisors will require special training (see the chapter "Supervisory Training") to help them identify the patterns of changed behavior, physical appearance and job performance that signal impairment. What are these patterns?

Absenteeism
- frequent unauthorized absences
- excessive sick days
- frequent absences of short duration, with or without medical corroboration
- frequent Monday, Friday, day before and day after holiday absences
- frequent use of vacation days to cover absences
- high absentee rate for vague ailments: colds, flu, headache

On the Job Absences
- frequently away from work station
- excessive tardiness after lunch, breaks
- frequent trips to the water fountain, parking lot, locker room, rest room

High Accident Rate
- accidents off the job that affect job performance
- accidents on the job due to carelessness
- failure to wear safety gear (helmets, gloves, etc.)

Poor Job Performance
- a pattern of diminished morning or afternoon performance
- complaints from coworkers, clients, etc.
- missed deadlines
- taking longer to do less
- wasting materials, damaging/losing equipment
- improbable excuses
- alternating periods of high and low performance, which becomes increasingly unsatisfactory
- difficulty with instructions, procedures

- difficuly recalling mistakes
- difficulty understanding new information
- difficulty with complex assignments
- uneven work habits

Changes in Personal Habits
- reporting to work in abnormal condition (drunk, dazed, vague, etc.)
- different behavior after lunch than before
- increasing lack of attention to personal hygiene
- increasing lack of interest in personal appearance

Poor Relationships with Coworkers
- over-reaction to real or implied criticism
- unrealistic resentments
- excessive talking with coworkers
- wide mood swings
- borrowing money
- avoiding coworkers and friends
- complaints from coworkers and friends
- increasing irritability
- increasingly argumentative
- inappropriate outbursts of anger, tears, laughter

Naturally, documentation requires documents. Supervisors should be made familiar with them prior to beginning any documentation procedures. You will want to devise documents suitable for your organization's need, but the examples on the next pages will give you some idea of the form they might take.

Below are some sample forms for documenting impaired work performance.

Sample Three is the most thorough of the documents and while this is seen by some employers as its advantage, supervisors who don't like the many pages and headings complain of "paperwork" and "bureaucracy." If you are concerned about the legal aspects of documentation and want to provide yourself and your supervisors with the maxiumum protection, this document is the best of the three. Also, when dealing with an employee whose denial is very strong, a document this detailed and precise can be an extremely powerful tool.

Documenting unsatisfactory job performance has been proved to be a successful means of eliminating the kind of impaired work behavior that costs companies money. Identification by documentation takes longer than blood or urine testing, but it is effective. We know of countless case histories illustrating the positive use of documentation.

One involved Tom, a man who had worked for a large aircraft company for more than 15 years, establishing in that time a record of valuable and reliable service. The

EMPLOYEE EVALUATION FORM

Supervisor:_____

Employee (name or number):_____

Instructions:
    Evaluate the employee according to the criteria listed
    below. Be specific. Note dates and times involved.

Absenteeism:
    Comment_____
_____
_____

Tardiness:
    Comment_____
_____
_____

Accidents:
    Comment_____
_____
_____

Difficulty in Concentration:
    Comment_____
_____
_____

Irregular work pattern:
    Comment_____
_____
_____

Reporting to work in an unsuitable condition:
    Comment_____
_____
_____

Lowered Job Efficiency:
    Comment_____
_____
_____

Relationships with Coworkers:
    Comment_____
_____
_____

Inappropriate Workplace Activity:
    Comment_____
_____
_____

EMPLOYEE EVALUATION FORM

Instructions: Mark each characteristic you have noted about the
employee.

Dates   Absenteeism
_____   _____ Repeated unauthorized leave
_____   _____ Excessive sick leave
_____   _____ Frequent Monday and/or Friday absences
_____   _____ Repeated absences
_____   _____ Excessive tardiness
_____   _____ Frequent long lunches and breaks
_____   _____ Leaving work early
_____   _____ Frequent unscheduled short-term absences

Dates   Work-post Absenteeism
_____   _____ Continued absences from post
_____   _____ Frequent trips to water fountain or restroom
_____   _____ Long coffee breaks
_____   _____ Excessive fraternization
_____   _____ Physical illness on the job

Dates   Accident Rate
_____   _____ Accidents on the job
                Details:_____.
                _____

Dates   Problems in Concentration
_____   _____ Work requires greater effort
_____   _____ Jobs take more time
_____   _____ Trouble taking direction
_____   _____ Trouble learning new routines/procedures
_____   _____ Difficulty recalling instructions, details
_____   _____ Other significant memory problems
                Details:_____
                _____

Dates   Irregular Work Patterns
_____   _____ Alternates periods of high/low productivity
_____   _____ Productivity impaired after lunch, Mondays
                           and Fridays

Dates   Reporting to Work
_____   _____ Coming to work in an inappropriate condition
_____   _____ Returning to work in an inappropriate condition
                Details:_____
                _____

Additional relevant comments:
_____
_____
_____

EMPLOYEE EVALUATION FORM

INSTRUCTIONS: Describe each problem and action precisely.

Date	Description of Problem	Action Taken	Date

INSTRUCTIONS:To visually track a
pattern of employee absences
and late days, use the calendar
and the following code.

Absence ✗
Late ○
Overlong lunch break ☐
Absent after lunch ⊠
Late more than fifteen minutes ⊗

JANUARY

S	M	T	W	T	F	S
					1	2
3	4	5	6	7	8	9
10	11	12	13	14	15	16
17	18	19	20	21	22	23
24	25	26	27	28	29	30
31						

FEBRUARY

S	M	T	W	T	F	S
	1	2	3	4	5	6
7	8	9	10	11	12	13
14	15	16	17	18	19	20
21	22	23	24	25	26	27
28	29					

MARCH

S	M	T	W	T	F	S
		1	2	3	4	5
6	7	8	9	10	11	12
13	14	15	16	17	18	19
20	21	22	23	24	25	26
27	28	29	30	31		

APRIL

S	M	T	W	T	F	S
					1	2
3	4	5	6	7	8	9
10	11	12	13	14	15	16
17	18	19	20	21	22	23
24	25	26	27	28	29	30

MAY

S	M	T	W	T	F	S
1	2	3	4	5	6	7
8	9	10	11	12	13	14
15	16	17	18	19	20	21
22	23	24	25	26	27	28
29	30	31				

JUNE

S	M	T	W	T	F	S
			1	2	3	4
5	6	7	8	9	10	11
12	13	14	15	16	17	18
19	20	21	22	23	24	25
26	27	28	29	30		

JULY

S	M	T	W	T	F	S
					1	2
3	4	5	6	7	8	9
10	11	12	13	14	15	16
17	18	19	20	21	22	23
24	25	26	27	28	29	30
31						

AUGUST

S	M	T	W	T	F	S
	1	2	3	4	5	6
7	8	9	10	11	12	13
14	15	16	17	18	19	20
21	22	23	24	25	26	27
28	29	30	31			

SEPTEMBER

S	M	T	W	T	F	S
				1	2	3
4	5	6	7	8	9	10
11	12	13	14	15	16	17
18	19	20	21	22	23	24
25	26	27	28	29	30	

OCTOBER

S	M	T	W	T	F	S
						1
2	3	4	5	6	7	8
9	10	11	12	13	14	15
16	17	18	19	20	21	22
23	24	25	26	27	28	29
30	31					

NOVEMBER

S	M	T	W	T	F	S
		1	2	3	4	5
6	7	8	9	10	11	12
13	14	15	16	17	18	19
20	21	22	23	24	25	26
27	28	29	30			

DECEMBER

S	M	T	W	T	F	S
				1	2	3
4	5	6	7	8	9	10
11	12	13	14	15	16	17
18	19	20	21	22	23	24
25	26	27	28	29	30	31

DOCUMENTATION OF UNSATISFACTORY JOB PERFORMANCE

EMPLOYEE'S DEPT._____
EMPLOYEE'S NUMBER_____
DATES COVERED BY THIS REPORT _____

Check the phrase(s) that best describes the current situation. Jot down specific details where appropriate.

(1) GENERAL APPEARANCE: DATES, COMMENTS

__ Significant inappropriate appearance _____
__ Significant lack of hygiene   _____
__ Other   _____

(2) WORKPLACE BEHAVIOR:

__ Talks excessively
__ Exaggerates self-importance   _____
__ Inflexible about procedures   _____
__ Argumentative   _____
__ Inappropriate emotional outbursts   _____
__ Excessive use of telephone   _____
__ Physically threatening   _____
__ Other   _____

(3) TEMPERAMENT AT WORK:

__ Withdrawn   _____
__ Suspicious   _____
__ Feelings easily hurt   _____
__ Agitated, edgy   _____
__ Excessively worried about illness
   and/or death   _____
__ Extreme variations of mood   _____
__ Other   _____

(4) JOB PERFORMANCE:

__ Forgets instructions,
   procedures, corrections, etc.   _____
__ Other unusual loss of memory   _____
__ Working abnormally slowly   _____
__ Erratic (high-low) productivity   _____
__ Missed deadlines   _____
__ Poor judgment   _____
__ Excessive complaints about job   _____
__ Intoxicated on the job   _____
__ Other   _____

EMPLOYEE'S DEPT. _____
BADGE NUMBER _____
DATES COVERED BY THIS REPORT _____

(5) RELATIONSHIP WITH CO-EMPLOYEES:

___ Abnormal reaction to criticism
___ Borrows money from co-workers
___ Resents other workers
___ Has unrealistic expectations
    (for salary, promotion etc.)
___ Imagines criticism
    where there is none
___ Receives complaints from co-workers
___ Receives complaints from customers
___ Receives complaints from community
___ Other

(6) ABSENTEEISM:

___ Excessive absences
___ Improbable excuses for absences
___ Frequent unscheduled absences
___ Absences follow a pattern
___ Excessive tardiness
___ Excessive trips to car, water
    fountain, restroom, etc.
___ Excessively long coffee breaks
___ Excessive sick leave for colds,
    flu, headaches, stomach problems,
    general malaise
___ Other

(7) ACCIDENTS:

___ Failure to wear safety gear
___ Abnormally casual about safety
    procedures
___ Complaints from coworkers about
    employee's safety standards
___ Near-accidents on the job
___ Accidents on the job
___ Other

FURTHER OBSERVATIONS REGARDING UNUSUAL EMPLOYEE BEHAVIORS:

DOCUMENTATION OF TARDINESS, ABSENCES, & REQUESTS FOR LEAVE

EMPLOYEE'S DEPARTMENT_____
EMPLOYEE'S NUMBER_____
DATES COVERED ON THIS REPORT_____

(1) Dates of Tardiness (over __ minutes) and Excuse Given:

_____ _____
_____ _____
_____ _____
_____ _____
_____ _____
_____ _____
_____ _____

(2) Dates of Absence and Excuse Given:

_____ _____
_____ _____
_____ _____
_____ _____
_____ _____
_____ _____

(3) Dates Sick Leave Requested and Reasons Given:

_____ _____
_____ _____
_____ _____
_____ _____

(4) Dates of Personal Leave and Reasons Given:

_____ _____
_____ _____
_____ _____

FURTHER OBSERVATIONS REGARDING EMPLOYEE TARDINESS, ABSENCE, AND
LEAVES:

changes in this man's work personality and job performance were quite subtle at first. He became less sociable and more short-tempered. His coworkers began to avoid working with him. During Tom's regular six-month evaluation the supervisor might have made some comment, but chose not to. He liked Tom and wanted to think well of him.

After the evaluation session the supervisor felt uncomfortable, as if he had not done his own job properly. He watched Tom more closely and documented increasing signs of impairment. Tom began dozing on the job, called in late several mornings a month and had trouble following directions. Eventually, after two warning interviews, Tom was told that he would have to get help for his "problem"—whatever it was—or lose his job. This was just the incentive Tom needed to make him face his disease.

When we were called in to assess Tom's case, we discovered that he was addicted to painkillers, originally prescribed to help him live with a painful lower back. It was not easy for Tom to break his drug habit, but today he is back on the job, at a new work station that permits him to sit down most of the time. His back still bothers him sometimes, but when it does he resorts to milder, nonaddictive medication.

Documentation of impairment is not a "quick fix" for today's chemical crisis. It isn't glamorous or dramatic enough to make the front page. In fact, documentation is a pretty fundamental and down-to-earth way to get the job done. It is based on the simple premise that if you tell a supervisor you want him to supervise and give him the tools to do it with, he will do a good job for you. And why shouldn't he when a clean and sober workplace is in the best interests of everyone, from the boss on down to the consumer.

7

WORKPLACE INTERVENTION

"I'll never do one! I wouldn't know what to say!"

"It's not my business to pry into an employee's private life."

"I'm not a doctor. How can I tell what's wrong?"

"I'm not looking to get sued!"

These responses are typical of supervisors when we first mention the word "intervention." Experience has shown us that in the workplace the intervention process is frequently misunderstood. Rather than seeing the procedure as a part of what they do every day—that is, "supervise employees"—many supervisors have the mistaken impression that a workplace intervention is a technical or meddlesome procedure that should be left to the "experts."

To counter the mistaken ideas and negative feelings attached to workplace intervention, this chapter will present a clear and simple definition of the term. We next lay out step-by-step the intervention procedures for supervisors to follow. We'll offer a set of guidelines to make those interventions as easy, direct and effective as possible. In a special chapter we will discuss the problems associated with intervention for executives and female employees.

By the end of this chapter, it will be clear that supervisors are the people most likely to manage workplace interventions successfully. They are, indeed, the experts.

DEFINITION

A workplace intervention is a sequence of job-performance reviews in which a supervisor uses documentation and job leverage to make an employee face and take responsibility for his deteriorating job performance. A workplace intervention emphasizes that an employee has a choice between getting help and continuing his destructive behavior to its inevitable result.

As mentioned in previous chapters, documentation of a worker's impaired performance is the crucial foundation of a successful intervention. It begins when a supervisor perceives a pattern of unsatisfactory job performance: too many days late, long lunches and coffee breaks, missed deadlines, forgotten appointments, excessive absences, and so on. Generally, four to six weeks is sufficient time to observe and document such a patttern, but variance between individuals and worksites can be expected.

There is nothing to be gained by postponing the documentation phase of the intervention process. In fact, supervisors who hesitate to take this responsibility may unknowingly be working against the best interest of both employee and company. Numerous studies show that if a drug- or alcohol-addicted person can get help early in his disease, chances of recovery are maximized. Furthermore, early interventions generally translate into shorter periods of treatment—which represents more cost-savings in terms of insurance payments and lost man hours.

Effective workplace interventions are managed in stages.

STAGE ONE: THE INFORMAL PERFORMANCE REVIEW

This first performance review is as relaxed and nonconfrontational as possible. It provides an opportunity for the employee who has allowed his performance to slip to correct the problem with a minimum of fuss. As every supervisor knows, there are times when the best worker will suffer setbacks that make it difficult for him to function at peak levels. In these cases, just a cautionary word or two from a caring supervisor will be sufficient to correct the problem. The supervisor takes an employee aside and mentions that he or she has been observed coming in late, or taking extended lunch periods, or missing compulsory employee meetings, or leaving work early without explanation.

At this point it is not necessary for the supervisor to tell the employee that the specifics of each tardiness, each missed meeting, have been documented on paper. The supervisor allows the employee to make excuses, but offers no solutions, and should resist the temptation to be a Dutch uncle eager to give advice. Concern is only over job performance and maintaining a well-run workplace. However, it is appropriate to mention the sources of assistance your company makes available to troubled employees, and to reassure the worker about confidentiality and job security if help is sought.

Following this informal review, the supervisor writes a brief report of the meeting and attaches it to the documentation. This report should include the date and time of the review and a recommendation that the employee get help if he needs it. If the pattern of unsatisfactory performance continues or if it reappears after a period of good performance lasting weeks or months, the supervisor will have the earlier record to refer back to.

An informal performance review might be similar to this hypothetical interchange between Bill and his supervisor.

Supervisor: Bill, you've been a mainstay in this company for almost five years but just lately I've noticed that you've had some trouble getting to work on time. You've also been taking longer lunch hours.

Bill: Last week my car broke down and my wife couldn't drive me because she had to be at the kids' school.

Supervisor: And we've missed your input at the last two employee meetings.

Bill: Yeah, well, I got behind and wanted to finish up some stuff. . . . Didn't figure you guys'd miss me.

Supervisor: You know, Bill, if something's bothering you, you could call the EAP rep and make an appointment. It's all confidential and . . .

Bill: No, there's nothing bothering me. I'm fine. I'll be on time. No sweat.

STAGE TWO: THE FORMAL PERFORMANCE REVIEW

The second stage of the intervention follows the informal review by four to six weeks—less if the supervisor feels the job impairment is severe enough to require fast action. As in the previous review, it is supported by the accumulated documentation of many weeks. But in several important ways, it is different. At the first meeting the supervisor made a conscious effort to keep the tone friendly and casual. In the formal review, it has to be made clear to the employee that he is being called on the carpet.

Prior to this review the supervisor should inform the employee's union representative that the meeting will take place and, if appropriate, give him the opportunity to be present.

Sitting face-to-face in privacy where interruptions cannot occur, the supervisor shows the employee the documentation of his impaired performance: that which prompted the first informal review and that which led to this one. He brings the worker's attention to the specific days and times of tardiness, absences, missed meetings, faulty workmanship or interpersonal problems that are adversely affecting work—anything that contributes to an overall pattern of unsatisfactory performance.

At no time should the supervisor mention any off-the-job incidents or suggest the employee might have a drug or alcohol problem. The supervisor must stick to what he is best qualified to judge: the worker's deteriorating job performance. Analysis and diagnosis are left alone. Deviation from this approach greatly lessens the chance of an effective intervention; moreover, if supervisors begin accusing employees of drug or alcohol addiction, they may find themselves at the center of a union dispute or a lawsuit.

This is just what happened in a Pennsylvania case involving an employee who was allegedly told by her supervisor that she had a drug problem and that if she did not enter a detoxification program she would lose her job. She later sued her employer, her counselor and the drug program for over $1 million, claiming she was not and had never been a drug abuser. As of March 1987, that case was still in the discovery phase. Even if the court eventually finds in favor of the company, the case will have cost them many thousands of dollars. This case is only one of many that make the point that managers and supervisors must not act as diagnosticians. To do so jeopardizes the company policy and program and perhaps its economic viability.

Some experts recommend that if your company has an employee assistance program, the formal review stage is an appropriate time for an "assumed closing." In an assumed closing the supervisor assumes that, faced with undeniable documentation of impairment and knowing that his livelihood is imperiled, an employee is motivated to get help for whatever problem is threatening his job. In the classic assumed closing scenario, at the end of the performance review the supervisor picks up the phone, dials the EAP number and then hands the receiver to the employee to complete the process by making an appointment for assessment and evaluation.

Many supervisors balk at the directness of an assumed closing. They prefer to tell the employee that help is available and provide him with a brochure or mimeographed sheet listing help agencies and their telephone numbers. Although not as immediately motivating, this approach can also be effective.

Regardless of which approach the supervisor feels most comfortable with, it is important that he again assure the employee that if he seeks outside help, his job status will not be jeopardized. On the other hand, it should be made clear that if the employee fails to improve his work performance he is risking his job.

At the end of the review, the supervisor and the employee agree upon a statement of immediate improved-performance goals. In contrast to the casual oral promise given in the informal review, this should be in writing on an official form similar to the one that follows.

Before signing the document, the supervisor reads it over with the employee, making certain he understands that this is a statement in which he promises to improve his

```
              AGREEMENT TO IMPROVE JOB PERFORMANCE
This agreement is made between _____(the employee) and
_____ (the supervisor.)

The supervisor has advised the employee of the following matters
that need correction.
    1._____
    2._____
    3._____
    4._____
    5._____

The supervisor has informed employee that assistance is available
through the company EAP (or other).

Employee agrees that the following corrective action will be
taken.
    1._____
    2._____
    3._____
    4._____
    5._____

A review of this plan will be made on _____,
at_____a.m./pm.

If at that time, these matters are settled as planned, this will
be noted.  If work performance continues to be unsatisfactory,
this agreement will be used as part of any disciplinary or
corrective action as may be necessary.



Signed_____     Date_____
               Employee

Signed_____     Date_____
              Supervisor
```

on-the-job performance, a statement that will become part of his permanent work record. Set specific dates for future progress reviews and make sure again that the employee understands that his job is at risk if he fails to live up to his commitment.

In this short example of a formal job performance review, Bill is once again being called to account for his actions.

Supervisor: Bill, you've been with us a long time and we value you as an employee. It's men like you I know I can count on. But over the last two months your job performance has not been satisfactory. We talked about this last month and I hoped that would be enough, but as far as I can see, except for a day or two right after our conversation, there hasn't been any improvement at all.

Bill: Well, I've had a lot of things going on at home and, you know, the kids and all . . .

Supervisor: Look, Bill, I've been keeping count of the days you've been late or absent. You've been late to work 28 times in two months.

Bill: A few minutes here and there . . . What is this, a police state all of a sudden? I've been with this company five, almost six years. Can't a guy punch in late once in a while without things getting heavy?

Supervisor: On one occasion—the 20th of last month—you came in 15 minutes late for work. The next day you came in 13 minutes late. Two days later you were almost 30 minutes late.

Bill: Yeah, and I made it up after work, didn't I?

Without responding to Bill's hostility, the supervisor goes on to mention each specific occasion when Bill came in late or missed work. Eventually, under the weight of this accumulated evidence, Bill runs out of excuses and listens sullenly.

Supervisor: It's not just absences and tardiness, Bill. I'm getting complaints from the other men. Two guys came to me last week and said they wouldn't work with you on that new project. They say you don't pull your weight anymore.

Bill: Who said that? Connor? He's out to get me anyway. You going to listen to him? I'm going straight to the union if you do.

Supervisor: I've already spoken to your union rep, Bill. He's as concerned as I am that something's bothering you and making it hard to put in a good day's work. He knows about this meeting and I've promised him a complete report when we're finished. Neither one of us wants to see a good man lose his job. Especially when there are so many ways to get help. Give the EAP a call, Bill. Here's the number. See if you can settle this problem somehow before you lose your job. I really don't want to have to let you go, but unless your job performance improves and stays improved, I'm going to have to do it.

Bill's response is a sullen agreement that he will do "something." He pushes his chair back, eager to end the meeting. But his supervisor isn't finished yet.

Supervisor: I've got a form here I'd like you to look at and sign. It says that you and I have talked this problem over and you've agreed to correct the problems we spoke about. It says here that I've advised you of certain problems like tardiness and not getting along with the other men on your shift. Now I'd like you to fill in the lines about corrective action. This way we both know for sure what happened in this meeting. And let's set a date right now to review progress.

STAGE THREE:
LETTER OF REPRIMAND

If the subsequent review shows that the employee's performance has not improved according to the terms of the signed agreement, the supervisor's next step is to write a formal letter of reprimand. Using as a model the sample letter that follows, include in this letter the date and times of previous reviews, notes of the employee's failure to keep his performance goal commitment, dates and times of continued impaired performance and a threat of specific disciplinary action such as demotion, suspension or termination. Finally, the letter makes a very strong suggestion that the employee seek assistance from either the company EAP or from an outside service. Copies of this letter go into the employee's file, to the employee, manager, personnel officer and labor representative.

```
                       LETTER OF REPRIMAND

Dear _____,
            On _____, we discussed the continuing
problem of your ___(note specific problems)_____.
You were told at that time that your job performance was
unsatisfactory according to the terms of your employment by this
company.  We agreed (copy of agreement to improve job performance
attached) that you would correct the following:_____,
_____,_____.

However, the problems have continued.  (Letter explains
particulars)

Persistent work problems such as those you are experiencing are
often the result of personal problems.  In recognition of this
fact, I strongly suggest that you contact _____ in an
effort to clear up these problems.

Unless your job performance shows a substantial improvement
within the next (week, month), I will have no choice but to
recommend that formal disciplinary action be taken against you.

Signed_____
```

STAGE FOUR:
DISCIPLINARY ACTION

Some managers worry that a disciplined employee may seek retribution by filing a law suit or union grievance claiming unfair treatment. However, there is a growing body of precedent *favoring* management in cases where supervisors:

1. Follow clearly mandated step-by-step procedures such as those outlined here.

2.   Address only the specific facts of impaired job performance and do not attempt to diagnose an employee's problem.
3.   On more than one occasion provide reminders of the general problem-solving program (EAP or similar) the company makes available to employees.

It should be noted that arbitrators have not looked favorably upon those companies that terminate acknowledged alcoholics and addicts without first offering them opportunities for recovery and resumption of work.

If it becomes necessary to suspend, demote or terminate an employee, it can be very discouraging to the supervisor who has made a good-faith effort at intervention. Many supervisors see it as a sign that they have failed. We strongly disagree with this view. We suggest that disheartened supervisors look again at the impaired employee's work record. The documentation will speak for itself: absences, tardiness, diminished performance, interpersonal problems, accidents, poor attitude. Discouraging as it might seem to a supervisor with a strong instinct to help, he or she is right to discipline an impaired employee who refuses to get the help that is available, offered and badly needed.

GUIDELINES FOR SUPERVISORS

Although there is no guarantee that each invervention attempt will work, there are techniques that improve the chance of success. Drawing from our own experience and that of other specialists in the field, we have collected the following set of guidelines for supervisors.

1.   Make documentation thorough and incontrovertible.
2.   Never diagnose or interpret. Stick to the facts of impaired performance.
3.   Whenever possible during performance reviews, make positive comments about an employee's areas of competence. By acknowledging the worker's strengths, you make it easier for him to admit his work impairment without a loss of dignity.
4.   Don't get involved in excuses, explanations or arguments. You are interested in one thing only: improved job performance. All else is irrelevant to a performance-based intervention.
5.   At each stage remind the employee that help is available for personal problems that may be affecting his work.
6.   Make it clear that it is the employee's responsibility to get help for his or her problems.
7.   At the stage of a formal performance review, use your supervisorial leverage. Make it clear that the employee's livelihood is at stake. This leverage is what makes workplace interventions the most successful way of getting help for im-

paired employees. Drug and alcohol addicts may be willing to sacrifice their families and their health, but they will do almost anything to keep from losing their income.

8. Beginning with the formal performance review, keep labor representatives informed at every stage of the intervention process. If you made a genuine effort to include labor input when you formulated your company's drug and alcohol policy, this is the time you and the employee will benefit from that congenial partnership.

A successful workplace intervention can be an immensely rewarding experience for the employee, the supervisor and the company. Here is the story of one that worked out well for everyone.

Adam is a supervisor in a suburban store, part of a large chain specializing in building products such as lumber, paint and glass. There are 12 men in his department. The owners of the company sought help from experts when they realized there was a high incidence of theft in certain stores where there also happened to be frequent accidents. All supervisors were given special training in documentation and workplace interventions.

I got so I was noticing little things that kinda passed me by before. Like the guys who always came in late and laughing real loud were some of the same ones customers complained about. I mean when a lady comes in and she wants to buy lumber for a bookcase and she doesn't know pine from mahogany, these guys were not the souls of patience if you get what I mean. Things like that started showing up and I kept records like the bosses told me to.

One of these guys is cutting wood one day and he saws off his index finger. Right down to the hand. Come to find out when I check the documentation, he's the same guy had been coming in late after lunch every day and leaving work early on Fridays. It was classic.

When he came back to work, I took him aside and said, real casual, that I hoped he could start off on a new footing without coming in late or missing work. I reminded him our company had an employee-assistance program and it was confidential. He laughed at me. Swear to God, if it'd been up to me at that moment, I'da fired the guy.

Instead, Adam continued to document this employee's impaired performance and after another month of absenteeism, tardiness and complaints, he held a formal job performance review. This time, the employee was a little less cocky, but he insisted there was nothing wrong with him.

When I told him to fill in the performance agreement, he got mad and started calling me and the company all kinds of names. I thought sure he was going to quit right then, but he didn't. After that, I kept my eye on him and for a while he was doing okay but after a couple of weeks it all started again. Late to work, absent, lame excuses for everything.

I was getting set to write a letter of reprimand when I got a letter from the employee-assistance program. It was a request to release the documents I had on this employee and it was signed by him. A while after that I got notice from Personnel he was going to be gone from work about six weeks and they were sending me someone temporary. I didn't know for sure, but I figured it was all connected with the problems he was having.

Andy's employee returned to work after six weeks and after a few days when he seemed agitated and ill at ease in his old position, he settled down. One afternoon when business was slow, he took his supervisor aside and thanked him.

He told me he was doing drugs and never woulda got help if I hadn't pushed him to it. He said he'd been in one of those residential treatment programs you hear about. He said he couldn't even drink beers with the guys anymore. Turns out, I like this kid. When he isn't all loaded up on drugs he's a good worker and I can count on his honesty. I wish I had more like him.

When a workplace intervention has been successful, the employee corrects his deteriorating job performance: there are fewer absences and tardies; complaints from coemployees cease; work product improves; use of medical benefits drops. These changes may have come about through self-correction or with the assistance of trained professionals. In either case, improvement occured because through workplace intervention the employee recognized his job performance was impaired and that failure to take corrective measures would cost him his job.

The supervisor can, like Adam, take satisfaction from having helped a subordinate and saved the company substantial costs, and knowing that his area of supervision will function more smoothly.

8

THE HARD TO HELP: EXECUTIVES AND WOMEN

There are many studies showing that male and female executives and females working at all employment levels are more likely than the general population to avoid a confrontation over their chemical abuse. In this chapter we will profile these members of the workforce and discuss strategies for helping them get the treatment they need.

EXECUTIVES

Until recently, little has been written about male and female executives as a subgroup of the chemically addicted. However, the Alcoholism Council of Greater New York not long ago completed a study of recovering alcoholic executives that not only treats executives as a group with particular problems where addictive chemicals are concerned, but also divides its findings into male and female categories. This gender differentiation is a remarkable departure from the usual unisex form of such surveys, and one that makes the New York Council's findings particularly helpful.

Sixty-two executives were surveyed and personally interviewed for the New York study. Of this number, 46 were men and 16 were women. The subjects were chosen from a field of almost 100 executives active in New York Alcoholics Anonymous. Each had at least two years of what the test givers evaluated as "quality" sobriety.

Half of the males were married but fewer than 20 percent of the women lived with husbands. Career categories included communications, finance, sales, service and manufacturing. Eighty-two percent reported having blood relatives who were alcoholics.

During the period of active alcoholism, these executives rose to prestige positions in *Fortune* 500 companies, major New York City companies and smaller firms as well. Better than half those surveyed had been promoted as high as vice president, 33 percent became general managers and 8 percent were either company presidents or CEOs. In sobriety, at the time of the New York Council interviews, 45 percent of the subjects were vice presidents, 32 percent were general managers and 23 percent were either presidents or CEOs. (The study cautions against the easy assumption that sobriety led many vice presidents to be promoted. Actually, job changes were much more complex than that. For example, some of those surveyed had gone from being vice presidents of large firms to CEOs of much smaller enterprises.)

Like all impaired workers, at the peak of their disease these executives had trouble coming to work regularly, were frequently late, failed to keep appointments, etc. But because these men and women were decision makers and figures of some authority, other symptoms of impairment caused problems—not only for them but for the many people with whom they worked and who were dependent on their competent functioning. Procrastination, the inability to make decisions, became a problem for 61 percent of the men and 56 percent of the female executives. More than half the women reported a severe loss of interest in their work; almost 40 percent of the men experienced the same feelings. Forty-one percent of the men and 56 percent of the women reported fatigue and sleepiness. A sense of being drained of all energy was another serious problem. Perhaps most devastating of all for this group of men and women who once took pride in their ability to meet and overcome all challenges, the recovering executives—about 60 percent of both men and women—described a frightening loss of self-confidence.

It is no wonder they lost confidence. Their description of their alcohol-related behavior makes clear just how sick they were. More than 40 percent of the men and women reported having memory blackouts at work. Fifty-nine percent of the men and 67 percent of the women told of inappropriate drinking at work—bottles in desk drawers and filing cabinets, three and even four martini lunches, early lunches, lunches that lasted all afternoon.

We know the stories told by these New Yorkers are not unique. An alcoholic woman executive with whom we are acquainted always drank too much at midday, and in the afternoon she routinely slept curled up on the floor under her desk. With the chair pulled in close and all her paperwork arranged neatly on top, everyone assumed she was at an appointment. The orderly desk and crisply efficient decor of her office were all the evidence most people needed to convince them she was doing a good job.

Chemically addicted executives are rarely confronted with evidence of their deteriorating job performances. Rarely are they made to face the truth of what chemical abuse is doing to their businesses. Last year, American commerce lost better than $100 billion because of chemical abuse. Impaired executives had a lot to do with that loss because when they stop making good decisions, their mistakes can cost hundreds of thousands—even millions—of dollars. Their disruptive behavior has the power to affect employees at all levels. The corporate image is damaged; productivity suffers. Furthermore, if a chemically addicted executive is in a position to influence company policy on such matters, he is very likely to block the implementation of an employee-assistance program with potential to help other employees. Without doubt, the impaired executive is a major problem for big business.

At the time he entered treatment for acute alcoholism, Charles was a vice president of a large office-products company with which he had a long and successful history, starting from the time he began working as a young man right out of Harvard Business School. He was aggressive, dynamic, charming, and endowed with an apparently inexhaustable supply of energy. He expected the best from everyone around him and better than the best from himself. He was married in his late 20s to an attractive young woman named Jill. They joined the right clubs and bought a summer place on a lake in upstate New York. When their two sons were old enough to attend the best schools, that's where Charlie made sure they went. As the years went by, Charlie and his wife and the two boys were seen as a model family: beautiful, bright and making more money every year.

He told us:

We were never as happy as everyone thought, but we put on this facade. It was never talked about, but we seemed to agree without saying so that when we were out in public, we acted like the happiest married couple in the country. And at home we always kept our voices low and controlled, even when we were angry enough to start throwing things. I grew up in a home where my dad and mom fought loud and mean and I didn't want that for my boys. I wanted their life to be as close to perfect as I could make it.

But I know exactly when it all began to fall apart. I remember the day like it was yesterday. Jill and I had been having arguments—just the usual stuff you expect when a couple's been together 10 or 12 years and they realize nothing's ever going to change and they're not getting any younger. On that particular day, it was a Sunday morning and the boys were staying overnight with Jill's mom and dad, we were getting ready to go to brunch at some friends'. We were going to watch football and eat and have a few drinks and I was looking forward to it. Jill was complaining about how she hated football and wanted to do something else. All of a sudden, it seemed like I was always doing what Jill or the boss or some client wanted me to do. And I felt this huge rage in me, like I could put my fist through the plate glass window, you know? I listened to Jill go on about how she wanted to go into the city for an art opening or to the ballet or something, anything to avoid that football brunch. And my anger got so bad, I really got scared by it. It seemed possible I might do something to hurt Jill or even myself. I don't to this day know where that anger came from all of a sudden, but I figure it must have been down inside me growing for years and years and just happened to emerge that morning. Anyway, I left Jill in the bedroom yelling at me and went downstairs and fixed a double scotch. I didn't even stop to think what I was doing. All I knew was I felt better right away. I didn't care if Jill stayed home or stood on her head. I was going to that football brunch.

I always did like drinking. People used to say I knew how to work but I knew how to play too. But I'd never been one to get drunk except once or twice a year maybe. Drunks were embarrassing. But after I started using the scotch to take care of my anger, it was hard to be moderate. I'd have a couple when I got home. Then I started having one while I waited for a later train. Then maybe I'd have two drinks and one on the train and a couple at home. Some days I'd order two on the train, just so I could stand to go home. It got so I was going to bed with a buzz most nights.

Then one night the drinks were not enough to keep Charlie's anger under control. He struck Jill during an argument and she left him, cleaning out the bank accounts and taking the boys with her. From that time, drinking began to affect Charlie's work. He had been miserable in his marriage, but living alone was even worse. He was lonely and too proud to admit it. He drank to keep himself company. The months passed and Charlie's alcoholism moved into high gear. His secretary imagined that she understood his unhappiness and went to lengths to cover up his inadequate job performance. She told herself he'd snap out of it when he got over his divorce. All around Charlie, his coworkers were beginning to take action to compensate for his problem. Gradually his subordinates took over more of his responsibilities. His superior suggested a vacation in the Bahamas. The company had business down there. Why not combine work and play and get a new lease on life?

I screwed up the whole deal. By the time the plane landed I was drunk and I never sobered up the whole two weeks. Missed every appointment. I even changed my hotel so if the office called they wouldn't be able to find me. When I got back to work I had a bunch of lies figured out to cover my tracks, but I was shaking like an old man. Anyone could see I was a drunk, even me.

Charlie went to the president of the company and promised to make everything up to him. "I told him I'd work like a son-of-a gun and he knew I could do it. I was one of his best men. He needed me and we both knew it." Charlie went on the wagon and for six months stayed absolutely clean and sober by the force of his tremendous will power. To make up for the damage done during his drinking period, Charlie worked twice as hard as he ever had before. But the same will power that kept his nose to the grindstone without a drop to drink also worked against him. Every time he rejected the urge to drink, the will to slip into a bar or buy a bottle was almost as strong. Eventually, he just gave in to it.

I was on another business trip, Toronto this time. And I remember I saw this family—a couple and two kids—and that got me thinking about Jill and the boys. I realized how much I missed those kids and I regretted not trying to work it out with Jill. So I got on the phone and I called her and I tried to tell her I wanted to start over again. She wasn't having any of it. She even asked me if I was drunk. After six months stone sober as a judge and hating every minute of it, that really pissed me off. I thought I might as well be a drunk for all the good it did me to stay off the juice. So I went into the hotel bar and tied one on. I made it to the meeting next day, but I was in no condition to do business. After that, I don't remember much except I ended up in Montreal with a woman I didn't know.

Charlie belongs to one of three executive alcoholic types described by R. W. Thoreson, PhD, of the University of Missouri, who has made extensive studies of executive alcoholics. Charlie is superpowered, work obsessed, high on energy and high on denial. A second type of executive alcoholic described by Thoreson is the worrier, an individual driven to perfection, obsessive about everything he or she does, a stickler for detail and precision. This is the quintessential bureaucrat who comes to work early and stays late, riding roughshod over subordinates who dare to be less obsessive than he. The third model is the adventurer, the risk taker, the man or woman whose creative high energy and sometimes antisocial periods of behavior alternate with pits of remorse and guilt. Employees in creative fields are often of this kind.

Stan is an example of the adventurer type who, after years of heavy but uneventful drinking, discovered he could no longer control what happened to him once alcohol was in his system.

Stan always liked taking risks. He said it made him feel alive. For several years he had worked for movie studios in a number of capacities doing mid-budget horror films and science fiction. He had earned a reputation around Hollywood as a man who could get the job done. It didn't matter too much what the job was because Stan was a quick study and seemed to have an almost instinctive understanding of Hollywood and the financial end of filmmaking. He knew how to make things happen.

Stan began mixing his alcohol with cocaine on weekends at the beach and in the mountains. It made him feel even more energetic than he naturally was and the doubts he had about his appeal to women disappeared when he was high. High, he knew he could sell anything! Over a period of a few months he began snorting every weekend and then on Wednesday for a midweek lift. When he was snorting cocaine every night and drinking from noon on, his disease began to show in his work performance. He took financial risks that made some important men look foolish. He promoted a high-budget fantasy film and managed by the power of his dynamic personality to convince backers it was a good investment. Then he lost interest, the picture failed, and Stan was penniless. No one returned his calls.

It would not have been easy to do a workplace intervention on either Stan or Charlie. Such interventions pose very special problems. Generally, executives are individualistic men and women who have a difficult time admitting weakness or asking for help. As they rise higher in the company structure and there are fewer trusted colleagues to whom they can speak candidly about personal problems, this trait becomes more pronounced and problematical. These executives perceive personal problems as potentially fatal character flaws, chinks in the armor of "executive machismo." Stan told us he knew if he confessed to anyone his fears about cocaine and alcohol, the word would be out overnight and no one would call him. Ironically, that's what happened anyway. To most high-powered executives, asking for help translates as weakness; weakness means inadequacy; and inadequacy means they will not get the next fiercely desired job promotion or assignment.

There are some situations when management knows about the abuse of chemicals and makes a choice to allow it to continue. To understand this better, we need to look at the connection between workaholism and alcoholism. The dynamic executive who is putting his company on the map at the same time he is drinking or snorting himself to death is—in the early stages anyway—a liability the boss may be willing to tolerate. Although the executive is not 100 percent reliable, he is still capable of a prodigious work effort most of the time. The boss in this circumstance fears that the executive cannot function (i.e., produce) without alcohol. From his point of view, it does not make good business sense to take away the elixir of success.

Judy is an account executive for an advertising firm.

Before I went into treatment, my job was the most important thing in my life and I poured everything I had into it, believe me. Maybe if I'd had a family, kids, it would have been different but my husband and I were both compulsive about making it big in advertising and we goaded each other on, being competitve about the accounts we landed and the size of our salaries and bonuses.

A partner in Judy's firm, Arnold, told us, "She was the most creative person on our team. And tireless. Most people start to slow down a little when they've been around a few years, I think, but Judy was the opposite. She worked nights, she worked weekends, she worked at home. And everything she did was dynamite."

Amphetamines were the secret of Judy's phenomenal energy.

It was a joke around the office. Arnold called them my genius pills. Everyone knew I was speeding, but who was there to tell me to stop? And why should they when I had the Midas Touch? My campaigns were bringing in money for the whole firm.

And then one Sunday I was in San Diego and I had to get back to L.A. in time for a meeting that night. Right around Disneyland, I hit the football traffic and I was furious because I'd forgotten all about the Raiders. Maybe that doesn't seem like much to you, but for me it was really unusual because I had my life planned down to the smallest detail. I had a car phone, but I couldn't reach Arnold or my husband. The tie-up was simply horrendous, and I got madder and madder and my blood pressure went into orbit! I didn't watch the guy in front and the next thing I knew I was in the middle of a five car smash with a bunch of drunk football fans yelling at me.

At the emergency room where the ambulence took Judy, the doctors were concerned about her elevated blood pressure. It did not take them long to realize that Judy was a very sick woman.

> Of course, it all came out about my taking speed and they told me I had to go into treatment. All I could think of were my accounts and all the money I wasn't going to be making. And looking like a fool, of course. I knew Arnold would be upset. And I was right. He told me to get all the help I needed, to take all the time off necessary. But I knew he didn't like it one bit. He knew all along about the pills and how they worked and he liked them. Why not? I was making him a rich man. The bottom line was what mattered to Arnold.

It is difficult to document executive impairment. Professionals like Charlie, Stan and Judy do not work under direct supervision. Their hours are flexible, making tallies of absences and tardiness irrelevant. They are often protected by the people who work around them: devoted secretaries, respectful subordinates and ambitious superiors. Nevertheless, experts like Dr. Thoreson who work with chemically impaired executives tell us that there are some early signals their colleagues can document.

The first is apt to be the erosion of credibility and trustworthiness within the executive team. Although the impaired executive still appears to be a valued member of the team, his colleagues begin to doubt he will produce as he promises. What he says carries less weight than it once did. His name appeared on promotion lists but no longer does. Other executives may feel he has to be dealt with in a special or careful way, which can generate resentment.

These are subtle changes in the workplace dynamic, but they can damage an entire business. If the company is a small one, the problem executive disturbs everyone's work pattern. He is a component in the business machine and he has ceased functioning as he should, with the result that all other parts must compensate.

Impaired executives often continue to work at a high level of quality until they are very sick indeed, but careful observation reveals that they do less work than before. Job shrinkage is one of the most common signals of executive impairment. They volunteer ideas infrequently, take on new tasks less eagerly. What they do seems to take longer than before.

Judy admitted to us that she often worked nights to make up for what she didn't get done during the day. "Sometimes, I was too fidgety to concentrate. Other times, I'd work like a house afire but the results were crap. I'd have to start all over again."

And consider the case of Oscar, an executive and computer engineer. Oscar was asked to speak before a prestigious conference of his peers on a subject on which he was the acknowledged expert. His speech was well received, he appeared on local television and was interviewed for several articles in newspapers and magazines. On the basis of this stellar performance, he might have received the promotion he expected.

It did not turn out that way, however. Oscar's immediate superior discovered that in order to prepare his address, he had let everything else on his desk slide for a month. He was late on some projects and behind schedule on others. His secretary was working overtime to cover Oscar's sloppy work. To protect her boss, she was not recording her hours.

Executives like Oscar are professional problem-solvers, but when they become addicts they lose their ability to generate fresh, creative solutions. They rely increasingly on old remedies that, though they may avert disaster, do not make optimal use of business circumstances and opportunities. But even as the quality of work deteriorates, the executive's impairment may continue to go unnoticed because of the "halo effect" created by his previous shining performances.

A businessman who helped finance Stan's debacle told an auditor, "I thought the idea was stupid from the beginning. But who am I? A real estate man from Nebraska. What do I know about movies? When Stan said it was going to make us all rich, I looked at his past success and figured he must be right."

A subordinate of Oscar's told us, "I used to wonder how he'd gotten so far in the company. He just didn't seem to have the energy and ideas a top man should have. But everywhere I went I kept hearing what a genius he was so I finally figured I must be wrong."

During the months before he went into treatment, Oscar's secretary assumed the protective role that is typical of the secretaries of impaired executives. She worked many extra hours to correct his work, made excuses when he forgot commitments and soothed his colleagues' growing irritation. She had come into Oscar's office when he was the wonderchild of the firm. He had taught her everything she knew about computers and for her the halo of the wonderchild remained in place despite overwhelming evidence it had long ago been sold to support Oscar's addiction.

It is difficult to identify the impaired executive, but it is not impossible. Surveys like that done by the New York Council on Alcoholism and the pioneering research work of Dr. Thoreson and Paul Sherman enable us to list certain workplace behaviors that may indicate an executive is having trouble with drugs and/or alcohol. Earlier in this book we gave you another such list for lower-level employees. All those characteristics apply to the executive as well, but it is unlikely you will notice them particularly. Remember, too, that you are looking for patterns of behavior repeated over a period of time. Isolated incidences of lateness or a failure to be a decisive mean nothing except that the executive in question is human.

- lateness, morning or after lunch
- excessive absenteeism or unexplained absences
- bizarre or unlikely excuses
- use of leave in small increments instead of one or two weeks at a time
- incomplete or faulty, incomprehensible instructions

- unavailability for decision making or critical discussions
- absence from important meetings
- indecisiveness, procrastination
- reluctance to take responsibility for projects
- large amounts of time on phone or working on vaguely defined projects
- failure to brief staff on important matters
- shifting the blame
- defensive behavior
- withdrawl, depression
- inappropriate behavior
- increase in discussions of a personal or embarassing nature
- inexplicable memory loss
- fatigue
- erratic work behavior
- hare-brained schemes, grandiose plots and projects that come to nothing
- failure to meet deadlines

Executive interventions require the cooperation of secretaries and other executives for the accumulation of documentation, and they are sometimes compared to family interventions because several people may participate and the tone of the interview is usually supportive.

Dale is a tenured professor at a large university. After the death of her husband, her drinking increased so that students began to complain about the clarity of her lectures, apparently arbitrary grading practices, and the fact that she was rarely available to them during posted office hours. The head of Dale's department, Vincent, did not know what had caused the change in his collegue's work performance, but he knew that before saying anything he would need plenty of proof that a problem existed at all.

For several weeks Vincent kept a record of complaints against Dale. He made it a point to observe three of Dale's lectures and, on a number of occasions and without warning, dropped in on her office during office hours. When he realized that the student complaints had merit, he took into his confidence another collegue as well as a senior secretary in whom he put great trust. They, too, confirmed the students' complaints and added some of their own. Dale had missed faculty committee meetings, failed to respond to memos and was not returning phone messages. She had become hard to get along with in recent weeks. She made unreasonable demands on the department's already overburdened secretarial staff. On two occasions, she had asked the least senior of the secretaries to lie for her and put her request in such a manner that the younger woman felt her job was at risk if she refused.

When Vincent had accumulated several pages documenting Dale's unsatisfactory performance, he arranged a private meeting with his friend, their colleague and the senior secretary. At this meeting, each spoke candidly about how Dale's impaired performance affected their own ability to work, the students' ability to learn and the reputation of the department. When Dale became defensive, pointing out what they already knew—that she was a tenured professor who could not be fired—the intervention team continued to present their facts. They knew Dale's history as a devoted and conscientious teacher. They hoped this, combined with the documented evidence of impaired performance, and their own determination to remain unmoved by her anger and intellectual excuses would break through her denial. Eventually, the intervention process began to work. Dale talked about loneliness since her husband's death, her unresolved anger at him for leaving her, and the shame she felt for being unable to master her emotions and behave rationally. She was, finally, relieved and gratified when her problem came into the light. She became willing to speak to a recovering alcoholic in the department who told her several of their colleagues from other departments in the university held a regular AA meeting one lunch hour a week. Dale was invited to join them.

Documentation that is thorough and irrefutable is crucial to convince the impaired executive that he or she needs help. Denial is supported by highly developed verbal and analytic skills. The creativity that once went into work now empowers that denial system, making it virtually impenetrable without strong, incontrovertible evidence. The most effective means of reaching impaired executives is by objective proof that their behavior negatively affects the whole company and puts their own career at risk.

Impaired executives may feel their entire identity is bound to the work they do. That was certainly true of Dale. Thus it is important to praise the contributions they have made to the firm and the value everyone places on their continued participation. Vincent stressed this point with Dale because he knew she had devoted her life to students and learning. Impaired executives whose jobs are threatened are frightened individuals—though they may never show it. Let them know that the company appreciates their unique abilities and assure them that if they get help for their problem—"whatever it is"—their rung on the career ladder will not be jeopardized nor will their opportunities for future advancement.

Jan is a partner in a Washington, D.C. firm specializing in international law. In the course of her work she spends a third to a half of the year overseas. She has been with the firm for almost 20 years. For half of those years she has been a recovering alcoholic.

> The senior partner was the one who blew the whistle on me. And thank God he did. He said my clerk was complaining, my secretary was tired of covering up, I was making stupid mistakes and then working overtime to cover up for myself. I was a mess and he said it was time to get help or lose my job. Period.
>
>   I was one of three women in my law school class, and to get ahead I had to give up a lot. I got a reputation as some kind of superwoman and I spent my life living up to that reputation. I never even considered getting married or having kids. There never was time.

My dad and my mom were both drinkers and I always swore I wouldn't be like them. When I woke up after my first blackout and I realized what was happening to me there was never a day from then on that I didn't worry about alcohol. But I kept on drinking. I'd tell myself I'd quit the next year at New Years and so I'd go on the wagon for a few days or a week or a month and then something would happen and I'd be back at it.

Both my folks died from drinking. I would have too if the boss hadn't stopped me in time. My job was everything to me and when I knew I was about to lose it, that's all it took to get me into AA. I've been there ever since.

It is estimated that executives who make it to recovery early in their disease have an 80 to 90 percent chance of staying clean and sober. An executive may be hard to help initially, but once his denial is overridden and destroyed, he will go at recovery with all the power of his considerable intelligence and energy.

FEMALE EMPLOYEES

Generally speaking, women who become alcoholics and addicts bring to their disease great emotional and psychological pain. A women's treatment specialist knows that once her patient has stopped drinking and using, she will be forced to confront a daunting number of other problems—anger, passivity, dependency, fear, low self esteem, guilt, shame. She is likely to suffer from acute loneliness and depression and to have a history of suicide attempts. Her history with the opposite sex may be stormy. Female addicts and alcoholics are often battered women with childhood histories of incest, molestation and battering.

Until recently the treatment of female addicts and alcoholics has paralleled that of men. Today, however, more and more specialists realize that in our society the chemically dependent woman has special recovery needs not generally addressed by traditional treatment models.

Betty Lou works in an expensive deparment store in Southern California selling cosmetics. She has twin sons.

Betty Lou began drinking in high school, where getting drunk was considered grown up and sophisticated. In those days she had a reputation for being able to drink almost everyone under the table. In high school she made only average grades but she was a beauty queen and a cheerleader, and when she graduated she was voted most popular girl in her class.

She went to work in the cosmetics department right after graduation, and by the time she was 20 she was representing a prestigious firm. She loved her work because it gave her an excuse to spend hours on her appearance and wardrobe. At the time she married Eric, a computer programmer, she had a designer wardrobe and was deeply in debt to several expensive department and specialty stores.

Eric and Betty Lou wanted a new house of their own and a pair of expensive cars, so there was never any question of her not working after the twins were born. It made her sad, though, to drop them off at the baby-sitter's house when they were less than two months old. She knew the baby-sitter didn't give them the kind of individual attention every baby deserves, but Betty Lou couldn't possibly stop working to care for them. She and Eric had bought the house they both wanted, and although she was still driving her old car, Eric had a new sportscar. There was never time to work in the yard, so they were going to hire a landscape service to put in the lawn and flowers. She had to work to pay for that, too. . . .

When the twins were three years old they still weren't toilet trained. The baby-sitter refused to change any more diapers, and Betty Lou had to find someone else to take care of them. Separating from the baby-sitter left each boy deeply disturbed; the toilet problems became worse and Eric blamed Betty Lou for not being an adequate mother. At about the same time, her supervisor told her she would have to spend more time on her personal appearance if she wanted to keep her job.

Betty Lou began drinking wine coolers. She was depressed and given to unpredictable crying jags that always infuriated Eric because they seemed so unmotivated. When she experienced trouble sleeping, her doctor prescribed Valium to help her cope. Betty Lou discovered that the diet pills she sometimes used made it possible for her to get up an hour or two earlier in the morning. This extra time was what she needed to put on her makeup and lose the droopy look that made her appear older than her 25 years. She was afraid of losing her position at the cosmetics counter now and worked harder than anyone else so she would not be accused of doing an inadequte job.

Betty Lou had always been likable. At work she had many friends who knew that something was the matter. They saw her taking pills on the sly, and when they all went out for drinks together after work Betty Lou was always the first to order a second round. It was one of these friends who finally intervened on Betty Lou's behalf. She was able to list the signs and symptoms of alcoholism and drug abuse and make Betty Lou realize that if she continued as she was, she would lose first her job and then probably her husband and sons.

Betty Lou's story has a happy ending. She has been sober several years now, and although she and Eric have divorced, the twins are with her. She still works and she is still exhausted a lot of the time, but Betty Lou understands now that drugs and alcohol offer her only misery. Unfortunately, for every happy ending there are countless unhappy stories of women trapped by chemical addictions.

The New York Council survey tells us that alcoholic women executives arrive at their drinking milestones (first drink, first drunk, first trouble from drinking, first awareness of trouble, readiness for help and recovery) at the same time or earlier than their male counterparts. In that study, the women judged they were ready for help 11 years earlier than men on the average. Most of the women entered recovery around the age of 38; the average age for men was 45. The Council study also underlines what students of alcoholism have known for a long time: women experience more severe symptoms of chronic alcoholism at an earlier age than men.

Dr. Stephanie Covington, of La Jolla, California, a psychologist working in the field of women and alcoholism, told us that one of the obstacles to understanding how the disease affects women in the workforce is the fact that until recently, studies of alcoholism and drug abuse have not been gender-differentiated. Dr. Covington and her colleague, Mary Dana Phillips, have made some important steps in correcting this omission, however, and we are grateful to them for sharing their insights with us.

The largest percentage of female alcoholics are employed. Married women with jobs have substantially higher rates of chemical abuse than do single working women and housewives. Like Betty Lou, they are also likely to be addicted to some kind of mood-altering prescription medication. Most likely, this woman is depressed but she does not see any relationship between the chemicals she injests and her persistent feelings of low self-esteem, frustration, fatigue and hopelessness. She experiences extreme mood swings but rather than connect them to chemicals, she lives with a vague sense of dread that there is something wrong with her mind. How often we have heard women in treatment say, "Thank God I'm an alcoholic. I thought I was going crazy."

If she thinks very much about the amount she drinks, the cocaine she snorts, the dope she smokes, she feels a sense of shame. Alcoholic women, particularly, feel stigmatized, for while our society may excuse and even glamorize the heavy drinking of men like Stan and Charlie and Oscar, women who drink must bear labels that identify them as sexually loose, morally weak, aggressive and neglectful of their families.

Although the female addict/alcoholic may be a highly paid executive or professional, she most frequently works at a job for which she is underpaid and overqualified. She has insufficient insurance coverage and is much less likely than a man to belong to a union.

These women rarely have just one job. Most are like Betty Lou. They are trying to be wives and mothers as well as wage earners. And since media and cultural norms decree that wives must be pretty and vivacious and sexually attractive at all times, gourmet cooks and pristine housekeepers, and that mothers must be creative and loving and patient and able to drive long distances without complaining, this working alcoholic/addict is under constant stress as she strives to fulfill the images society has given her as models. To compound her confusion, the message from the media is that if she is modern and fully human she must love working, thrive on the stress, smile through the pain. As women like Betty Lou try to reach these unrealistic goals, they fail repeatedly. With each failure they feel less and less worthy as women.

"I felt like I was being cut up and divided like a piece of meat," Betty Lou wrote in a self-evaluation. "Drugs and alcohol made me feel together again."

Even among an executive population, the alcoholic/addict woman perceives herself as being alone in this struggle. As our society is structured, she receives little or no emotional support even when she is able to make her needs known. Physical support is generally missing as well. Most of the housework is her responsibility, as is the preparation of meals, carpooling and child nurturing. Eric believed he was an enlightened modern man, but it never occured to him that he might share the task of toilet training the twin boys. Betty Lou was the woman; it was, therefore, her job.

A woman may deny the evidence of her illness because of the problems posed by recovery. If the female employee has an uncooperative spouse or no one to care for her children, she may reject a period of hospitalization *even when health benefits exist to pay for it*. Furthermore, while never easy, the critical break from denial, the acceptance of one's chemical addiction and the willingness to accept help, is much more difficult if the woman feels she must act alone and without social support. A 1980 study supports the hypothesis that low social support is most often the case among women who combine the roles of mother and employee. While this is true across all occupations regardless of salary or status, it is most true for female blue-collar employees. They are likely to be stigmatized by their family and friends if they admit to being chemically dependent. They find it difficult or impossible to arrange their lives to accommodate a period of hospital treatment. Their recovery is made more stressful by spouses and children who do not welcome the behavioral changes in their newly sober wife and mother.

If you employ women in your business, alcoholism and drug abuse are a problem that must be acknowledged. At present, chemical addiction is on the rise among working women, with the most conservative estimate putting the number of afflicted women at between 8 and 10 percent. But at all professional levels, women employees are hard to help.

There are four general problems associated with interventions on chemically addicted women.

1.   Inadequate Insurance. Once the woman is informed of her inadequate job performance, many employers have nowhere to send her for help because there is no third-party money available. While the majority of women today are employed, their employment patterns and economic situations are generally very different from those of men. Despite the advances of recent years, they tend to be concentrated in low-paying, low-prestige, nonunionized positions. They often work part time or sporadically, according to specific family need, and therefore have access to fewer medical benefits. Frequently employers keep impaired female employees in place, allowing them to work at ever-decreasing efficiency, until they either quit or can be fired.

     Even when benefits for treatment are available, a woman may be reluctant to make full use of them. The executive women in the NYCA survey were more likely than men to turn for help to a health-care specialist; but while 53 percent of the men surveyed actually got professional treatment for their disease, this was true for only 25 percent of the women. The survey does not make clear the reasons for this disparity. However, it has been theorized that even at the executive level, women believe their jobs are less secure than those of their male counterparts. Rightly or wrongly, they fear that taking a month off for treatment jeopardizes their professional security. Another theory for the reluctance of women to seek treatment relates to the shame borne by women who acknowledge they are alcoholics and addicts. Seventy percent of the women executives (as opposed to 43 percent of the men) depended upon AA alone for their recovery. Perhaps it was only in the uncritical environment of AA that they felt comfortable and safe acknowledging their disease.

2. Type of job. Many addict/alcoholic women never demonstrate impaired work performance until they are very far gone in their disease. They are often overqualified for the jobs they hold, and it is not difficult for them to perform adequately when the work takes little thought or concentration. Except for full time homemakers and those in executive and highly placed academic and professional positions, women do not generally identify strongly with the work they do. One woman in recovery for alcoholism told us, "Being a dental assistant is no big deal. I mean, one office is about the same as any other. The way I always worked it was, if I knew there was trouble and I might get fired, I'd just quit before the ax fell. Usually, they were so glad to see me go without a fuss, I could even get a good letter of recommendation. I just kept drinking and changing jobs that way for years."

3. Manipulation and disguise. It is not sexist to say that a female employee who is an addict or alcoholic will consciously or unconsciously manipulate her male supervisor in order to get him to tolerate her many absences, her tardiness, her frequent illnesses. She may hide behind a manner that makes her supervisor unwilling to confront her professionally. Perhaps she plays the needy, helpless little girl to his big, capable and generous daddy. Or she may use sexual bribery in exchange for his tolerance. If her supervisor is a woman, she may again act the needy little girl to engage the other's motherly instincts or to manipulate the woman's need to be well liked.

Some female employees disguise their problems with hints of vague female illnesses or family problems too emotional to talk about. What research exists in this area indicates that most male supervisors are embarrassed by what they think of as strictly female problems. They expect women to be victims of their biology, to be emotional and moody. Therefore, they accept a female employee's excuses in an unquestioning way that would not be the case if the employee were male.

4. Gender-linked motives. Some male supervisors disapprove of working women and underestimate their intelligence. These supervisors never really take their female employees seriously enough to bother to document their deteriorating job performance. In such work situations, the impaired employee is only doing what is

expected of her. Perhaps the supervisor cannot look at a woman without seeing his mother—and he would never be able to reprimand his mother! Or maybe she is so young she reminds him of his daughter—and he's always been soft on his little girl.

Overall, it must be acknowledged that standard workplace interventions based on job performance work less well for women than for men. In Betty Lou's case, it was the fear that she might lose her children that forced her into treatment. Although she enjoyed the money her job brought in and it was fun to wear a lot of expensive clothes and makeup, she did not identify with her job as her husband did with his. The *core* of her identity was with her home and children.

What will work then? Keith McClennan, executive director of Tri-County Employee Assistance Program in Akron, Ohio, believes that volunteer referral agents—he calls them "key employees"—are especially helpful in companies with many female employees. Invariably, women will talk to their friends about their problems, and a good listener will often have the best opportunity to intervene. Women are strongly influenced to seek treatment when, like Betty Lou, they fear they may lose the love, respect and companionship of family members.

Your workplace drug and alcohol policy can also encourage women employees to seek out the help they need by emphasizing the ease and privacy of self-referrals. Many women are willing to refer themselves for help if they are sure that their stories will remain confidential.

But there is a larger social problem here. Simply stated, so long as women shape their lives in accordance with the media vision of working womanhood, a vision that leaves no room for disappointment, failure or exhaustion, they will continue to experience the kind of emotional pain that makes them vulnerable to the chemical "quick fix." To shatter the power of the false images of womanhood by which so many working women are guided, it has to be okay for women to say aloud that they are unsatisfied with their lives. To ease the pain and make the emotional confusion tolerable, there needs to be honest and straightforward talk, less hiding behind illusions and pretense.

Betty Lou said it very well:

I don't have any more money now. The kids still worry me. But now that I'm in AA I have friends I can talk to about all this and they don't criticize me for being so damned imperfect. Before I was trying so hard to be what everyone wanted me to be, I wasn't a real person at all. And I've got my values straight now. That big house with the perfect lawn . . . they didn't mean anything when I thought I might lose the boys. Now I'm just me and it feels good. Warts and all.

9

CHOOSING A TREATMENT FACILITY

A manager's first important decision in this area is to develop and implement a drug and alcohol policy in the workplace. The second is choosing a treatment facility that will meet the needs of employees. Whether your company develops its own help program or contracts with an established employee-assistance program, you will have a considerable investment in the quality of treatment your employees receive. For this reason, you will want to be well-informed about the theory and specifics of treatment.

Jerry, the manager of a prosperous family-run business in Southern California told us, "I came into the tire business right after high school because my dad expected me to. And I do a good job because I learned from the time I was a kid. I've added innovations like computers. I'm comfortable with the new technology. But what do I know about hospitals and clinics and therapy? No more than my dad does. This is all new stuff to both of us. Some fly-by-night outfit could tell us anything and we'd probably believe them."

Unfortunately, there are many treatment facilities that promise marvelous cures. At these facilities the highest line item in the budget is advertising and marketing. Their television and print ads carry powerful emotional messages. They hire shrewd salespeople to convince you that if you buy their treatment program all your troubles will be over. Business people without knowledge of treatment theory and the varieties of care available are easily convinced by the sales pitch. Then, when treated

135

employees relapse repeatedly, these same business people lose their faith in the concept of recovery and—in the worst cases—revert to their old methods of dealing with impaired employees.

With this chapter we hope to keep you from being one of the disillusioned. We begin with a discussion of how addicts and alcoholics recover.

THE THEORY OF RECOVERY

It is important to know that recovery is a developmental process. Just as all of us went thorugh a number of "stages" in growing up, so a recovering addict/alcoholic must pass through periods of emotional growth marked by particular problems and behavior. To demonstrate the practical application of these stages, we've chosen two case histories—Pat and Glenn—to follow through the process of recovery.

RECOVERY STAGE ONE

This is the stage at which an addict/alcoholic enters treatment. At this point he or she may have acute physical and/or neurological problems that require monitoring by medical personnel, as withdrawal agony requiring prescribed medication. At this stage the individual might also have severe behavior problems. Most common of all are the psychological problems.

Pat combined all of these characteristics. For many years she had been employed as a bookkeeper/secretary for a large supermarket chain. When she suffered a mild heart attack, her addiction to Valium was discovered. Her dependency was so great that she had to be withdrawn from the drug gradually, putting as little strain on her heart as possible. For weeks, she was unable to sleep for more than a few minutes at a time. During this period, she had to be put in an isolation room to keep her from waking up the other patients whose ability to sleep she noisily resented. She underwent such a serious loss of appetite that her caloric intake had to be monitored by nurses. Her behavior was so bizarre at this time that her husband wondered if she had lost her sanity for good. She spoke of divorce one moment and in the next proclaimed her love. She wept and laughed without apparent motivation. Her conversation was garbled and confused. Her psychological problems ranged from extreme fearfulness to a suppressed but potentially volcanic rage directed at God, her husband, father and mother.

Glenn was 19 when he came into treatment. He had been employed by the same fast-food chain for almost two years and up until just before he began treatment he had received fair to good performance evaluations. Then his supervisor began noticing that Glenn was making mistakes. He confused the wrappings on the burgers so that people ordering one kind of meal often got another. He forgot orders altogether, disappeared for long breaks, and when a new intercom was installed at the drive-through window, he was totally inept at its simple operation despite several explanations from the supervisor.

At the treatment center, Glenn's medical evaluation determined that he was suffering from neurological damage caused by acute marijuana addiction. Although doctors and therapists promised he would recover eventually, for a time—for his own safety as well as that of others—he was unable to do anything requiring motor skills. His psychological profile indicated he was extremely immature. Like Pat, Glenn had trouble sleeping during the first several weeks after he stopped using marijuana. His behavior was moody. He was nervous and anxious.

RECOVERY STAGE TWO

When a patient reaches this period of recovery, his or her physical and neurological problems have been stabilized but in many cases they must still be monitored by medical personnel. The patient has also become emotionally stabilized to the point where he or she can make the all important volitional commitment to recovery. At this point, the patient begins—through the guidance of trained therapists—to attain the beginning of self-awareness and insight into the role chemicals have played in his or her life.

It was almost two months before doctors monitoring his progress indicated it was safe for Glenn to drive his car again. For Pat, whose case was complicated by a heart condition, some level of medical scrutiny was necessary for many months after she stopped using Valium. Both the individuals expressed a desire to "get well" and this was considered a hopeful sign by their therapists. In Pat's case, she very quickly came to see how she had used Valium to keep from expressing the rage she felt might alienate her from her family and the world. In theory, she acknowledged that in order to "get well" she would have to explore the roots of that anger. Glenn spent several weeks making excuses for his marijuana abuse: everyone smoked grass; his job was boring; dope was preferable to alcohol; the world was too stressful to survive without chemical assistance. His therapist felt Glenn was making progress when he admitted his attitudes were immature. Gradually both these individuals began to recognize their denial and the way it worked to keep them sick.

RECOVERY STAGE THREE

At this phase of recovery, medical and neurological problems continue to be stable, and with the help of regular group and periodic individual therapy, the patient begins to take significant steps in personal growth, steps that were previously impossible because of the deadening effect of drugs on his or her personality. Now the connection between chemicals and behavior is understood. The patient is ready to experiment with new ways of coping with life situations and to examine personal and family issues despite the knowledge that these examinations will be emotionally harrowing. He or she has begun to experience some of the benefits of recovery and is wlling to venture further.

For Pat this period meant getting to know herself and exploring the wellsprings of her anger. In the process, she discovered something she had never known. Pat was mostly angry with herself for her failure to stand up for herself, for always doing what her mother and father and husband wanted of her, for following the demands of a strict Protestant religious denomination. She learned how Valium made it possible for her to endure the stress of a lifestyle that would otherwise have been unbearable. Her first experiment with a new coping style occurred at Thanksgiving, six months after she first entered treatment. She told her parents that she and her husband would be spending the holiday in Hawaii and did not plan to include either a turkey or a church service in their celebration. At about this time Pat also reported to her therapy group that she was enjoying her work for the first time in years. She had recently reorganized the filing system in her office, and the supervisor was interested in having her go around to all the branch offices and do the same.

Glenn's physical recovery was swifter than Pat's. But emotionally he was so slow that his therapists sometimes wondered if he would ever "get with the program." He returned to his work at the fast-food restaurant and there were no further complaints from his employer. But in group therapy he was stubborn and unwilling to open up as his growth and recovery required. The treatment team decided to try him in a special group where he would be encouraged to explore some issues left over from his childhood. It was at this point that Glenn's true recovery began, for he was able in that protected environment to examine for the first time the damage done to him by his bruising and bitter stepfather and a mother too timid to intervene on his behalf.

RECOVERY STAGE FOUR

A treatment specialist we know calls this stage "Onward and Upward." It is an excellent way to describe this high-growth period in recovery. The recovering addict/alcoholic is in fair to excellent physical health at this point. Life skills are strengthening with each successful sober day. The patient has more than average personal insight and a growing independence and is willing to rebuild relationships where necessary and to continue to experiement with new ways for coping with life. He or she is apt to see problems as challenges rather than roadblocks to personal development.

Pat had to go through a lot of anxiety before she was able to work through her family problems. In time, however, she was reconciled with her mother and father, who reluctantly accepted the fact that their daughter was determined to shape her life according to her own, not their, wishes. Pat and her husband entered a therapy group intended for couples and with the help of that group they learned they could live together without either of them sacrificing a sense of identity. Pat never did reorganize the filing systems for her company. Instead, she was promoted.

Glenn remained in therapy of one kind or another for almost two years. During that time he moved from his mother's home into his own apartment and entered into a stable relationship with a girl he met in treatment. He is still employed by the fast-food restaurant and does not aspire to a more grandiose position at this point, although he has been told that if he wants to go to managers' school his application will be given serious consideration. For now Glenn seems happy with life as it is. He told us:

> If I was to start pushing, pushing, pushing, worrying about the future and making a million bucks, I think I might do drugs again. I mean, I know for a fact I don't do good with lots of pressure. I used to think I had to be a hotshot and when I wasn't it meant I was no good. That's part of why I did drugs, see? I feel way different now. I'm just being me and right now me feels like cooking burgers and fries. Maybe next year I'll want to be a brain surgeon, maybe not. I'll just take it as it comes.

TREATMENT PERSPECTIVES

The four stages of recovery are generally approached from one or more treatment perspectives.

MEDICAL

The medical perspective on treatment is concerned with biological, chemical and genetic factors of addiction. From this point of view a family member's drinking habits, a family pattern of depressive mood swings, and the presence (or lack) or certain brain chemicals are all significant. The patient's level of health must also be considered. What is the extent of damage to the liver from alcoholism, to the nervous system from drugs such as cocaine and marijuana?

PSYCHOLOGICAL

The psychological perspective on the treatment of chemical addiction focuses on the disease as a form of motivational and emotional disfunction. According to this theory, the disease is sustained by a pathological family environment. From this point of view, the apparently high statistical correlation between alcoholic women and women who were sexually abused as children would be regarded as significant. According to Dr. Ann D. Clark, PhD, research indicates that perhaps as many as 75 percent of alcoholic women have endured some form of sexual abuse. Of that number, more than half were rape victims. Between 1/3 and 1/2 experienced incest at some time in their lives. Also very important is the influence on children of parental drug and alcohol abuse.

SOCIOCULTURAL

This point of view sees drug and alcohol abuse as the result of living in a particular social or cultural environment. The improper use of chemicals is regarded as a learned behavior in which such elements as ethnicity, age, class, etc. are contributory. According to this school of thinking, a child raised in a neighborhood where drugs are sold on the corner and addicts shoot up behind the dumpsters is more likely to use drugs than a child from the suburbs. A girl raised in a home where most of the women take pills as tranquilizers will likely use such pills herself. By contrast, but still to prove the point, in certain cultures where drinking is frowned upon, alcoholism is low on the list of pathologies.

Just as there is no single cause of the disease, *there is no one way to treat the person who suffers from it*. After studying many programs, we can say without hesitation that the good ones utilize all three perspectives when treating alcoholics and addicts. In the next part of this chapter, we will discuss the varieties of treatment available today, and you will note how the three perspectives are applied.

CHOOSING A RECOVERY FACILITY FOR YOUR EMPLOYEES

GOAL SETTING

It is surprising how many people come to us without a clear idea of what they want for their employees. They know what they want for their organization—safety, productivity, profitability—but when we ask them their goals for their employees they are usually stuck for an answer. We tell them it will be impossible to evaluate treatment programs without exploring this point. There are two options to consider: abstinence alone and abstinence coupled with a lifetime program of recovery.

Option One: Abstinence Only

If impaired employees will simply abstain from drinking or taking drugs, there is bound to be some improvement in their work performance. But it is likely that this improvement will be marginal. Their accident rates will drop, of course. They will probably come to work on time and stay until closing.

They may, however, continue to suffer from maladies that keep them away from work the maximum number of days and run up the insurance rate. Personal relationships both on and off the job may not show any improvement. Without drugs and alcohol, they may even deteriorate.

For some employees, the threat of job loss alone is sufficient to force a sustained period of abstinence. Several years ago, we knew Al, a man in his early 60s who had worked for a large defense contractor for many years. Now as he approached retirement, his drinking became a problem at work and he was told that if he wanted to make it all the way to retirement, he would have to stop drinking. He went home and threw out all his liquor bottles and remained abstinent until retirement. He started drinking again at his retirement dinner, and six months later he was dead from liver disease brought on by acute alcoholism.

Another way an employer can try to force abstinence is by making attendance at meetings of Alcoholics Anonymous, Narcotics Anonymous or Cocaine Anonymous a requirement of continued employment. In chapters 10 and 11, "RE-ENTRY" and "RELAPSE," we explore the methodology of AA and other "twelve step" programs. At this point it is sufficient to say that for some impaired employees an extended exposure to the wisdom of the AA principles will be sufficient to keep them sober in the workplace. It may even improve the quality of their relationships.

The weaknesses of the "abstinence only" option are obvious. In the first place, abstinence alone—abstinence like Al's—generally does not work for an extended period. The addiction to chemicals is a disease, and one cannot will it away by abstaining any more than one can will diabetes or cancer into remission. Furthermore, because it is a progressive disease it will always be worse if the addict begins to drink or use again. Poor Al. He had worked hard for that retirement pension, but he lived to enjoy very little of it. Abstinence alone, without insight and the support of friends, is a hard, lonely way to go. It rarely lasts for long.

A second weakness is that the kind of abstinence that is forced on an employee so that he can keep his job may have little or nothing to do with what the employee wants for himself. It will never break through the wall of denial we talked about in earlier chapters. Instead, it is likely to make the abstinent alcoholic/addict bitter and bad tempered, convinced that he is being victimized by a brutal and uncaring world, a burden to his family and coworkers. If there was one thing treatment specialists we spoke to could agree on, it was simply that if an employee is not *self-motivated* to stop drinking or using, the chances of successful recovery are virtually nil.

In a treatment center, the first weeks are spent breaking through the denial and developing the vital motivation to recover. Sometimes attendance at AA meetings can achieve the same thing. Those who find AA on their own and take the risk of walking into a roomful of strangers and admitting aloud, "My name is ——— and I'm an alcoholic" have already overcome denial and taken the first step toward recovery. For them, treatment may never be necessary so long as they remain abstinent, attend meetings and listen to the wisdom of other recovering addicts and alcoholics. By contrast, employees coerced into AA are likely to enter the room with a grudge. Chances are their ears will be closed to everything except the slow ticking of the clock. For these people, there can be no hope of long-term recovery without treatment.

Option Two: A Lifetime Program of Recovery

Most employers understand that it is in the best interests of their company, the employee and his fellow workers to aim for a recovery goal that is more than mere abstinence. Recovery of an employee's emotional and physical health requires extended care in either an inpatient or an outpatient program or a combination of the two.

FINDING A TREATMENT FACILITY

This is the simple part! To discover the names of drug and alcohol treatment programs operating in your area, all that is required is a phone book and telephone. The following headings in the classified listings will give you an idea of the number of programs that will welcome your inquiries: Alcohol, Alcoholism, Drugs, Drugs and Alcoholism, Hospitals. If you prefer, a phone call to your county's health or mental-health department will also give you this information.

If you wish to find a facility outside your own area, you will be interested in the *Drug and Alcohol Treatment Program Directory* published annually by the U.S. Journal of Drug and Alcohol Dependence, Inc. This directory includes an alphabetical listing of facilities with the address, phone number and name of a contact person. In a second section, all programs are listed in a state-by-state geographical section that provides an easy-to-read, "grid" format noting many of the services at each facility:

Typical duration of stay in days
Number of beds available
Hospital-based program or not
Free-standing facility or not
Inpatient treatment provided
Outpatient treatment provided
Detoxification services provided
Family services available
Adolescent service available
Insurance coverage for treatment

The *Directory* currently costs $5 and may be obtained by writing or calling

The U.S. Journal Inc.
1721 Blount Rd. Suite 1
Pompano Beach
Florida 33069

Toll Free call: 1-800-851-9100

Call the facilities that interest you and ask to speak to the program managers or directors. Make it clear that you are a person in business, shopping for a program suitable to the needs of your employees. You will find that the representatives of drug and alcohol recovery programs—those connected to hospitals as well as private clinics and centers—will be delighted to speak with you. Take time to explore every aspect of each treatment program. Ask questions and speak your mind if something seems not quite right.

CHARACTERISTICS OF A GOOD PROGRAM

A good treatment program looks after the emotional and physical well-being of the alcoholic/addict and his or her codependents—those people closely linked to him or her through upbringing or marriage. Fancy premises and promises have nothing to do with what makes a good facility. Amenities may even act as a screen to disguise a lack of substantive programs.

On the following pages we explain in detail the factors you should consider when choosing a treatment site.

ACCREDITATION

In most cases, the best programs are connected to fully certified hospitals. Because of the certification and licensing requirements of hospitals, in this setting you will find a higher level of staff skill, a more complete knowledge of pathology, and personnel equipped to treat physical as well as emotional problems. As a minimum standard, an in-treatment facility should have a board and care license from the state.

Occasionally even this is lacking. During our research for this book we heard the story of one such mistake. For several years a large hospital in the Midwest had been sending patients to a nearby residential facility when they were not sick enough to require inpatient treatment but still needed care and supervision. The administrator of the facility was a physician with an excellent grasp of treatment fundamentals. Several people at various levels of hospital administration assumed that all the residence's legal papers were in order. Since hospital staff and personnel—as well as patients—were pleased with the care level at the residence, no questions about legality of operation were ever raised. For many months things went smoothly. Then one day the hospital administrator was visited by an official from the state licensing board who informed her that not only did the recovery residence lack proper state approval, its director was not now and had never been a medical doctor.

If you visit a treatment center and are hesitant to ask about licensing and credentials, bear this story in mind. Although no one was harmed by his sojourn in the unlicensed recovery residence, a tragedy might have occurred. You do not want to take that risk.

QUALIFIED STAFF

Credentialed doctors and nurses are always available in the first-class programs because drug and alcohol addiction are frequently accompanied by physical ailments that must be monitored from the first stage of treatment. Conselors must be certified under some kind of license. This will vary from site to site. Some will be licensed clinic social workers, others will be licensed psychologists or marriage and family counselors.

There are also what is known as "life experience" counselors. These men and women, themselves recovering addicts and alcoholics, have received some professional training and demonstrate such impressive skills working with their fellow addicts and alcoholics that a fully licensed doctor or therapist is willing to supervise and take responsibility for them. It has been our experience that mere training and book learning are rarely sufficient to qualify a therapist in the field of chemical addiction. Frequently, the "life experience" therapists are the best in the business, for they possess the insight that can only come from having "been there" and recovered. The bottom line in determining the effectiveness of any therapist or counselor is his or her knowledge of the disease of chemical addiction.

To explore this point further, most addicts and alcoholics initially view their own chances of recovery as pretty hopeless. "I know I can't stay sober more than a week," a woman named Jan told us at her intake interview. "I want to, but I know I can't because I've tried, I've really tried." Jan was put in a group run by a skilled life-experience counselor, Laverne. Laverne told Jan her own story—omitting none of the details of several wretched marriages, blackouts, parenting failures and public humiliations. Jan was astonished. When we saw her a few weeks into therapy, she told us, "I knew if Laverne could be sober, so could I. My life wasn't half as screwed up as hers."

Patients frequently bond with life-experience counselors as they do with no others. The counselors act as role models and for some there is an early period when staying sober like the special counselor becomes a matter of pride, of wanting to make the right impression on a particular therapist. Pride and wanting to make the right impression will not keep anyone sober for long. Often, however, it will keep an individual in early recovery long enough to break through the denial. Beyond that, they must build a sober, drug-free life on their internal motivations.

It is important to add that life experience counselors are often able to see through the cons and manipulations of the addict-alcoholic in early recovery. The old saying, "you can't kid a kidder" takes on important meaning in the context of therapy. Addicts and alcoholics are usually skillful liars, adept at getting people to do what they want. No one knows this better than a life-experience counselor who has only to look back a few years to be reminded of the liar and cheat he or she once was. These counselors know that in early recovery a patient will say or do anything to protect and shore up the denial of his or her addiction.

In an adult-treatment facility, a ratio of therapists to patients of between seven and 10 is adequate. In adolescent-treatment units, where the need for one-to-one care is intense, a ratio of five to one is recommended.

AFFORDABILITY

Whether you and your employees can afford a particular treatment program depends on the style and scope of medical benefits made available through your company. Although at least 29 states have laws requiring health insurers to offer coverage for psychiatric care—the heading under which the medical illness of chemical dependency is archaically listed—many do not. When available, it is always less generous than other medical coverage. Less than half of all privately insured employees have inpatient coverage for psychiatric problems that is equal to their medical coverage. Less than ten percent have equal outpatient benefits.

Here are a few financial facts you should be aware of.

Inpatient treatment may run as high as $500 a day. Six thousand dollars for a 28-day stay is not uncommon. Some even call it reasonable. Outpatient care may be as much as $150 a week for three to four evening sessions. In some programs, one-on-one sessions with a therapist are charged for in addition to the base rate, as are family groups, codependent groups, couples groups etc. Thus, if a whole family is in outpatient treatment, the expense may be as high as $500 a week. A residential treatment facility that furnishes meals and includes a resident therapist will rarely be less than $100 a day.

The cost of psychiatric benefits has always been expensive, but the expense of not providing them is proved even higher by a survey conducted by the Washington Business Group on Health. "Insight," a counseling program conducted by Kennecott Copper Corporation, is credited with bringing about a 53 percent reduction in absenteeism and a 55 percent reduction in hospital/medical/surgical utilization. Blue Cross of Western Pennsylvania reported that for 136 persons utilizing outpatient psychiatric benefits, medical costs dropped by more than half.

Since 1979, more companies have added psychiatric coverage to their benefits packages. However, these dollars are in most cases restricted by limitations on days of treatment or dollar coverage. And there is a trend toward a greater involvement of the insurance carrier in the treatment process itself. For example, Minnesota Blue Cross reviews each case and pays only for medical treatment considered "medically necessary" by a review team. Cost overruns become the financial burden of the hospital rather than the covered employee. Under other plans, individual cases are closely monitored by psychiatric nurses and physicians who review all medication and treatment plans.

As you formulate your company's plan to help employees impaired by drug and alcohol abuse, you will need to consult your insurance carrier about the creative options his company offers. Because the effective treatment of chemical dependency is highly individualized, we recommend benefits that include both in- and outpatient coverage. Going back to the cases of Pat and Glenn for a moment, full hospitalization was absolutely necessary for Pat because of her heart condition and the difficulty of withdrawing from Valium. Glenn, on the other hand, could have been much less expensively treated as an outpatient while living in the protected environment of a special residence until his neurological problems stabilized and he could be trusted to drive a car or cook at a grill again.

SUCCESS RATE

Beware of any facility that makes exaggerated claims for the success of its program. At this stage in the history of treatment there are few reliable statistics connecting treatment and recovery. Directors of the best facilities will tell you this without equivocation. But if a program director insists the behavior modification (or biofeedback, neuroelectric therapy, psychoanalytic or group therapy) approach of Facility X has a 78 (or 65 or 100) percent success rate, we suggest that you remain skeptical.

Although there is little reliable data about the recovery rates of patients treated by specific facilities, theoretical models of recovery rates exist based on a hypothetical population of 100 men and women who abstain from use of chemicals:

- *Twenty* of the 100 will recover on their own the first or second time they make the effort. For them recovery will be relatively easy thanks to four specific factors: strong family and social ties, stable employment, strong goal orientation and early diagnosis of disease.
- *Forty* will be able to recover only after a struggle and with the help of trained therapists.
- *The last 40* will never recover from alcoholism, although they may be "on and off the wagon" for many years. They will suffer from arrested development, have one or more secondary pathologies (brain or liver damage, for example), a pattern of repeated relapse, and disturbed work, family and social relationships. Eventually they will die of drug- or alcohol-related causes.

Instead of regarding these numbers in their most dismal light—40 percent of the people who try to stop drinking and taking drugs will never make it—we prefer a positive approach. *Sixty percent* of the people who try to stop drinking can be helped. And although no *program* can claim to have cornered the market on treatment, many *companies* are proud to point to the success of their drug- and alcoholic-treatment programs. These are the statistics of greatest interest to managers.

- *The Sheraton Corporation*'s retention rate for treated employees is 84 percent.

- *Firestone Tire and Rubber Corporation*'s Executive Vice President David L King estimates that the typical alcoholic loses 17 work days a year. This number is typically halved after treatment, dropping later to 1.4 per year. For every dollar invested in treating impaired employees, the company estimates a $3 to $5 return.
- At *Kimberly-Clark*, Darwin Smith reports that in a study of one group of treated and recovering alcoholic employees there was a 43 percent decline in absenteeism and 70 percent fewer accidents.
- At the *University of Missouri* 200 employees who received treatment showed an 89 percent positive change, which was estimated to represent a net savings of over $50,000 to the university.
- *General Motors Corporation* studied 117 employees who received treatment. A full year later accidents had decreased 82 percent. Grievances were down by 79 percent and discipline problems by 67 percent.

MEDICAL CARE

Patients in a treatment center must receive a complete medical evaluation at the time they enter the program. This may include, although usually at a later time, a psychological profile. This complete physical checkup provides baseline information that tells doctors and therapists the extent of physical and neurological damage an individual has sustained through the abuse of drugs and/or alcohol. On the basis of this information, a preliminary course of treatment is devised that may or may not include detoxification.

DETOXIFICATION

It is not uncommon for people to enter treatment drunk or high on drugs. The last fling is often a whopper, and it may take several days or a week for the chemicals to lose their potency. During this time the addict/alcoholic may need prescribed sedatives, around the clock medical supervision and a special diet. Patients are sometimes violent. Because "detox" can be messy and requires medical doctors and certified nurses, many facilities are not equipped to accept patients unless they are sober at the time of admission.

FLEXIBLE PROGRAM DESIGN

The best treatment programs recognize and prepare the recovering addict/alcoholic for the world outside the hospital, the world of work and play and family. Through flexible program design the patient can be helped at each stage of recovery. What is a truly flexible program like?

AA/NA/CA

There was a time when treatment facilities were considered to be in competition with self-help Twelve Step programs like Alcoholics Anonymous, Narcotics Anonymous and Cocaine Anonymous. That is no longer the case. AA and its associated programs are now regarded as essential for maintaining healthy sobriety. The former manager of TWA's EAP, Mary Bernstein, believes AA is crucial to the care and treatment of employees impaired by drugs and alcohol abuse. In her experience, those recovering addicts and alcoholics who are active in AA perform better on the job than those who merely abstain. During treatment the best facilities make every effort to forge a link between the patient and AA by taking patients to several meetings a week and by using AA terminology in therapy sessions.

Programs for Women

Good therapists realize that recovering women have specific prolems. Let's briefly look at three of these.

For some women, accepting their disease is a major effort, for there is a powerful stigma attached to female alcoholics and addicts: the dated and erroneous "barfly" image that assumes that a woman with a drug or alcohol problem lives on the fringes of society and is lax in her morals and personal appearance.

For those who buy this stereotype, it may come as a surprise that, far from being lax, many female addicts are driven by the demands of perfectionism. For these women it is not enough to be good mothers, good wives, good artists, good workers; they must be the *best*. If they are not the best then they fear they are nothing at all. How difficult it is for them to accept that not only are they not the best, they are addicts in the bargain.

Finally, despite the best efforts of the women's movement, there are still many women who are unable to assert themselves. They have learned they are helpless and hopeless and, in a sense, they have given up on trying to make their lives better. Often these are the women who were sexually abused as children or who grew up in homes with physically abusive fathers. In treatment they have to learn that they have the power to change their lives.

Many women will be unable or unwilling to face these issues of recovery without the assistance of female therapists. In fact, for many there will be subjects they cannot speak of in a mixed group. Studies of how men and women react and interact in therapy groups support this. In groups mixing men and women, the women have minimal interaction with one another and generally allow the men to dominate. By comparison, in women-only groups the sharing is often intense, particularly when the discussion relates to their histories of sexual abuse—often a serious problem for recovering alcoholic and addicted women.

As well as being helped by conventional forms of therapy, a woman's recovery can often be assisted by classes in assertiveness training, career guidance, makeup, clothing and color advice. These topics may seem trivial but, on the contrary, they can be immensely helpful for these women who without exception suffer from low self-esteem. When she returns to work after a month in treatment, the newly recovering woman addict/alcoholic is likely to feel as raw and fragile as if she had just had major surgery. It is a great help if she at least knows she looks good: a more flattering hairstyle, a wardrobe and makeup that suit her new self-image.

Recovering Executives

The work obsession, the reluctance to surrender the illusion of control, the typically high verbal and analytical skills—these characteristics of the addict/alcoholic executive can confound the work of unskilled therapists bound to a single therapy mode. A therapist must be willing and able to drop the confrontation method often used in groups for a more flexible and educative approach which allows the executive to—in time—"discover" his own problem.

A therapist we know in San Francisco had been working with a young insurance executive for almost six months in outpatient care. Week after week Ray attended therapy groups where he maintained either a morose silence or adopted an argumentative posture. Vince, the therapist, admitted to us that he was often very irritated by this man, but he managed to preserve his calm exterior. Dealing with Ray, Vince became almost passive—a behavior mode quite unlike his usual self. He encouraged Ray to talk about the role of alcohol in his life and kept quiet while the group corrected him or pointed out his denial. "I knew he was smart," Vince told us. "I knew that if I just gave him enough rope, he'd eventually haul himself in." And that is exactly what happened. One afternoon Ray paid Vince a surprise visit in his office. The man's face was alight as if he had just discovered The Truth. Well, in fact, he had. "I just realized I've been an alcoholic since I was in high school," were almost the first words out of his mouth.

Vince and Ray worked together for many months. During all this time Ray continued to work at the insurance company and did very well. Recovery was going well for him until one day when—as oldtimers in AA like to say—he fell off his pink cloud. Overnight he was made miserable. He told Vince he knew he would never feel any better. He was truly afraid that his mood of despair would motivate him to drink again.

At this point in Ray's recovery, Vince tried a creative approach that often works well for executives who are motivated to succeed. The approach is sometimes called a contingency agreement, others call it "self-blackmail." For Ray it worked this way. In Vince's office he typed out a letter to the head of his company informing him that he had begun to drink again and was unfit to work for a reputable insurance company. The letter was a formal resignation with a specific request that under no circumstances should he be given any letters of recommendation to another firm. The letter was given to Vince for safekeeping with the provision that if Ray relapsed he would immediately mail it to the insurance company.

Although we favor separate therapy groups for women to encourage them to share freely, it is probably best to mainstream executives to avoid issues of exclusivity. Discussing this with a local specialist, he was adamantly opposed to special executive groups because, he said, "an addict is an addict is an addict, but one of the problems some of them have is they think they're a better class of addict."

Whole Family Treatment

Unfortunately, recovery from any addiction is not as simple as merely treating the addict in isolation. True recovery requires several kinds of treatment for both the addict/alcoholic and his or her family. Experts we spoke to agreed that failure to get this kind of total care increases the chance of relapse. It is essential to remember that the addict/alcoholic is part of a family system. In response to his illness, this system of relationships has warped and become diseased itself. *The spouses, parents, children themselves are now also ill.* If only the addict/alcoholic is treated, he or she returns to a family system that remains poisoned. Slowly—but almost certainly—there will be regression to old patterns of thinking and behaving, the old patterns that were part of the addict's drinking and using days. Without the enlightened support of family, it is likely the addict will relapse into a diseased state.

The best treatment facilities provide programs for the whole family. What does whole family treatment involve?

Codependent Treatment

By definition, a codependent is a spouse, parent, child or sibling who is locked into a system of dependency with the addict/alcoholic. Put another way, "codependency is the impaired ability to freely think, feel, relate or act secondary to a relationship with a chemically dependent person or another codependent," according to Dr. Max Schneider, a noted authority on the effect of alcoholism and addiction. The system of intertwined dependency to which the addicted person has become accustomed and to some extent comfortable requires that he continue to practice his disease. If that changes, if he begins to get healthy, the codependent is often thrown into emotional confusion. Suddenly the codependent is oarless, rudderless, without a compass or even a destination, stranded in a new and troubled sea. To regain a sense of certainty, the codependent will sometimes unconsciously sabotage the addict/alcoholic's recovery.

From a manager's point of view, the untreated codependent is a threat to an employee's sobriety and, by extension, to the success of a company's drug and alcohol program.

Frank and Anna represent a fairly classic case of codependency. Prior to his treatment, Frank worked on the line for a manufacturer of automotive products while Anna stayed home and tended the house. Both were raised in traditional homes where a man's worth was determined by his physical strength, his paycheck and the number of male children his wife delivered. Anna's model of a good woman was her own mother who came from Italy at the age of 16, promptly married and thereafter devoted her whole life to church, raising babies and taking care of Anna's father and their home. Although they wanted a large family, Anne and Frank were never able to have children.

When Frank was drinking his pattern was this. He came home from work and sat down before the television set. Anna brought him a glass of red wine and turned on the news. Dinner—with more vino—was on the table promptly at 6 every night. Throughout the evening Anna supplied him with more wine until, around 11, he passed out. Then she would drag or walk him to bed. In the morning she had coffee and a screwdriver ready as soon as he awoke. Neither of them ever mentioned the fact that he drank too much. Weekends he watched more television and drank beer and wine with his friends at a local bar.

When Frank was drunk he sometimes fell, and when he did Anna soothed his aches with linament. If he smashed the taillight on the car, Anna ran it down to the repair shop without a word of complaint. In short, Anna made mothering Frank and covering up for his alcoholism the center of her life. She was totally preoccupied with making his way smooth. She called the plant when he was too sick to work. When he was rude to their friends or family she made excuses like, "He works so hard" or "Poor Frank, he's not feeling well today." Sometimes he made fun of his "little woman," calling her stupid or boring or nagging, but she never defended herself, never complained. She also never wept or laughed or expressed an opinion.

Frank had an accident at work and broke his hand. After his recuperation he came back to find his place on the line taken by another man. Frank's supervisor brought out the documentation of Frank's poor work performance over the last six months and he was told to get help for himself or lose his job. Since Frank's masculinity was defined in part by his work, this coersion was effective. He quickly acted on his supervisor's ultimatum.

In treatment he learned the role of alcohol in his life and now has had over a year of sobriety. Anna too has blossomed. She has come to understand that for years she *enabled* Frank to be a practicing alcoholic, coddling and catering to him as if he were a needy child. She has discovered that she can, with love, detach herself from him, his disease and his needs without destroying either one of them. She does not have to depend on Frank's dependency to shape her identity.

How is Anna's recovery relevant to Frank, the employee? It is worth saying a second time that codependents like Anna, left untreated and perpetuating the same sick dependency, are a real threat to the sobriety of a recovering addict/alcoholic. When one person in a family begins to get well, the rest of the family—unless they too are getting healthy—is likely to be resentful and angry about the change.

At first, Anna reacted to Frank's sobriety almost as she would have to the loss of a child. And she did what she could to return that child to her care. Although she knew Frank's job depended on maintaining sobriety, she offered him wine, called him half a man because he could not drink, and on one occasion got drunk herself as if by doing so she could lure him from his program. Until her own treatment began she felt unnecessary, extraneous.

Now Frank understands that Anna enabled his alcoholism for years. He also understands that if he were to begin drinking again she would make him bear the responsibility alone.

Couples Treatment

Couples often need help learning how to communicate in recovery. There are old grudges and resentments that should be expressed aloud in a protected clinical environment. In a couple's group Anna finally told Frank how much she hated him for being sterile. At home alone she never had the courage to express herself but in the clinical setting she did so for the first time. And he got to tell her that he was sick of having a mother for a wife.

Like codependent treatment, couple's treatment strengthens the family unit, which in turn strengthens the recovering addict/alcoholic's ability to remain sober.

Children's Treatment

The children of alcoholics are also codependents who need treatment. Their personalities have developed in reaction to the presence of alcoholism in their home. If the alcohol is taken away the old rules no longer seem to apply. This often results in difficult and angry behavior.

Mike was accustomed to his father being a drunk. He knew how to behave when the old man was around. He kept quiet and he kept out of the way. When Father got sober, he realized that for years he had been neglecting Mike and so he tried to make it up to him. When Mike entered treatment he was furious about this sudden interest. It was an invasion of his adolescent space for which no previous relationship with his father had prepared him. To show his resentment, he was acting out by failing in school, using drugs and staying out all night.

If Mike's father is your employee, he may be coming to work sober but he is not giving work his full attention. His thoughts are on Mike and Mike's well-being. The father feels like a failure with his son; he is angry with the boy and with himself, with his codependent wife. He is apt to miss work as he tries to mend old fences. He may develop psychosomatic illnesses as a result of constant worry. Unless his family gets help, the father will probably drink again just to escape feelings of failure and helplessness.

ACA Treatment

The initials ACA stand for Adult Children of Alcoholics. Many addicts and alcoholics are themselves the children of addicts and alcoholics and grew up in disfunctional homes. In the workplace ACAs are likely to behave in certain rather predictable ways. They are often perfectionists who have a hard time listening. They like to be in charge and go off on their own tangents. Or, they may be rigid rule followers, the perfect bureaucrats, the kind of employees who will not bend for anyone.

ACAs take criticism personally. To them it seems like a form of rejection. Their response to a few kindly words of advice may be extreme hurt or anger that is way out of proportion to the comments given. They look for faults in their supervisors as a way to tolerate their own inadequacies.

On the positive side, ACAs are often able to handle any crisis and for this reason they are frequently given a great deal of responsibility. Unfortunately, this responsibility frightens them—though the employer will not realize it—because they have a great fear of failure.

For this group of alcoholics (and codependents), a rich and lifelong recovery requires that volatile childhood issues be acknowledged and examined, defused and then put away. For many addict/alcoholics this is the most painful part of treatment but also the most beneficial.

Greg is a furniture manufacturer in upstate New York. He entered treatment when his partner confronted him with evidence that his misuse of money was hurting their small company. Greg responded well in treatment but he was not happy in his sobriety. His partner and employees complained that he was morose and hard to get along with. He lost interest in socializing and kept more and more to himself. He developed a whole repertoire of aches and pains and always seemed to be complaining. Not until he was enrolled in an ACA group did positive changes occur in Greg's life and attitude.

In the ACA group Greg talked for the first time about his alcoholic father, whom Greg had seen physically abuse his mother and molest his sister. He spoke about the guilt he felt for not stepping in to stop the man. "But I was a little boy, see, and he was a big, mean man. I knew what he was doing was wrong, but I was helpless." He talked about his father's death, of the joy he knew then, but also the shame because he always believed he should have been able to make things better. Greg had never told this side of his story to anyone, but in the group he not only talked but felt again those old pains. He was permitted to grieve for himself as a child. "I felt like part of me was set free for the first time," Greg wrote in a program evaluation months later. "It was like the little kid in me was getting a second chance to live."

It is clear that a variety of treatment groups geared to enlarge the alcoholic's understanding of his past as well as his present, groups that involve members of the whole family system, are crucial to the successful treatment of chemical addiction.

Also parts of a flexible program design are an educational, physical and spiritual component.

Educational Component

Everyone in treatment needs to learn as much as possible about the way alcohol and drugs affect the human body. There should also be at least two lessons in basic nutrition and health.

Physical Component

A good treatment facility will include some kind of physical exercise in its program for recovering alcoholics and addicts. A full gym and tennis courts are not necessary, although some of the expensive facilities in the country offer glamorous frills like these. Actually, all that is needed is somewhere to do aerobic exercise, a volleyball court, a Ping-Pong table, a chance to go for a run or a walk.

Outward Bound

Outward Bound is a demanding outdoor program that had its beginnings in the Rocky Mountains of Colorado. Today, Outward Bound programs are available in many parts of the country and they have activities tailored to the needs of the recovering addict/alcoholic.

To find out more about Outward Bound, we spent four days in the desert of the Southwest with a therapist, two guides and a dozen patients from a treatment center. It was easy to see from this exhilarating experience how physical challenge coupled with frequent small intense therapy groups can help the patient grow in sobriety. After four days of rock climbing, repelling and hiking, the patients in our group had bonded and taken leaps forward in self-esteem. The women patients especially seemed to benefit. One told the group that she had been brought up to believe that she was awkward and clumsy. What a surprise it was for her to discover she was actually quite the opposite. "I feel like I can do anything now," she told the group.

Spiritual Component

We believe that every good program has a spiritual component. Men and women entering treatment have been described by therapists (and sometimes themselves) as "spiritual bankrupts." Apart from drugs and alcohol, their lives have lost all meaning. Many of these patients yearn to be connected to a power greater than themselves. The founders of Alcoholics Anonymous recognized this yearning. For this reason, the program has a strong spiritual (as opposed to religious) component emphasizing every individual's need to establish a relationship with a higher power. People without a close knowledge of AA may have the mistaken idea that "higher power" means the Christian God or Jesus. In fact, it means only whatever the recovering person chooses it to mean. We have known men and women in AA for whom the higher power is the fellowship of AA itself. Others in recovery return to the religion of their childhood. A great many others create their own individualistic concept of a higher power. It is often said, and appears from our experience to be true, that although belief in a higher power is not a requisite for membership in AA, there are no atheists in the organization. Many members begin their tenure believing in nothing more powerful than the bottle or the fix, but few can sustain that point of view once they acknowledge the miracle of their own recovery. Some recovery facilities have a spiritual advisor on the staff, a priest or minister able to talk about a higher power in a nondenominational, nonthreatening way. Other facilities encourage and teach meditation as part of their basic recovery program.

In summary, a flexible treatment program is designed to meet the physical, educational, spiritual and emotional needs of the addict/alcoholic and his or her whole family. Anything less than whole family treatment will make true recovery difficult—and perhaps impossible—for your employee in treatment. We believe that attempting to treat addiction with less than this family approach can be likened to treating diabetes without dietary controls or hay fever in the middle of a meadow in spring. Of all the factors you should consider when choosing a facility for the members of your organization, there is probably none more important than a flexible program design.

OUTPATIENT CARE

The availability of outpatient care is another factor to consider when choosing a facility. For many years, outpatient care was the orphan child of drug and alcohol treatment. But recently experts in the field are realizing that many addicts and alcoholics do not need full-time care. Far more can be successfully—and less expensively—treated on an outpatient basis. With this care plan the patient remains part of the world as he goes through the stages of recovery. From the very beginning he learns to monitor and manage his own recovery.

A good inpatient facility is characterized by a concern for the addict/alcoholic's educational, physical and spiritual needs. It does not treat the addict/alcoholic alone but as part of a disfunctional family system in which each member is to some extent impaired by codependency. These characteristics apply equally to the best outpatient treatment programs. However, there are additional criteria specifically relevant to care programs in which the recovering addict/alcoholic is free to come and go and which rely upon his determination to seek out and sustain a program of treatment without the constant supervision and care available in residential treatment.

Hours, Frequency and Location

There is no advantage to contracting with a facility offering outpatient care at a time when your employees are hard at work or that is located so far from the worksite that commuting to treatment becomes an ordeal. Nor is it wise to choose a program that meets only once a week for a few hours. Even twice a week is too little time to spend on treatment in the early stage of recovery. Generally speaking, a good early recovery outpatient program will meet a minimum of four times a week for a mixture of group therapy and education.

Appearance of the Treatment Facility

One weakness associated with outpatient programs is the high rate of patient attrition. In a 1983 pamphlet from the NIAAA Division of Alcoholism Services Development entitled "Attrition Factors in Alcoholism Treatment," it was reported that 64 percent of clients at NIAAA centers dropped out before completing treatment. According to a 1977 study, the average patient stops attending treatment before the fourth session.

One of the reasons cited as contributing to the high dropout rate is the appearance of the treatment center itself. If it is a labyrinth of corridors and featureless doors, if the walls are drably colored, if it smells bad or is noisy or poorly lighted, if the building is not pleasantly landscaped, if parking is difficult, if the patient must enter the center under a large and embarrassing sign, he or she may decide not to bother with outpatient treatment.

Use of Desensitizing Agents

Some outpatient programs rely heavily on desensitizing agents to maintain sobriety. You should be familiar with the arguments for and against these drugs.

Daily use of Antabuse (pharmaceutical name: disulfaram) is prescribed for alcoholics to inhibit their use of alcohol. The existence of a desensitizing agent for alcohol was discovered when workers in a rubber factory reported they could not drink without becoming violently ill. After World War II, Danish researchers found that one particular chemical used in the production of rubber—tetraethyliuram disulfide—was the culprit. In turn, this discovery led to the production of what some think of as the "anti-drinking" pill—Antabuse. With virtually no prior testing, it was first prescribed for alcoholics in the late 1940s.

Alcoholics have been the guinea pigs for Antabuse for over 30 years. Researchers are just beginning to appreciate the dangers in it. Recent studies indicate that alcoholics who rely on Antabuse over an extended time period may develope seizures or cardiovascular and nervous diseases like Parkinson's. A May 1979 article in the *Journal of Studies on Alcohol* reported a possible connection between Antabuse and mood disorder such as mania and depression.

The advantage of Antabuse is that it permits the alcoholic in the first stages of recovery to renew his vow of abstinence one day at a time as he takes a pill. He knows he cannot drink for the next 24 hours because Antabuse modifies the way his liver metabolizes alcohol. Normally, liver enzymes change alcohol first to acetaldehyde, second to acetate, and then to carbon dioxide and water, which the body eliminates easily. When alcohol is taken with Antabuse, the metabolic process breaks down after acetaldehyde is produced. The level of acetaldehyde rises to toxic levels, causing acute discomfort: respiratory problems, chest pains, vertigo, nausea, sweating, weakness and palpitations, blurred vision and a number of other reactions. According to the 1980 *Physicians' Desk Reference*, "The intensity of the reaction varies with each individual, but is generally proportional to the amounts of Antabuse and alcohol ingested."

The specialists with whom we spoke were in agreement about Antabuse: It is a crutch that cannot take the place of the varied treatment programs described above. Although it may temporarily help some recovering individuals by preventing impulse drinking, Antabuse is at best a short-term solution. Long-term sobriety requires a change of lifestyle and mindset that a pill can never provide.

Another well-known desensitizing agent is Methadone, which is used to help heroin addicts break their addiction. Although it was initially heralded as a great treatment breakthrough, most specialists now acknowledge that Methadone creates as many problems as it solves. Like Antabuse, it is a crutch. Unlike Antabuse, it is just as habit forming as heroin itself.

WHAT DOESN'T WORK

Before closing this chapter, we want to briefly mention some of the treatment methods which, though proven ineffective in the long run, are sometimes touted as miracle cures. Psychoanalysis—hours spent on the psychiatrists couch free associating and analyzing one's dreams—is of no help curing the disease of chemical addiction.

For years, psychiatrists controlled the field of alcoholism, which was considered a mental-health problem. Since 1970 this has been changing, and today there is increasing attention to the biological, genetic and neurophysiological aspects of the disease. There is a growing understanding that the treatment of alcoholism and addiction is highly specilized. Doctors and therapists without expertise, operating from general knowledge or merely a strong point of view, may actually harm patients by increasing their guilt and shame, strengthening their denial system and prompting them to delay meaningful treatment while their disease continues its inexorable progression.

At a meeting of the National Association of Alcoholism Counselors, David Ohlms, himself a psychiatrist, put the situation quite bluntly. He told his assembled colleagues, "As long as the mental-health field insists on viewing alcoholism as a symptom rather than a primary disease that creates its own symptoms, it should keep its nose out of this [alcoholism] field."

Some psychiatrists can admit their failure to treat the disease successfully. In a survey of members of the Southern California Psychiatric Association, one half of those questioned admitted to having no record of success treating addicted patients. The other half estimated their success at 10 percent. Nor is there any indication that hypnosis, vitamin therapy, behavior modification or biofeedback are suitable treatments. In fact, they probably do more harm than good for they raise the addict/alcoholic's expectation of an easy cure.

Despite what a few exploitive men and women in the treatment business may say, there is no easy or simple way out of this disease. Recovery comes only with time and painful personal assessment coupled with total lifetime abstinence.

TREATING ALCOHOLISM AND ADDICTION IN THE FUTURE

Will there ever be a quick sure cure for alcoholism and addiction? Certainly not in the near future. There is, however, interesting technology for treating the disease now in the early stages of development. Some scientists are studying the feasability of blocking alcohol's pleasure message to the brain. Others are experimenting with substances that alter the chemical balance in the brain and thereby appear to decrease the patient's need for alcohol. Most significant and likely to achieve far-reaching results is the growing body of research connecting chemical addiction and heredity. This avenue of research may eventually lead to specific genetic markers indicating those for whom alcohol is a potentially deadly substance.

One day in the future therapists may be able to structure treatment precisely to the needs of the individual by the use of photoelectron photography or magnetic resonance imaging. By means such as these, it will be possible to determine the exact nature and extent of the physical and neurological damage suffered by a chemically addicted person coming into treatment. One specialist told us, "These days we're seeing a lot of young adults who've been smoking pot since they were nine, 10 years old. Either this particular population is pretty slow witted or we're seeing some extensive brain damage. If we're ever going to help these kids function in the adult world, we need to know more about how certain chemicals damage the brain and just how reversable that damage is. As far as this kind of information is concerned, medical science is way behind the times. But that's changing. One of these days we'll be able to study a kid's brain with a scanning device and know exactly the job ahead of us. And if it can be done at all."

Wonder chemicals and machines may eventually revolutionize the treatment of addicts and alcoholics. For now, however, nothing is more effective than abstinence, a skilled and caring counselor, and a lifetime program of recovery.

SUMMARY

In this chapter we have explained what you need to know about the theory of recovery and treatment to enable you to choose a facility for your employees. With this material in mind, you cannot become the target of one of those polished and persuasive salesmen we talked about at the beginning of the chapter.

To summarize the chapter, we suggest you bear these five simple standards in mind.

1. A good facility treats the addict/alcoholic *and* his codependents.
2. A good facility works with AA/NA/CA and other twelve step programs.
3. A good facility treats the addict/alcoholic from the medical, psychological and sociocultural perspectives.
4. A good facility does not make grand claims for the success of its method.
5. A good facility is concerned with the health of both body and spirit.

10

REENTRY

For employees fresh from treatment, reentering the workplace is one of the most courageous steps they will make in sobriety. Employees are understandably apprehensive. Outside the sheltered circle of a therapy group, the world looms as a mixture of dangerous shadows and temptations. They have worked hard in treatment and learned more about themselves than most people learn in a lifetime. At reentry the employee knows he or she is only one drink or line or joint away from returning to the dead end way of life before treatment. Wholeheartedly, he or she wants to stay clean. At the same time, it is known that relapse, a return to alcohol and drugs, is a risk to be faced on a daily basis and against which the only protection is years of sobriety and a solid program of recovery.

The apprehension is not one sided, however. Employers and supervisors are also nervous when the recovering employee resumes work. We believe that uncertainty and unease should be expected and accepted as a necessary part of reentry. It may even be interpreted as a good thing because it makes everyone try a little harder. The more a supervisor knows about this time in the recovering employee's life, the easier for everyone.

HAZELDEN FOUNDATION STUDY

Hazelden Foundation is a Minnesota based not-for-profit chemical dependency center with an international reputation for the quality of both its treatment and research in all areas of chemical addiction. Among many studies it has supported over the years is one examining the problems of employees and their supervisors at the time of reentry. It is worthwhile to take a close look at the Hazelden research.

One hundred and fifteen graduates of inpatient treatment were included, and at the time of the study all had been out of treatment for a minimum of one year. These individuals (83 percent were men) had come to Hazelden as a result of work related problems. Of the total number, 41 percent actually believed their jobs were in jeopardy. A wide range of employment was represented with just over half being professionals and managers—including nurses, priests, pilots, physicians and executives. Employees from clerical, sales, technical, manual labor and unskilled trades were also represented in the sample. Eighty-four percent had full-time jobs. Almost three quarters of the total number had stable employment histories with three or more years at the same job.

These employees and their supervisors were asked what problems they experienced when the recovering employee returned to work. From the employees' point of view, the most commonly reported reentry problem was their coworkers' lack of education about chemical addiction. Over half the employees surveyed reported discussing their treatment with coworkers (67 percent), supervisors (66 percent) or workplace counselors (52 percent). Yet their second most commonly cited problem was a lack of confidentiality at the workplace. A significant inference may be drawn from this fact and the accompanying figures. While workers may choose to take others into their confidence regarding treatment, they resent it when this is done for them. Thus, an employee may if he or she wishes announce on the office public address system that he or she is a recovering cocaine addict. But if a supervisor tells one person even in the utmost secrecy, the recovering addict feels betrayed and resentful.

The remaining problems endorsed or described by the recovering employees in the Hazelden study can be grouped together. In general, a large number—almost half of those surveyed—did not feel trusted or respected when they returned to work. They felt they were being watched, that coworkers and supervisors were just waiting for them to lose their sobriety. They believed their coworkers were uncomfortable in their presence or that they had to work harder than others to regain management approval.

William is a real estate salesman who entered treatment after a series of mistakes that almost cost his employer his license. This is how he describes his reentry problems.

I was nervous about working again. I could admit that to my AA friends and my therapist, but I didn't want my boss to know because he wouldn't have confidence in my ability if he knew I was scared. Of course, he knew I'd been in treatment. It was he who made me realize I had to get help in the first place. And I never really tried to keep it a secret from anyone else. I didn't care if the secretaries and all knew. There's a lot of boozing goes on in real estate and at first I wasn't sure I could handle drinking soda water while the rest of the guys were tossing back scotch and martinis. I did okay though and I was starting to think I had nothing to worry about. Then I began to notice that every time I'd come back from a business lunch or a meeting over drinks, my boss's secretary would find some reason to come and hang over my shoulder. She'd say she had papers she wanted me to check or something that seemed legitimate. Only it wasn't. Finally I caught her sniffing and I knew she was checking to see if I'd had anything to drink. I don't know how to explain the way that made me feel. Like a freak or a criminal. There I was busting my ass to make sales and bringing in thousands of dollars, but they were treating me like a bad little boy who couldn't be trusted near the cookie jar. I went to my boss and confronted him with what I knew and he got all hot under the collar. I could see he was embarrassed I'd figured out what they were doing.

As a part of the Hazelden study, supervisors were asked to express their concerns about the recovering employee. In general, their responses showed great sensitivity to the employee's problems.

Many were unsure of what their role should be: unconcerned, trusting, watchful, protective? They worried that the employee would not be fully accepted by his peers, that he would be apprehensive and unable to take pressure. One supervisor wondered which came first, job stress or drinking. Or was there any cause-and-effect relationship? Did the urge to drink just come out of nowhere? Overall, supervisors acknowledged they knew very little about alcoholism. They expressed a desire to learn about it and about treatment specifically.

In this chapter, we will examine how employers can help the reentering employee.

IMPLICATIONS OF THE
HAZELDEN STUDY: EMPLOYEES

The Hazelden study tells us that a recovering employee requires a support group that can help him or her deal with the problems experienced at reentry. While an "aftercare" treatment group might fill this requirement for a time, treatment is not a lifetime condition. Instead it should be seen as merely a starting point in a recovery process that lasts the life of the addict/alcoholic. After treatment, the recovering alcoholic/addict needs to develop a dependable support network. For this job, there is no better organization than Alcoholics Anonymous.

Alcoholics Anonymous

AA began in 1935 when two alcoholic men named Bill and Bob, a stockbroker and a doctor, met in Akron, Ohio. The two made a startling discovery. By talking to one another about their drinking problem and by seeking out other alcoholics and trying to get them sober, they could keep from drinking themselves. From this simple beginning came a volume entitled *Alcoholics Anonymous* in which the basic tenets of AA are explained. The anonymous author of the original forward to the first edition of the book put it this way: "To show other alcoholics precisely how we have recovered is the main purpose of this book." Today, more than 50 years after Bill and Dr. Bob met, AA has hundreds of thousands of members of all races, classes and creeds. Three hundred and sixty five days a year, AA meetings are held in places as remote as Dar es Salaam, Tanzania and Alice Springs, Australia.

The principle that makes AA work is identification. The point of AA is to learn from shared experiences how to live soberly. How often one attends meetings is a matter of choice. Commonly, AA members talk about the need for a person new in recovery to attend 90 meetings in 90 days. The reasoning behind this stems from the principle of identification. The more meetings a recovering person attends, the more quickly he begins to feel a part of the group and to make friends. The more meetings he attends, the more stories he hears. And the more he listens to other people tell about how the disease affected their lives, the more he will identify their experiences with his own history. Gradually, the feeling of strangeness, of being out of step with the sober world, diminishes in a new feeling of community.

Some people call AA a form of community group therapy, but from our observation that description is not apt. It is more valid to say that in AA recovering addicts and alcoholics learn to help themselves as they hear how others have solved their problems and been able to live comfortably in their own skins through the use of the Twelve Steps of Alcoholics Anonymous. These steps are a group of spiritual—but not religious—principles which, if they are made part of a recovering alcoholic's daily life, can make possible a full, useful and meaningful life.

The Twelve Steps

1. We admitted we were powerless over alcohol—that our lives had become unmanageable.
2. Came to believe that a Power greater than ourselves could restore us to sanity.
3. Made a decision to turn our will and our lives over to the care of God *as we understood Him.*
4. Made a searching and fearless moral inventory of ourselves.
5. Admitted to God, to ourselves, and to another human being the exact nature of our wrongs.
6. Were entirely ready to have God remove all these defects of character.
7. Humbly asked Him to remove our shortcomings.
8. Made a list of all persons we had harmed, and became willing to make amends to them all.
9. Made direct amends to such people wherever possible, except when to do so would injure them or others.

10. Continued to take personal inventory and when we were wrong promptly admitted it.

11. Sought through prayer and meditation to improve our conscious contact with God *as we understood Him*, praying only for knowledge of His will for us and the power to carry that out.

12. Having had a spiritual awakening as the result of these steps, we tried to carry this message to alcoholics, and to practice these principles in all our affairs.

AA members speak of "working" or "taking" the steps. How this is done varies considerably from person to person and points up one of the reasons for AA's success. There is only one hard and fast rule in the organization and that is an honest desire to live a sober life. Apart from this deceptively simple requirement, members are given the widest possible leeway in determining the shape and style of their own program. For some, the first step, in which the alcoholic acknowledges powerlessness over alcohol (or, by extension in groups like Narcotics Anonymous and Cocaine Anonymous, drugs), may be done in the silence of the heart. For others, it is necessary to do a lot of writing and talking about the ways that powerlessness has affected daily living.

Generally, an AA member works the steps with the guidance of a sponsor, a person with an extended period of sobriety who has already worked the steps. A sponsor may be the recovering addict/alcoholic's best friend in AA or it may be someone only called in emergencies. What matters is the connection, the identification that is possible between these two people. The newcomer in AA may think he is making a pest of himself if he calls his sponsor when a fellow employee irritates him, when he gets passed over for a promotion, when he feels uncomfortable at the office Christmas party. Actually, his calls help the sponsor to strengthen his own program by giving him a chance to talk about the ways he handles his own similar situations. There is a saying in AA: "We only keep what we give away."

The truth of the saying goes back to the earliest members of AA, who discovered that by working with other alcoholics they were able to maintain their own sobriety. It is no less true today. Even very new members are encouraged to make "twelfth step calls" in the company of more experienced members. In this way they meet and tell their stories to "wet" alcoholics who have called for help. Sometimes the setting is the drunk tank of the city jail. Other times it is an elegant home. As part of this twelfth step outreach, representatives of AA go into prisons and hospitals to tell their stories. Those who are willing to break their anonymity may even speak to professionals and school groups. Without exception, the AA members we spoke to told us that whatever form it takes, twelfth step work brings them out of their own problems and makes them willing to do whatever is necessary to live a sober life.

Having said all this, it is important to add that a recovering addict/alcoholic is not required to do anything in AA. Although any AA member of long standing is likely to attribute his sobriety to the Twelve Steps, neither reading nor interpreting them is a requirement. There are no dues. Chemical addiction is the only rite of initiation. In no way is AA to be confused with a religious program. If the addict/alcoholic is made uncomfortable by references to a higher power, he or she is encouraged to speak up and say so in no uncertain terms. It will become apparent that there are plenty of other members who identify with that particular point of view.

Every employer should know that an employee in early recovery will benefit from membership in AA. It will keep fresh what is learned in the treatment center. It will help the recovering addict to make friends who do not use chemicals. It will provide a place to go where problems at home and on the job can be discussed without fear of reprimand or reprisal. After William, the real estate agent, discovered his boss's secretary smelling his breath for liquor, he was tempted to quit his job. At the AA meeting where he felt most comfortable, he vented his anger and hurt over this lack of trust. His friends in the group listened and after the meeting were able to convince him that quitting was unwise.

> Thank God I listened to them. What happened was I didn't blow up at my boss and I just kept on working. Every time I felt myself getting ready to blow, I'd call my sponsor and he'd talk me down. After a few weeks my boss came to me and apologized for doubting my ability to stay sober. We work pretty well together now and I don't bear him any grudges. He was doing the best he could. He didn't know any better.

IMPLICATIONS OF THE
HAZELDEN STUDY: SUPERVISORS

Supervisors should know better than William's employer if they want to make reentry as comfortable as possible for the recovering addict/alcoholic. For supervisors, the major implication of the Hazelden study is that their *attitude* is crucial.

The following guidelines for supervisors can make reentry more pleasant for everyone involved.

- Be knowledgeable about drug and alcohol addiction and its treatment.
- Realize that if an employee returns to work and encounters the same problems—lack of personal achievement, lack of recognition, unchallenging work—chances are he will have a difficult recovery.
- Be willing whenever possible to switch shifts, departments or jobsites for the recovering employee if that switch will remove him from the situation that puts his sobriety at risk.
- Be supportive of the recovering employee but do not single him out for special treatment.
- Assure the recovering employee that he and other employees have equal promotion opportunities.

• Maintain strict confidentiality regarding the recovering employee regardless of how much the employee himself may share details of his addiction and recovery.

IMPLICATIONS OF THE HAZELDEN STUDY: MANAGERS

In this section we will discuss the steps which you as a manager can take to make reentry less traumatic. You may wish to devise methods specifically suited to individual employees and for this the assistance of his treatment counselor will be invaluable. A skilled EAP counselor will also be able to give you valuable insight into ways to help an employee stay sober.

AA may be the most sustaining aspect of an employee's recovery. Because it promotes a lifetime program for sobriety, we believe employers are wise to strongly encourage attendance. How strongly is a matter of individual choice. Signed proof of attendance at certain required meetings is a strict way to assure an employee will go to a minimum number a week. If you require meetings for one level of employee, you will need to do so at all levels to avoid accusations of discrimination. Sex discrimination must also be avoided. This may mean that in communities where meetings are few, male and female executives and rank-and-file employees attend the same meetings. While this leveling is likely to cause some awkwardness initially, it will benefit your company's drug and alcohol policy as well as management/employee relations in the long run. In some work settings it may be sufficient to allow time off at lunch for a meeting in the neighborhood. If your company has two or more recovering addict/alcoholics you may wish to provide a private conference room on the premises or nearby.

It is helpful if there is someone at the worksite to whom the recovering employee can speak in complete honesty. It may be an EAP counselor or a volunteer employee who is a recovering addict/alcoholic. Whoever is chosen to act as a workplace sponsor (as opposed to an AA sponsor), it should be a person whom the employee can trust to maintain confidentiality.

AT&T has eased employee reentry and enhanced the commitment of skeptical supervisors by instituting back-to-work conferences. These are generally held at the treatment center and are attended by the supervisor, the employee and his therapist. Although these conferences raise important confidentiality issues, advocates maintain that they succeed on a number of levels by addressing the reentry problems of both the employee and his supervisor. In the environment of the treatment center both the supervisor and the employee are encouraged to candidly express their apprehension about reentry. Furthermore, supervisors get a valuable first-hand view of the treatment site and are encouraged to ask questions about what goes on during treatment. After the conference, the supervisor is encouraged to use the therapist as an advisory resource. The result is a feeling of teamwork between the employee, his therapist and his supervisor.

Duane Rogers, President of Personal Assistance Services, a large EAP in Southern California, does two things to make reentry less difficult. When confidentiality is not an issue, he sometimes meets with supervisors and employees prior to the recovering employee's return to work. In a relaxed conversational environment, he gives them an idea of what they can now expect from their colleagues, answers questions and allays fears. Rogers also believes that an "icebreaker" is helpful for all concerned. A day or so before the recovering employee returns to a full-time work schedule, he and Duane "drop by" the worksite to pick up a check or a work schedule or go through the mail or a full in-basket. The ostensible reason doesn't matter as long as it gives the employee a chance to say hello to coworkers and show them that he or she is well, clear-eyed, not a freaked out bundle of nerves. It will also be reassuring to find that he or she has been missed and fills a valuable niche in the workplace. When returning for a first full day on the job, some of the strangeness is gone for everyone concerned.

Based on the Hazelden study, we believe every workplace should have a program to educate employees to the facts and fantasies about alcohol and drug addiction. In chapter 13, "Primary Prevention," we will explore some of the ways you might choose to go about this education process. Certainly, it is clear that the likelihood of a successful reentry increases when the recovering addict/alcoholic's coemployees understand something of the disease from which he or she suffers.

And what of the employees whose reentry is unsuccessful? In the next chapter we will discuss the relapse syndrome. By knowing how this syndrome works and is manifested in workplace behavior, a supervisor can act to keep an employee clean and sober.

11

RELAPSE

"More than anything else, I told myself, I wanted to stay sober."

Grace is a young woman in her early 30s, fashionably dressed, who moves and speaks with confidence. On the day we interviewed her she had just returned from vacation and looked tanned and healthy.

I was a customer service rep for a big oil company. I spent all day at the computer trying to figure out what had gone wrong with people's statements. Half the time, I couldn't see the print in front of my face. I was doing coke in the bathroom every chance I could and on the weekends I never came down long enough to get my act together.

I wasn't crazy about my job, but I didn't want to lose it either. I'd been there almost six years and I knew the work. The money was great. That's why I got help. The first time. I just plain didn't want to lose my job.

After treatment, though, it was the same stuff all over again. Nothing changed except I didn't have drugs and alcohol anymore.

It was hard not to keep thinking about all the fun times I had before I got sober. At least when I recalled them they seemed like fun. After a while, I started feeling like some kind of mutation. I remember I took some days off and just holed up in my apartment staring at the ceiling. I knew I had to do something but I couldn't figure out what. See, I didn't stick around AA long enough to make friends so I couldn't just pick up the phone. I didn't feel like I could anyway. I just laid there and thought how I was a good-looking woman, not even 30 years old and already my life was over. No guy'd ever be interested in someone who couldn't even drink champagne at her own wedding.

So, eventually, having a drink seemed like a reasonable option. As far as I could tell, it was the only thing I could do to make myself feel better. I went out and bought a pinch bottle and drank the whole thing. When I came to I was stretched out on the bathroom tiles and I couldn't remember anything except that first drink. I wanted to die. If I felt bad before, this was much worse. I was a failure and I couldn't excuse that. I had blown my sobriety and that was the worst thing I could do.

I called the treatment center where I'd been and they called AA for me. A woman my age came by and got me, took me to a meeting,. I was a wreck and I didn't want to go. I remember I made her stop at the drug store so I could get some hairspray. There I was looking like someone had walked on my face, and I was worried about hairspray.

My company gave me a second chance at treatment. This time, I really paid attention. Now I was doing it for myself and not just so I could keep my job. I knew I never wanted to be drunk again. I learned that what started my slip was isolating, shutting myself off from people. I know now that I can't ever do that. People, AA people, are vital to my sobriety. I've been sober four years now and I go to five meetings a week. Right around the anniversary of my slip, I go to one meeting a day. I don't ever want to relapse again.

THE THREE STAGES OF RELAPSE

Terence T. Gorski, in his paper "The Dynamics of Relapse in the Alcoholic Patient," defines relapse as a progressive pattern of behavior that allows symptoms of the disease to become reactivated in the recovering addict/alcoholic. According to Gorski, who directly and indirectly observed more than 700 recovering men and women over a period of several years, relapse behavior can be broken down into three phases.

(1) First stage relapse behavior is characterized by a change in attitude toward chemicals and addiction. For example, an employee who has stayed away from company gatherings where alcohol is served—office parties, after work meetings at favorite pubs or bars—begins to attend and vociferously announces that it isn't a bother to be around alcohol. He is convinced that alcoholism is no longer a priority issue. Other things—providing for the family, getting out of debt—are more important. There will be signs of impatience with the thoughtful, time-slowing slogans of recovery: "Easy Does It," "One Day at a Time." He may talk a lot about "getting on with life" in the "real" world.

There is probably no single trigger for the first stage relapse behavior. However, a phenomenon called Post Acute Withdrawal (PAW) may explain why many alcoholics relapse despite their good intentions. Dr. Gorski defines PAW as "symptoms of addictive disease that occur as a *result* [authors' emphasis] of abstinence from addictive chemicals." It occurs because there is damage to the central nervous system of the addict/alcoholic, and generally manifests itself from the first to the sixth month of sobriety. Most centeral nervous system damage reverses itself with time; but until it does, it increases the risk of relapse. Some symptoms of PAW are emotional outbursts and difficulties with sleeping, coordination, and memory lapse, emotional outburst or a lack of emotional affect. There is also likely to be a heightened sensitivity to stress factors in the environment. Thus, if your employee in early recovery seems to have difficulty concentrating on a task or recalling new instructions, if he responds to stress by becoming tense or irritable, it is highly likely that he is experiencing PAW—a condition that will correct itself with time.

(2) In the midst of second stage relapse behavior the addict/alcoholic abandons the positive problem-solving strategies learned during treatment and adopts old behaviors which, in turn, cause a resurgence of old problems including denial. An employee who has made frequent use of his workplace sponsor to manage the stress of working with a belligerent and verbally abusive coemployee begins, in relapse, to avoid the workplace sponsor altogether and to argue loudly and publicly with the bully. Happy hour haunts are revisited and pals are told by the addict/alcoholic that he can handle things as well as the next person. There certainly isn't a need to go to a sponsor and cry on his shoulder.

(3) The final stage of relapse behavior occurs when something happens that creates intolerably elevated stress in the recovering individual. Because of behavior in stages one and two, the addict/alcoholic's judgment is impaired and drinking or using seems like a desirable alternative to feeling bad. The recovering employee who has begun to attend happy hour again (although drinking only soda) has had a very bad day. On and off all day long the bully has been ragging about the least thing and the recovering addict/alcoholic has had it up to here. This afternoon he has a pounding headache and can't seem to silence an agitated mind and is so mad as to hardly be able to contain his anger. He need help but he has lost the habit of calling on the workplace sponsor for help. At a happy hour the recovering individual watches the person behind the bar pull beer from the tap, and suddenly it seems that only a beer will help. He walks to the bar and orders one.

SYMPTOMS OF RELAPSE

Accompanying this progressive relapse behavior Gorski has observed a number of symptoms of relapse which can act as flags to a concerned supervisor, a key employee or a workplace sponsor. It must be noted, however, that one or two of these behaviors in isolation are probably of no consequence. Like anyone else, the recovering person has days when he is critical, touchy, fearful, distracted, etc. When a supervisor observes impaired work performance, continuing patterns of behavior are examined. An occasional late day or missed deadline probably means no more than that the employee is a normal, imperfect human being, prone to make occasional mistakes. It is the same with spotting relapse behavior. The key is, again, continuing patterns of behavior.

1. There may be an adamant commitment to sobriety without any accompanying commitment to AA/NA/CA or treatment.
2. There is a focus on other people's drinking habits.
3. In relapse, the recovering addict/alcoholic is defensive, touchy.
4. The recovering person begins to overwork and to show a tendency to rigid, repetitive obsessional behavior. If he has employees under him, he may make unreasonable demands for perfection.
5. In relapse there is a tendency for the abuser to isolate himself, particularly from friends made in recovery.
6. Stressful situations become increasingly difficult for her to tolerate.
7. The reaction to stress is often impulsive and apparently out-of- control behavior. We know a recovering woman who actually threw a chair at her husband when she could no longer tolerate his persistent questions about her failure to follow her therapist's advice.
8. Symptoms of depression become apparent. There is listlessness, sleepiness.
9. She is inattentive to detail, fails to plan her work sufficiently and does not follow through on assignments.
10. More time is spent daydreaming.
11. Failure, inadequacy, a fear of the future become obsessions.
12. He is more and more easily angered by things that might not have bothered him a few weeks earlier. He flies off the handle when things do not go his way or when stress pushes him beyond the narrowing borders of his tolerance.
13. She may lose interest in her appearance and eat and sleep poorly.
14. When help is offered, he refuses it, probably insisting that he is doing fine. No problem.
15. It is difficult—even impossible—for him to initiate any action.
16. She may talk about drinking or drugs.
17. He lies.

INTERVENING ON A RELAPSING EMPLOYEE

What can be done to help the employee who is trapped in the dangerous downward spiral of relapse? Like so many aspects of treatment and recovery, there are no sure answers when it comes to relapse. A workplace sponsor, preferably another recovering person, can be an effective intervener if he knows the symptoms of relapse. A supervisor educated about the relapse syndrome might act to intervene when he believes the employee is endangering his sobriety. However, such an intervention has scant chance of success. More likely, it will make the employee angry and raise the hackles of his denial. There is one way a supervisory intervention at this stage may work, however.

When the recovering employee reenters the workplace, a supervisor, a key employee, or a workplace sponsor might cosign what is known as a "relapse contract." Under the terms of this contract, the employee specifically asks the cosigner to tell him when he is observed to be in the midst of the relapse syndrome. Not only that, the employee gives the cosigner permission—in advance—to act on his or her behalf by calling a therapist or a particular AA friend. In some workplace settings it is possible to make adherence to the relapse contract a condition of continued employment.

TREATMENT AFTER RELAPSE

Unfortunately, treatment does not always take, and for some employees, relapse and a return to drinking or using drugs is inevitable, perhaps even necessary to convince them that they suffer from a progressive fatal disease over which they are powerless. Treatment specialists who are the first to acknowledge this inevitability tell us that what happens after relapse depends on several factors.

If the addict/alcoholic perceives a relapse as fatal, it may ultimately prove to be that. If they believe all is lost, that they are worthless failures, that there is no hope for them, then long term recovery is unlikely. If, however, they pick themselves up and go looking for help, they will find there is plenty available and their recovery chances will be good.

The attitude of the therapist is a vital factor at this point. If it is punitive and intolerant, even the most resilient addict/alcoholic will lose hope the second time around. More than merely understanding the addicts'/alcoholics' problems, therapists should make every effort to let them know that they respect the tremendous effort it takes to admit to a relapse and try again. No one—and least of all an addict/alcoholic—cares to admit failure.

A new treatment program will have to be devised. It must take into consideration the fact that this is an individual prone to relapse. If the first treatment period was as an outpatient, inpatient treatment is now definitely indicated. Only in an intense 24-hour program of several weeks' duration can the relapsed addict/alcoholic find the kind of care required.

As part of this intensive treatment, patient and therapist will need to study the relapse pattern. What triggered it? Where did the patient first begin to go wrong?

What can be done if it happens again? The patient will need to make a thorough listing of the factors that pointed him toward relapse. When aspects of work, family, social and emotional life have been examined, the therapist may then assist the patient in figuring out healthy ways of coping with these stressors in the future. In this way, the recovering person learns to expect, accept and prepare for relapse symptoms at certain times, under certain conditions.

Let us return to the hypothetical case of the man who relapsed at the office happy hour. When he and his therapist studied his relapse dynamic, they discovered that the first sign of trouble occured right after he reentered employment and was put in a position where he could not avoid contact with an individual (the bully) who deeply upset him. He was afraid to speak up for himself at that point. He felt guilty for taking a month for treatment; the perfectionist in him said he should be "cured" after that much time. He wanted more than anything to regain the respect of his supervisor and coworkers, respect he was certain he had lost by acknowledging his alcoholism. He could just imagine what everyone would say if he started right in making complaints and asking for favors. Had he summoned his courage and asked for a transfer or a shift change, admitting quite honestly that the bully caused him immense stress, he may have been able to stay sober. As part of his treatment program, his therapist should include stress management and some assertiveness training as well as deep-level therapy to explore his guilt and the emotions triggered by the bully.

Recovery after relapse also depends on the strength of the employee's support systems. If their family is 100 percent behind their efforts to stay sober, they are indeed fortunate. Along with job security, a strong family support system is the most important positive indicator for long-term recovery. But we believe that more than family support is needed.

The individual in recovery needs friends to go to; friends who can be depended on to listen and understand and—if necessary—tell the individual when his or her behavior is endangering sobriety. Alcoholics Anonymous, Narcotics Anonymous, Cocaine Anonymous: these twelve step fellowships can be the linchpin of successful recovery. In some areas of the country there are even special AA groups whose membership is made up of "slippers" or those who fear they may experience a slip and want to take special precautions to see that it does not happen.

The final factor in determining the chance of recovery after relapse is the duration of the relapse itself. The longer the period of relapse, the more there is danger of serious and perhaps permanent neurological damage. The longer the relapse, the greater risk to the addict/alcoholic's overall health. And finally, the greater the likelihood that support systems will be irrevocably damaged. A spouse's or lover's hope or patience or tolerance may be destroyed beyond rebuilding. There may be a divorce or the kind of intrafamily warfare that leaves a permanent residue of guilt and grief, such as rejection by children. After an extended relapse resulting in the loss of a job, a boss may refuse a bid to be rehired.

CREATING A RELAPSE POLICY

Realistic employers must expect that some of their recovering employees will relapse. Therfore, to avoid accusations of unfairness or discriminaton, a company is wise to have a standard response to all employees who do so.

Although you will wish to decide which policy best suits your own workplace, the three examples that follow will give you some idea of the variations that are possible. A word of caution is appropriate here. If yours is a union shop, be sure you confer with your own attorney and representatives of the unions involved prior to publication of the standard. This may save you a great deal of trouble in the future. If you have kept the union involved at all stages of developing and implementing the drug and alcohol program, you will not find it difficult to reach a point of agreement.

DISMISSAL WITH NO CHANCE
OF REEMPLOYMENT

You may decide to "show no mercy" where relapse is concerned. If you decide this way, we caution you on two counts. First, make it clear exactly to whom and at what point this standard applies: is it for employees who have been through inpatient treatment? outpatient? Selfhelpers who have joined AA or those who have "white knuckled it" without any support group? At what point can it be said that the employee received a first and only chance? During the job performance review? After treatment? At the time of reentry? Arbitrators agree that it is good policy to spell out these details precisely.

Our second caution has to do with the nature of the disease we are talking about. Alcoholism and drug addiction are no respecters of rank and authority although the general public is inclined to think of addicts as young, blue collar and uneducated and alcoholics as old and derelict. Actually, the percentage of addict/alcoholics may be higher in white-collar professions. Abraham J. Twerski, MD, of the Pennsylvania Medical Society Committee on the Impaired Physician, a nationally recognized authority in the field, estimates that between 5 and 10 percent of doctors are impaired by chemical abuse. Over a five-year period, fully half of Paul Sherman's executive clients earned better than $125,000 a year. If you have a "show no mercy" policy at your company—and mean it to stick—it will have to be democratically applied. If the vice president of your company is treated for addiction and then relapses, there can be no question of a second chance for him or her anymore than there can be for the most junior stenographer.

DISMISSAL WITH
CONTINGENT REEMPLOYMENT

You may chose to dismiss employees who relapse after treatment with the provision that they may be reemployed, contingent upon a set period of self-motivated rehabilitation. Again, it is essential that you be absolutely precise when writing this standard. Not only must you be able to answer the kinds of questions noted above. You must also make it clear what period of time you are talking about and exactly what is meant by "self-motivated" and "rehabilitation."

LAST CHANCE AGREEMENT

A last chance agreement allows an employee a second full period of treatment following relapse. Under this condition of employment, after relapse but before resuming treatment, the employee signs an agreement stating very clearly that this second treatment will be the final chance at rehabilitation the company is willing to allow, and it is fully understood that remaining sober is a condition of continued employment. The signed agreement states that a second relapse will be grounds for dismissal.

In their excellent book *Alcohol & Drugs: Issues in the Workplace*, authors Tia Schneider Denenberg and R. V. Denenberg cite such an agreement in the case study of Andy Y., a steel mill employee.

CONDITIONS OF EMPLOYMENT

I understand that my reinstatement to employment by the corporation is based upon and constrained by the following terms:

1. I accept admission to the Employee Assistance Program.

2. I recognize that my reinstatement is contingent upon the participation of my spouse and adult children in my recovery through the Employee Assistance Program.

3. I will comply with ALL of the program agreement requirements to their successful conclusion.

4. I recognize the adverse impact that working overtime may have on my recovery and waive my rights to assignment to overtime. For the same reason, I will accept supervision's decisions regarding requests for payment in lieu of vacation time off.

5. I understand that my previous job performance warrants close supervision for an extended period of time upon my return to work and will accept such supervision as a constructive part of my recovery.

6. I understand that upon return to the workplace I must meet all established standards of conduct and job performance and that I will be subject to the company's disciplinary procedures for any failure to meet the standards.

7. I understand that I will be subject to the terms of this condition of employment until I have completed at least twelve months of work. Upon completion of twelve months of work the appropriate parties will review my job performance and recovery progress and determine if the terms of this condition of employment will be removed, modified, sustained or added to.

I UNDERSTAND AND AGREE THAT MY REINSTATEMENT AND CONTINUED EMPLOYMENT ARE CONTINGENT UPON MY MEETING SATISFACTORILY ALL THE ABOVE TERMS OF THIS CONDITION OF EMPLOYMENT AND THAT MY FAILURE TO DO

SO RELINQUISHES ALL DEFENSE ON MY PART AND SUBJECTS
ME TO IMMEDIATE TERMINATION OF MY EMPLOYMENT WITH
THE CORPORATION.

Under the conditions of a last-chance agreement, an employee may also be required to sign a separate but equally binding program agreement. Again, we quote directly from Denenberg and Denenberg and the case of Andy Y.

I, Andy, fully understand and agree to the terms of my total participation in the corporation Employee Assistance Program.

This program may include, but is not limited to:
1. Detoxification in the designated facility for a designated time according to my needs;
2. Returning to work immediately after detoxification and/or residential treatment (hospital or other) in accordance with the appropriate procedures;
3. Attending a minimum of four . . . meetings of Alcoholics Anonymous (AA). One weekly meeting will be the AA Sunday night meeting[;]
4. Keeping weekly counseling and consultation appointments with the counselor[;]
5. When requested, providing the medical director [with] the information necessary (including required releases of information) for him to assess my medical status [and] to consult with other medical resources such as my personal physician concerning my treatment and recovery;
6. Making sincere efforts to recover from my alcoholism with the understanding that failure to adhere to this agreement will continue to be subject to the company's disciplinary procedures, not for my alcoholism but based on the effect the continuation of alcoholism may have on my job performance and work behavior[;]
7. Persons participating in the program are expected to meet existing job performance standards and establish work rules. No preferential treatment is shown employees on program.
8. In the event I do not abide by the above, I realize there will be no additional opportunity to return to the program.

Andy's company realized that without the cooperation and support of his wife, Andy would not be likely to maintain his sobriety. For that reason, she was asked to commit herself to participation in a program designed for the families of addicts and alcoholics.

I, spouse of Andy, fully understand and agree to all terms of family participation in the Employee Assistance Program. This program will include:
1. Compliance with all facets of family treatment offered during spouse's stay at treatment center;
2. Compliance with all facets of . . . after care sponsored by the treatment center;

3. Keeping weekly counseling and consultation appointments with the counselor;

4. Attending a minimum of 3 Al-Anon meetings weekly, one of which will be the Al-Anon Sunday night weekly meeting.*

The validity of last-chance agreements has been challenged on occasion, but arbitrators have upheld them. Two reasons are generally given. In the first place, the last-chance agreement is supported by consideration and taken as a modification of any otherwise binding collective bargaining. In the second place, arbitrators have found that last-chance agreements should be upheld as a matter of public policy because they are a means whereby an employee who might otherwise be unsalvageable can be coerced into rehabilitation.

The disease of chemical addiction has a tendency toward relapse. Uncomfortable as this fact makes everyone involved in treatment, it must be faced squarely if it is to be handled effectively. Any manager with one or more recovering addicts/alcoholics on the payroll needs to understand this.

Occasionally, it has been suggested to us that alcoholic/addict employees are not worth taking trouble with if there is a chance they will thank their employers by relapsing. We believe the opposite. It is both inhumane and bad business practice to fire skilled workers who happen to suffer from a frequently fatal disease called chemical addiction, a disease that has as one of its characteristics a tendency to relapse. A drug and alcohol policy that calls for treatment and reentry *after* relapse allows experienced employees to stay with the jobs they know and can do well. Additionally, it creates a pool of employees loyal to the company that did not give up on them when they were down on their luck. This kind of experienced and loyal workforce is the core support of our country's business and industry.

* Reprinted by permission from *Alcohol and Drugs: Issues in the Workplace* by Tia Schneider and Richard V. Denenberg, pages 139-141, copyright © 1983 by the Bureau of National Affairs, Inc., Washington, D.C.

12

ESTABLISHING AN EMPLOYEE-ASSISTANCE PROGRAM

INVESTIGATING THE EAP CONCEPT

An employer we know once complained, "The only thing wrong with people is they're human! Give me a machine any day." We asked him to explain himself and he went on to say that when a machine breaks down, there are manuals and procedures for fixing it and returning it to work. But when an employee breaks down there is nothing to do but ignore the problem and hope it goes away or live with the costs. "Or fire the guy."

Our friend must have been living with his head in the sand because a mechanism does exist to fix broken employees. As a matter of fact, it has been around—in one form or another—for most of this century. Today thousands of businesses of all sizes utilize employee-assistance programs.

It has been our experience that there is a great deal of misinformation about these programs. Many employers think they have to do without one because of the expense. Others think employee-assistance programs are for corporate giants only. Actually, the size of your payroll has nothing to do with the viability of an employee-assistance program. As this chapter will explain, any solvent company can afford some form of one.

In an earlier chapter, we showed how employers can cope with employees who receive poor job performance reviews *without* the aid of a formal employee-assistance program. If your supervisors are provided with orientation meetings and a manual telling how to handle documentation and intervention and if they are given plenty of employee-oriented brochures listing community agencies that provide assistance for all variations of family and emotional problems, then you have an employee-assistance program. It's not much like the one operating at the 3M Corporation or Time Life Incorporated, but it may be adequate to your needs. The material in this chapter may give you some clues as to how you can expand and increase the effectiveness of your small program without adding appreciably to its cost.

If you already have an in-place, fairly elaborate employee-assistance program and occasionally wonder if it is adequate, the next page will give you the information you need to do a comprehensive study of the program. We also recommend a little book published by the Hazelden Foundation entitled *Performance Benchmarks for the Comprehensive Employee Assistance Program* and written by Donald Jones.

Hazelden Educational Materials
Box 176
Center City
Minnesota 55012

800-328-9000

If you do not have an employee-assistance program and feel slightly daunted at the prospect of beginning one at your organization, the material in this chapter will make you practically an expert on the subject. You will be able to decide for yourself exactly how extensive a program you want and the best way to go about getting it.

This part of the chapter explores the background and theory of employee-assistance programs and will help you decide whom to serve and how.

Part Two takes you step-by-step through the development of a broadbrush employee-assistance program.

Part Three examines the implementation and evaluation of your program.

DEFINITION

As we use the term, employee-assistance programs (EAPs) provide business and industry with the means to identify employees whose job performance is negatively affected by personal problems. The EAP arranges for structured assistance to solve those problems with the goal of reestablishing the employee's effective job performance. The services of an EAP may be contracted for or the program may be something of your own creation, designed to fit the unique needs of your company.

EAPs help the employer and employee in four ways.

- First, by identifying the troubled worker. This may be done by supervisory referrals such as those described earlier in this book but they are not limited to that route. EAPs encourage entirely self-motivated referrals as well as self-referrals prompted by the influence of volunteer employees.
- Second, by education and job leverage, EAPs motivate employees to get the help they need.
- Third, by providing short term crisis management.
- Fourth, by assessing each individual and charting a plan of action suited to his need. This requires an ability to uncover the employee's primary problem, his weaknesses as well as the strengths he has to build on. The course of action designed for his needs is what will, ultimately, make it possible for him to again work at peak levels of performance.
- Fifth, the EAP assists the employee in actually getting help. This demands a wide knowledge of the help resources available in the community.

HISTORY

No one knows when the first employer offered counseling and social work services to his employees. But in 1917 Macy's Department Store in New York opened an office specifically devoted to helping employees deal with personal problems. Metropolitan Life and Western Electric were also early pioneers in the field; but it was not until the years immediately following World War II that a limited form of EAP became relatively common.

In those days Alcoholics Anonymous was a fledgling organization gaining widespread attention. For the first time, alcohol abuse was perceived by business to be a problem in the workplace. Many companies—Eastman Kodak, DuPont, Armco Steel, Illinois Bell, Consolidated Edison, North American Aviation, Standard Oil of New Jersey—started alcoholism programs for their workers. Usually, these programs were staffed by recovering alcoholics who trained supervisors to "spot" alcoholics by symptoms such as shaking hands, bleary eyes and whiskey breath. These early programs produced gratifying results.

But they were severely limited in that they only identified "late stage" alcoholics. Those in the early stage whose hands did not shake and who did not drink at work were passed over. It was not until the 1950s that a new method of identification—supervisory referrals of impaired job performance—was pioneered at the Chino Mines Division of Kennecott Copper. By this means the Chino program identified over 8 percent of the total employee population as either problem drinkers or outright alcoholics.

The Chino experience pointed to what has become an axiom in the identification and treatment of alcoholic employees: if supervisors are trained to go looking for addicts and alcoholics, they will help fewer employees than if they simply do their job—that is, supervise and evaluate job performance.

THE MODERN EMPLOYEE
ASSISTANCE PROGRAM

Today's EAPs have grown in both size and sophistication. In some places EAPs are operated through employee associations like the International Longshoremen's Assocation, Amalgamated Clothing and Textile Worker's Union and the National Maritime Union. Sometimes professional groups or like businesses and small industries unite to form a consortium. The "housemother" Metropolitan Life hired to counsel employees back in 1919 would be lost in the maze of service and benefits many of today's employees enjoy through the modern EAP.

Although all EAPs aim to help management and employees, there are differences in how they do it. Boiled down to the essentials, these differences come under two headings: who is helped and how that help is provided.

Single-issue programs aim to help only employees impaired by drugs and alcohol. Their focus is clear and they are generally small enough to cost the employer relatively little. If you are considering an EAP for your company, these are important to keep in mind. But you should also know the disadvantages of a single-issue program.

Your program will be stigmatized because of the negative connotations addiction and alcoholism bear. People will be afraid to use the program for fear of being labeled drunks or addicts. Since the per-person cost of your EAP decreases with the number of people who utilize it, this stigmatization is an important negative point to consider. Furthermore, no matter how many times you tell them not to, supervisors will continue to look for overt signs of abuse instead of concentrating on declining job performance, which is an earlier indication of the problem. They will see symptoms where none exist while completely overlooking otherwise significant signs of impairment like absenteeism and tardiness.

A midsize women's wear company in New Mexico had a drug and alcohol prevention program that included counseling and treatment. The director of the program told us, "Our utilization was low and our relapse rate was high because everybody who came through the program was in the late stage of alcoholism where the relapse risk is the greatest. Management wanted to can the whole thing but I got them to give me 90 days to do an evaluation, to see if I could figure out what was going wrong. Come to find out, you practically had to be falling down drunk to get the supervisors to refer you. Meanwhile, there's absenteeism and accidents and all the rest of it going on all over the plant. But nobody's paying any attention to it even though I had personally done two trainings on job-performance skills. Seems like none of it got through to them, though. Supervisors were too busy smelling breath and checking to see if the forklift operator had fresh track marks on his arm."

This may seem like an extreme example, but it is actually fairly typical of single-issue programs.

From the standpoint of both employer and employee, the greatest weakness of single-issue programs is their lack of preventive power. As the program director from New Mexico said, late-stage alcoholics and addicts have the highest relapse rate and the least chance of permanent recovery. Single-issue programs tend to find these late stagers while not even recognizing those in the early stages for whom help can be most effective.

Broadbrush EAPs offer help to employees suffering from all kinds of problems as well as chemical dependency. For example, a broadbrush program may provide crisis management services for those employees whose problems can be dealt with over a short term—say, six to eight weeks. This service is of special benefit to female employees who, more than men, increase their use of chemicals during periods of crisis such as financial hardship, illness or the death of a loved one. Sometimes all that is needed at such times is the chance to talk a problem through with a sympathetic listener. The great advantage of broadbrush programs is their ability to uncover drug and alcohol problems in their early stages when the chances of successful treatment are highest. According to Duane E. Rogers of Personal Assistance Services, a broadbrush program will bring in three times more chemical abusers than a single-issue drug and alcohol program. It happens this way. Early stagers come to their EAP presenting problems that make no mention of alcohol or drugs. At first clients complain about financial woes, a disturbed marriage, or children acting out. It is only after working with a skilled counselor that the truth reveals itself: cocaine is bankrupting an executive, a marriage is hell because the husband drinks and the wife enables him, desperate children act out because their mother and father are stoned all the time and can't give them the care and nurturing they need.

The only disadvantage we connect to broadbrush programs is the fact that they are usually more expensive than single-issue programs. But there are ways to minimize costs by designing a program suited to your workplace or in conjunction with other businesses. If you are creative and willing to shop around for the most flexible EAP and the best insurance coverage, there is no reason why you can't have an effective broadbrush program at your workplace. In the long run, the program is bound to save you money by making your business more efficient and productive, by reducing accidents, by raising employee morale and decreasing grievances, and by cutting back the number of frivolous or unnecessary insurance claims.

The second major difference among today's EAPs is the mode of service they deliver. It would be impossible to describe all the variations that exist, but a short description of several of the most common varieties will give you an idea of the possibilities.

- Some EAPs are just a hotline. Employees are encouraged to call a particular number and ask for help. The person on the other end provides the names and numbers of local public-service and mental-health agencies. Alone, this just barely qualifies as employee assistance. However, a hotline in combination with other services may prove helpful in drawing out fearful employees for whom anonymity is essential. And hotlines can be extremely beneficial at the holiday season when depression is a serious problem for many people.

One EAP coordinator we spoke with told us, "The phone is the most important piece of equipment I have. One man called me once or twice a week for six months just to talk about the trouble he was having with drugs. He never told me his name, and when I suggested he come in for assessment, he always got defensive. But he kept on calling and talking to me. I could tell he wanted help but he wasn't ready to trust the system. After six months he finally came in on his own.

- Other EAPs amount to no more than a single individual operating out of a cubbyhole in the personnel department or the medical office who can direct an employee off-site on the basis of his apparent problem. This is not much better than the hotline, and you may find that employees avoid going anywhere near the cubbyhole for fear of being labeled "sick" or "crazy." Employees required to report there because of poor job-performance evaluations and the fear of losing their livelihoods will complain loudly about the lack of confidentiality. Furthermore, the help they get may prove useless in the long run since individuals in such superficial programs rarely have the expertise needed to assess an employee's real problem.

- A few very large companies or companies situated in remote areas have elaborate on-site EAP divisions with full staffs including doctors and nurses.

- Companies with like concerns, products or geography (all situated in the same industrial complex, for example) may join together to form a consortium that makes a single contract with an EAP to provide services to employees from each site.

- The most adaptable service model for an EAP is one in which posters, cards, pay-envelope stuffers, brochures, supervisors and trained volunteers refer employees to an assessment and referral agent off-site. Using this broadbrush service model, the next chapters will take you step-by-step through the development, implementation and evaluation of a program.

Every day thousands of employees are being helped to more productive personal and professional lives by the services of their company EAPs. Going back to our friend the businessman who preferred machines over humans—he was wrong when he said there was no way to fix broken people. EAPs do it all the time.

But EAPs differ from social-service agencies found in the community. Such agencies have one concern and that is the health and well-being of the client/patient. The EAP's unique ability is to effect a balance between the needs of the employee and those of the employer. People connected with the program speak the language of the workplace and know how to use job leverage as a motivational tool. They make the human services of the community available to company personel so that the employer can protect his or her investment in human resources. The EAP is a risk management tool.

DEVELOPING A BROADBRUSH PROGRAM

Although you may elect not to follow each step prescribed in this chapter, your EAP will be less likely to founder during its developmental stage if you keep the steps in mind as an informal guide. The needs of each workplace will be different and, therefore, the developmental process will vary somewhat from site to site. You may find some of the steps can be done almost casually while others will require analysis, collaboration and strategic planning.

1. Getting an Overview
2. Deciding on Shape and Scope
3. Making a Preliminary Proposal
4. Enlisting Support
5. Forming a Program Advisory Committee
6. Hiring a Coordinator

GETTING AN OVERVIEW

From startup to program implementation will take anywhere from six to 18 months depending on the size of your organization, the scope of the program, and the motivation and expertise of the planners involved. Some of the specific tasks involved are report and proposal writing, advocacy, agenda planning, interviewing and budgeting. After reading this short overview segment you may decide that creating and implementing an EAP is a task for which you lack necessary skills. Or you just may not have the time to spend doing the job. It is perfectly appropriate at ths early stage to hire an expert who can come into the workplace and establish your program from start to finish, leaving you free to deal with business as usual.

Many EAPs are prepared to manage program development for you, but you may prefer the advice of a professional who does not have a vested interest in the ultimate style and size of the program. Advice is available from occupational program consultants (OPCs). The amount charged by an OPC will vary anywhere from 50 or 60 to several hundred dollars an hour. Some OPCs will charge nothing for a preliminary needs assessment and then if you decide to go no further with the program, you pay only expenses.

If you wish to locate an OPC in your area, you can write to the organizations listed below. Although these resources are presumed to maintain standards of qualification, you must decide for yourself if a consultant meets your needs. The material in this book will enable you to ask informed questions of any consultant regarding experience, training and philosophy.

The Administration of Labor-Management Administrators and Consultants on
   Alcoholism
1800 North Kent, Suite 907
Arlington, VA 22209

Occupational Program Consultants Association
10 Longview Avenue
White Plains, NY 10601

The Occupational Program Branch
National Institute on Alcoholism and Alcohol Abuse
5600 Fishers Lane, Room 11A05
Rockville, MD 20857

SHAPE AND SCOPE

To determine the shape and scope of your EAP, you must acquaint yourself with three areas.

1. Employee needs
2. Organizational Determinants
3. Available Resources

Employee needs are best determined by surveys and by interviews with representative employees and key employees. An anonymous needs-assessment survey can be given to all employees. On it, ask for demographic data such as age, type of employment and marital status. Allow space for employees to check off areas of concern: family problems (e.g. children, spouse, parents, siblings), alcohol/drug problems, stress, depression, housing etc.

On the needs assessment, explain what an EAP is and ask employees if they would use its services if it were totally confidential and guaranteed not to jeopardize their employment. If they respond negatively, leave space for an explanation.

In general, interviews should cover essentially the same information. They should be friendly and relaxed and conducted with as many employees as possible. You may find that informal discussion groups of 8-12 employees give you the candid feedback you need. Encourage employees to share anecdotes. Listen for what is not being said as

```
                    SURVEY OF EMPLOYEE NEEDS

This survey is entirely confidential.  It is intended to help
management develop a free and confidential Employee Assistance
Program to serve the needs of employees at all levels.

Job Classification

_____Supervisory
_____Nonsupervisory

Age

____18-25          ____25-35          ____35-45          ____over 45

Marital Status

Single     Married     Divorced     Separated     Widowed

As you know, people are often troubled on the job by
situations and problems not directly related to their work.  If
you feel that your ability to fully concentrate on work is
never/sometimes/or frequently affected by any of the following
problem areas, please mark the appropriate area of concern.

_____Family Problems              Never   Sometimes   Frequently
_____Alcohol and Drug Abuse       Never   Sometimes   Frequently
_____Gambling                     Never   Sometimes   Frequently
_____Compulsive shoplifting       Never   Somemtimes  Frequently
_____Depression                   Never   Sometimes   Frequently
_____Stress                       Never   Sometimes   Frequently
_____Anxiety                      Never   Sometimes   Frequently
_____Feelings of Inferiority      Never   Sometimes   Frequently
_____Grief                        Never   Sometimes   Frequently
_____Job Dissatisfaction          Never   Sometimes   Frequently
_____Getting Along with Others    Never   Sometimes   Frequently
_____Financial Problems           Never   Sometimes   Frequently
_____Legal Problems               Never   Sometimes   Frequently
_____Immigration Problems         Never   Sometimes   Frequently
_____Housing Problems             Never   Sometimes   Frequently
_____Overspending                 Never   Sometimes   Frequently
_____Overeating                   Never   Sometimes   Frequently


Would you use the program if it were available to you, entirely
free and confidential?

If your answer is no, please take a moment to explain your reasons.
```

well as directly mentioned problems. Make sure anyone you speak with understands there are no right or wrong answers.

A survey of *organizational determinants* will provide you with information about your company which will be relevant to the design and style of your EAP. Consider this question: how many men and women do you employ? The number obviously has important implications for your program. If you have 50 employees you know it is fiscal insanity to design a full-service on-site EAP. On the other hand, if you have 10,000 on your payroll, it might be the most practical way to go.

To help with your survey of organizational determinants, we have made a list of the questions for which you will need answers. Any professional you hire to develop your EAP should ask these same questions.

(1) What type of organization is yours?

If your company is a union shop operating under a collective-bargaining agreement, this will affect the style and implementation of your EAP. As we have said elsewhere several times, union representatives must be fully involved. If, on the other hand, yours is a social-service agency operating autonomously and with no particular ties to any employee organization, you will have greater flexibility in the design and implementation of the program.

(2) What is the structure of yor organization?

Are you a home office responsible for setting policy for hundreds of smaller offices all over the country? Or is yours a branch office unable to implement major employee policies without prior approval from management in another city or state? Will it be possible to start the program throughout the company or will the first stage be a pilot or experimental program serving one location?

(3) What is the management structure?

Is management oriented toward profit or some humanitarian objective as in a social-service agency? How are jobs classified? How rigid are the lines between employees, supervisors and management? How will EAP positions fit into the management structure? The director of a postal EAP told us hers was considered a very low prestige position. What effect is this likely to have on the success of the EAP?

(4) What is your service or major product? If public safety is involved, this will affect the urgency with which job-performance evaluations must be carried out. You may need to consider testing for drug use. If there is a great deal of line production at your worksite, it will be easier to document impaired performance than in those sites employing a large number of professionals who operate more or less independently.

(5) How old is your organization?

The length of time a company has been established affects the emphasis it places on image. A company with a long history in a particular community may be more concerned with its "family" of employees than a younger, less stable company. Also, younger companies are often in shakey financial condition and may feel that an extensive EAP organization is prohibitively expensive.

(6) What unions or employee organizations operate within your company? Which employees are covered by special agreements? Who will be chosen to assist in formulating policies and procedures? What problems may be expected to arise? Who are the influential union members whose help you will need to enlist?

(7) What specific data is known about your employees?

If you have a hard time answering this question you will have learned something important about your company's record-keeping procedures, something you will need to change if your EAP is to function smoothly. Do you know how many people you employ? Of that number how many are salaried; how many work on an hourly basis? How many are part- or flex time? What is the number of male and female workers and what are their average ages? What is the average length of employment? What is the average annual wage?

Data such as this will help you project patterns of EAP utilization. For example, experience has shown that the majority of production referrals come from hourly employees. If you employ a large number of men in their late teens and early 20s, marijuana is likely to be a problem. If your employees are predominantly female, your EAP will offer the kinds of services women find most helpful—like crisis management or noontime brown bag seminars on subjects relating to budgeting, health, family and childrearing. Alcoholism is generally more of a problem with middle-aged male employees.

(8) What is the rate of problem behaviors for the last year? In other words, how impaired is your workplace? How frequently has the company been involved in the following?
- arbitration
- disciplinary actions
- grievances

How frequently do the following occur?
- accidents
- job turnovers
- absenteeism
- customer or client complaints
- utilization of medical benefits

This baseline data will help you to gauge the success of your EAP after 18 months or two years of operation.

(9) Current personnel policies, procedures and contracts

Any conflicts between old and new policies will have to be ironed out before the new policies and procedures are put into effect. What contracts are currently out? Will they affect the EAP? How will employees be informed of new policies and procedures?

An EAP professional told us, "The worst thing management can do is drop a new policy in the supervisor's lap without preparing him. And it's the same for the supervisor. He can't all of a sudden start documenting tardiness and sloppy performance if he's been tolerant of that kind of thing for years. Before any new policies get put into practice, everyone has to be alerted. Fair warning is essential."

(10) Finally, the type and limits of health insurance coverage should be studied.

Health insurance is one of the most important determinants to consider when you are planning your EAP. Today the majority of firms provide health benefits for their employees but not all include provisions for treating drug addiction and alcoholism. There is a split of opinion about the value of such treatment stemming from a traditional reluctance on the part of insurance companies to provide coverage for certain *types* of illnesses of which addiction is just one.

- illnesses to which a stigma is attached
- illnesses that are difficult to detect
- illnesses that are considered either incurable or curable only outside the mainstream of medical treatment
- illnesses associated with a lifestyle subject to attack on "moral grounds"
- illnesses in which most health-care providers are not interested
- illnesses where treatment is labor-intensive rather than relying on medical technology
- illnesses that are difficult to classify according to medical speciality
- illnesses where the prevention and successful treatment require social intervention and a sustained effort by a number of disciplines

Sometimes an additional reason is given for the failure to include addiction and alcoholism treatment under health benefits. Many people believe it will be overused. However, there is no indication that any kind of mental-health benefits are ever overused. Denial and the stigma attached to treatment work to keep the numbers down. A 1976 study of the insurance utilization of 337,000 potential beneficiaries in California found that during one year only 300 used the benefits allowed for treatment of chemical abuse.

Experts tell us that, one way or another, employers end up paying dearly for untreated addicts and alcoholics. These are the employees who never feel really well, who complain—not of drinking or using drugs—but of secondary ailments like gastritis, headaches, liver disorders and palpitations. Estimates are that this population takes up between 15 and 20 percent of hospital beds at any given time. They use eight times as many hospital days as the general population. Members of their families use three to four times the total health benefits. This can hardly be called efficient health care. It is as if a person periodically drank poison and repeatedly spent time in the hospital being treated for the symptoms of poisoning—sweats, stomach cramps and blurred vision—but never for the poisoning itself.

Increasingly, cost conscious employers are realizing it makes economic sense to treat the primary disease of chemical addiction. A 1979 review reports that alcoholism treatment alone is linked to declines in sick days between 38 and 47 percent. In medical utilization the decline is between 26 and 60 percent. A 33 to 48 percent improvement is seen in dollars paid in sickness and accident benefits.

There are many kinds of health coverage available. To find out the specifics as they apply to your region of the country, check with a carrier who can put together a benefits package that suits your needs. The larger your company, the more choices will be available but even a small organization can afford a decent drug and alcohol treatment plan. If you are presently covered by some form of health insurance, it will be easy to add treatment to the basic package. It will probably cost no more than a few dollars per employee.

The most complete coverage provides for 30-day inpatient treatment (usually with a twice in a lifetime limitation), enhanced outpatient treatment, and followup care of from 20 to 40 visits for the employee and his family. A much less complete treatment package of the sort generally offered by HMOs (health maintenance organizations) includes detoxification and 20 to 40 therapeutic visits. Other choices fall within these extremes.

Ford Motor Company's health-care costs rose 240 percent between 1972 and 1980. In 1980, Ford spent roughly $2,300 per employee on health care. In 1960, General Motors spent $38 million on health care. In 1979, GM spent $500 million. In 1980, the company spent more for employee medical care than it did for steel for its automobiles.

In 1985, one dollar out of every 10 in the national economy was spent for health care. Clearly, it is no exaggeration to say that it represents the largest unmanaged cost in business today. But failing to provide adequate coverage for employees in need of treatment for chemical addiction will not improve the situation. As we have shown, it only contributes to the problem.

In December of 1983 the President's Commission on Drunk Driving recommended that state insurance commissioners should require and/or state legislators should enact legislation requiring health-insurance providers to include coverage for the treatment of alcoholics and other drug-dependent persons in all health-insurance policies. "In the long run, insurance carriers and society end up paying more if coverage is not provided."

Resources that concern you as you plan your EAP are of two types: internal and community. Whenever possible during the early planning phase of your EAP, make full use of internal or in-house resources to save both time and the expense of hiring outside consultants. Employees who have been with the company for some time—perhaps longer than the current management—will know whether the company has ever tried to establish an EAP in the past and, if so, why it did not succeed. It may be possible to integrate some of the previous plan into the new one. It will certainly be possible to avoid the mistakes that were made in the earlier effort. Obviously, only the largest companies will have the full range of resources listed below, but even a small firm will have some.

Insurance Consultants

To a great extent, the shape and size of your company's EAP will depend on the kind of insurance coverage available to your employees. Your staff consultant will have records of insurance utilizaton and know if different employees have different kinds of coverage and why this is so. Insurance is a complicated and changing field, one in which it will take an expert to get you the best coverage for the least money. That expert may already be your employee.

Employee Benefits

Probably your company insurance consultant knows exactly what employees are entitled to under coverage. Does your insurance carrier pay only for traditional medical services or are treatments for chemical abuse included? Will the insurance cover treatment after relapse? Is the employee's family covered?

Labor Relations Department

Labor should be involved with the EAP from the very beginning, for the obvious reason that it promotes a safe and harmonious workplace. Since union representatives have to spend a disproportionately larger amount of time with troubled members, a strong, active EAP actually makes their jobs easier by streamlining the grievance process and ensuring fair treatment of all employees. Failure to include labor will work to the detriment of your EAP. "The more the EAP is tight with management, involved with management and excluding labor," the Director of a Sacrementao EAP told us, "the more it's seen by the union as a *tool* of management."

Training Staff

Implementation of your program will involve educating employees in a variety of ways. Although your own training staff may not have the expertise necessary to do this, it can still give qualified trainers the kinds of background data they need to reach the greatest number of employees in the most efficient way.

Company Magazine or Newsletter

A company publication is an excellent vehicle for disseminating information about new policies and programs. You will want to know how often it is published, how wide is its distribution and what kind of articles and features the editors will accept.

Financial or Legal Services

Consult your financial experts before deciding the size and shape of your EAP. To determine how cost-effective a program should be, financial and insurance experts can give you a dollars-and-cents evaluation of the cost of such things as employee absenteeism, accidents, suits, grievances, tardiness, complaints, sick leave, disability, retraining and so on. And what will be your legal liability if you institute an EAP? How will it affect your procedures for firing employees? If you decide to test employees for chemicals, what are your rights and restrictions?

Medical Services

If you have medical services located on the company premises, you will want to know how employees use this service and how it can be made an integral part of the EAP package. What are the legal risks involved in such a service? Is it cost effective?

Public Information Officer

This valuable resource person knows what community agencies and services will be responsible to employee needs and probably has contacts with helping institutions, hospitals, treatment centers and educational facilities.

Employee Recreational Program

If your company has such a program it may have potential for encouraging a company wellness philosophy. The director of an EAP serving 3,000 utility company employees in the Far West told us that at her worksite the recreational program has been particularly cooperative in setting up activities on the company premises, activities aimed at alleviating the kind of employee stress that can eventually lead to problems either directly or indirectly associated with chemical abuse. "Six years ago, the idea of being sensitive to employees' emotional issues was alien to most managers," she told us. "But that's changing now. I've had requests for a lunchtime yoga program and my boss has given me a go signal."

To determine what community resources are available to your EAP, use the headings checklist below. The classified pages of the phone book are a good place to begin making a list. In some communities the chamber of commerce prints a resource booklet. Directors of agencies such as the YMCA, Planned Parenthood or NOW can also be helpful. You may be surprised to discover the dozens—perhaps hundreds—of agencies, committees, self-help groups, services and programs that exist within your city limits. And if you do not know the full extent of help available, it is virtually assured that your employees do not either. It will be one of the services of your EAP to guide them toward the appropriate source of help.

Legal Aid Agencies

Most communities have agencies and programs designed to give legal advice to persons of modest economic means. If a legal problem is making it difficult for your once-reliable employee to function well in the workplace, if he is distracted at his task, difficult to get along with, perhaps drinking too much to relieve his stress and worry over a legal matter, he needs to speak to the company EAP counselor who can put him in touch with a legal advisor.

Budget Counseling and Debt Management

An EAP representative from Southern California told us, "I worked with an employee who was falling apart on the job. She'd gotten two warnings from her supervisor and knew the third one meant she was out of work. Turns out she'd got into debt at Christmas, using plastic, and was trying to pay off everything by working another job nights. She did complicated electronic piece-work for us, and believe me, it's the kind of stuff you can't do when you're exhausted. We sent her to a budget counseling service that helped her consolidate her bills and set her on a payment schedule she could manage. She quit moonlighting and things have been okay with her since."

Educational Services

Adult education, remedial education, vocational guidance and tutoring are only four of the educational services available in many communities. If an employee feels stuck in a dead-end job, he or she may begin to drink excessively to relieve depression or may take euphoria-producing drugs that induce a false sense of confidence. The employee's not chemically addicted—not yet, anyway. If impaired performance is identified early, education may be all that is required for a turn-around.

Services to Children

If an employee is troubled about his children over an extended period, his work will reflect it. If he is in the early stages of alcoholism, this home problem will probably cause him to drink more. If the problem is one of communication, the drinking (or drugging) will intensify it. One of the things a fully functioning EAP counselor can do for this employee is familiarize him or her with the services offered for children in your area. Under this heading we include such things as latchkey programs, day care, family-counseling services, court-diversion programs for affected youth, abused children's services, shelters for runaways, child-tracing services, child and youth oriented self-help groups like Alatot and Alateen for the children of alcoholics and addicts, tutoring, recreation programs and many more. Exactly how many more will depend on where your company is located.

Services to Families

What agencies, programs and services aimed at helping families are in operation in your community? Are there counseling centers where the facilitators are trained to deal with such issues as whole family counseling, marriage counseling, divorce arbitration?

Self-help Groups

Make a complete list of the self-help groups in your area. You will probably be surprised by the variety of these groups. In one community studied, we compiled the following list by merely talking to women active in AA: Alcoholics Anonymous, Alanon, Alateen, Alatot, Cocaine Anonymous, Emotions Anonymous, Potsmokers Anonymous, Gamblers Anonymous, Overeaters Anonymous. Besides these anonymous groups, we were also told about support groups for the adult children of alcoholics, battered women, incest victims, women who love too much, widows, parents without partners, grandparents separated from grandchildren, diabetics, epileptics, and colostomy patients. We have been told this list is far from complete.

Women's Services

Sex, contraceptive, abortion and birthright counseling exist in most communities, as do clinics for battered women, women alone, women seeking specific help with divorce, alimony, child support and related issues.

An EAP director told us this story:

> I had a client come in who was an executive secretary. She said she didn't know what was wrong with her but she was having a harder and harder time with just the basics of the job she'd been doing for years. She knew her boss was beginning to get fed up with her, but she claimed she didn't know what the matter was. She was bad-tempered a lot of the time, and some clients had complained about her manner on the telephone. She didn't talk about her drinking problem then. That came out later, during the evaluation, when we realized she actually had a pretty heavy alcohol habit. Anyway, we got her into treatment for alcoholism, and then, as part of her recovery program, we encouraged her to link up with some of the women's support groups in our region. She'd had a miserable childhood—father beat her, mother left her alone for long periods of time, no encouragement from any adult. She told us she'd basically been on her own since she was six or seven years old. Anyway, she found a couple of women's groups where she felt comfortable enough to go down deep into all that stuff that she'd been carrying around with her since childhood. And it worked. She's still sober after almost four years and she's an excellent employee.

Drug and Alcohol Treatment Centers

Today all areas of the country have facilities to treat the chemically addicted. However, if yours is an urban area, you will probably discover dozens of treatment centers within easy driving distance of your workplace, and the problem will be choosing the best one. Using the criteria discussed in an earlier chapter, you will easily be able to evaluate which meets your particular needs.

MAKING A PRELIMINARY PROGRAM PROPOSAL

With all of the above information well-digested and collated, you are ready to write the preliminary proposal for your EAP. This proposal will be an educational tool. Remember, many of the people whose support you will need to make your EAP fly have very little knowledge of any aspect of either the problems of employees or their solution. With this preliminary proposal, you will be teaching them what you yourself have learned.

Before you are through, many others will wish to contribute to the design of your company's EAP. For this reason—and for the sake of diplomacy—make plain at the outset that this document is a preliminary draft only. It is acceptable to state what you feel is best for the business, but examine other options as well at this stage.

What is Included in the Preliminary Proposal?

The answer to this question will vary according to the needs of your business. The preliminary proposal of a multimillion dollar chain of sporting goods stores will differ from that of a manufacturing organization with 125 full-time female employees and the same number of seasonal employees working part-time.

However, some topic headings have generalized application.

State the Problem

The information in the first chapters of this book, the facts and figures appearing regularly in newspapers and newsmagazines as well as specific statistics from your workplace should be enough to convince anyone that American business has a problem with drugs and alcohol.

Present Different Program Models

If you favor a broadbrush EAP shared between a half dozen small businesses located in the same neighborhood, say this directly. But also include other ideas, airing the advantages and disadvantages of each. There are many creative ways to design an EAP that suits your needs and the better informed others are of the options, the more likely you are to come up with something that works for your company.

Coverage

Will only full-time employees be eligible? What about their families? From what you have read so far in this book, you will be able to state the case for including families in the coverage. How adequate is your current insurance coverage? What will be the cost of adding a treatment benefit? What is the chance it will be abused? If you do not answer questions such as these in the document, you will have a hard time selling your idea.

Advisory Committee

Who will this be and what will it do? Why is it needed?

Assessment and Referral

How might this be handled? On-site or off? Again, state your own preference but discuss the options available.

Program Administration

Will the administrator be a full-time in-house employee? Can you do without one?

Counseling

Do you favor contracting with an outside agency for counseling or hiring a full-time person to do so on the work premises? What are the advantages and disadvantages of these service models? How do the unique features of your business affect the choice of counseling mode?

Orientation

Who will attend and why? How many employee hours will be involved? Who will handle such an orientation?

Supervisory Training

Who will attend and why? How many employee hours will be involved? Who will handle these trainings?

Role of Volunteers

Who are they and what kind of training will they need? How will they be used?

Employee Followup

What should be evaluated and when? What are the options in the event of one, two, three unsatisfactory evaluations?

Costs

Be able to give a realistic estimate of how much the EAP program you favor will cost the company. Depending on the model you have in mind, you may need to quote costs and salary figures for one or more of the following:

- the program administrator
- on- or off-site counseling service
- assessment and referral agency

- office staff
- administrative costs
- increased health benefits

Expenses will vary greatly. The more employees who utilize a program, the less it will cost per employee and the more you will save through prevention. Duane E. Rogers in San Diego suggests that in his territory most companies can get a good working EAP for in the neighborhood of $10,000 a year but in another part of the country the cost might differ considerably. We suggest that the best way to estimate costs is to contact a nearby company about the size of yours that has had in operation for a year or more an EAP similar to the kind you hope to implement.

ENLIST SUPPORT FOR YOUR PROGRAM

You will use the preliminary proposal to inspire others with your enthusiasm for the EAP concept. If you have already recruited a team to put together a drug and alcohol policy, you will be halfway to the mark on this aspect of EAP planning. Many experienced program consultants consider that the failure to involve key people early and to keep them informed and involved in the planning process is the chief reason why some programs never get off the ground.

Ask yourself this question: "Whose support do I need to implement an EAP?" Your answer will include members of management, the board of directors, junior staff or union representatives, supervisors and rank and file employees.

Then ask yourself a second question: "Who can help me convince these people that an EAP is the way to go?" This answer may include a key member of the management team who is already supportive. But you might be better off if you consider enlisting the aid of someone your colleagues will perceive as unbiased or possessing special expertise in certain areas: industrial engineers, occupational program consultants, medical doctors, psychologists, executives who have been involved with similar programs elsewhere, someone from the insurance department or personnel, an accountant prepared to show the red-ink losses cause by impaired employees.

Do not attempt to convince everyone at once. Instead, meet separately with members of management, staff, labor and supervision. Present your proposal and be prepared for the questions you are bound to get. If your workplace is at all typical, questions will center on the following points:

- *expense*: How much will it cost to start the program and keep it going? How much will supervisor training sessions cost? Are employee health benefits adequate? How much money will the program save the company?
- *efficiency*: Will an EAP save the company time and money? How? What changes can be anticipated?

- *legal issues*: What is your company's liability relative to employee drug and alcohol abuse? What happens if your company adopts a do- nothing posture?
- *labor relations*: Will the program and its policies be applied fairly to all employees? Will employees have to sacrifice other benefits in exchange for having an EAP? Will EAP procedures harmonize with existing union grievance procedures? What steps will be taken to ensure employee confidentiality? Can or will the EAP be used as a management tool to harass employees?
- *employee utilization*: Will the program make more work for supervisors? How can extra work be minimized? Will time off and seniority be affected? Will program use affect an employee's opportunities for promotion? Will supervisors have to become involved with employees' emotional lives?
- *procedure*: Will the EAP mean extra paperwork and responsibilities for supervisors? Will referral procedures include a union representative? At what point in the performance review will a union representative be brought in? How will the employee be informed of EAP services? In case of employee complaints, who will be responsible? Will your company use relapse agreements? Second chance agreements?

Although you are convinved that your organization needs an EAP, some of your colleagues will need a lot of convincing to go along with you. This is because most of them are unaccustomed and uncomfortable with discussing the personal/emotional problems that are central to an EAP. They are at home with more concrete data and naturally they dislike the feeling of ignorance they get when trying to talk about problems for which they feel they do not even have an appropriate vocabulary—let along a sure-fire solution. Your colleagues will need to be shown how personal/emotional problems affect an employee's job performance. Also, be prepared to restate the specific details of your program many times before they feel the need as acutely as you do.

FORM A PROGRAM ADVISORY COMMITTEE

When you have won the necessary support from management, labor and supervisors, appoint a representative committee to iron out the details of the EAP.

At this point the advisory committee will make its most important decision. Is the company going to design and staff its own EAP or will it contract with an outside agency? For example, employers contract with Duane Rogers's Personal Assistance Services to do all the assessment and referral work with their employees. His staff is trained to tell the difference between an employee's apparent problem and an underlying, more central, problem. They know their region's social-service and human-resource pool and exactly where to send an employee to get needed help.

There are advantages to contracting out EAP services in this way. Many employees seem to trust that their confidentiality is best protected when all services are offered away from the worksite. This separation may increase rates of employee utilization, making the program more efficient and cost-effective. From management's point of view, there is the reassuring certainty that employee assistance is in the hands of specialists capable of diagnosing a variety of employee problems.

The disadvantages of an independent EAP are apt to seem like advantages to an employee concerned about his privacy. All records remain the property of the EAP. Except when special arrangements are made, there is little contact between the EAP and supervisory personnel. If management wishes to evaluate the effectiveness of the program, only general information will be made available. Actual followup evaluations can be difficult or impossible.

An in-house program has the advantage of being directly tailored to the needs and resources of the individual company. It works closely with personnel services, employees, supervisors, union officials and management, as appropriate. An in-house program can design a relapse agreement between the supervisor and the employee—something an independent may be reluctant to become involved with if it maintains strict rules of separation from the workplace. On the negative side, the cost of such a program can be prohibitive. A full-time counselor will command a salary of more than $20,000. He or she will need an office, equipment and 25 percent secretarial services to start with. Unless special arrangements are made, there will be no 24-hour phone-referral service. Finally, and most damaging of all, employees are reluctant to use an in-house service because of their fear of being identified as problem employees.

The full-time counselor at a major shipbuilding company employing many thousands of workers told us, "When I first came on board, no one would speak to me. I'd walk around the plant and I felt like the invisible woman. No one wanted to be seen talking to me for fear of being labeled 'sick.' I've been here six months now and just gradually that's changing. Generating trust is the hardest part of my job."

Four to six thousand employees are needed to justify hiring a full-time EAP professional. If your payroll is between 2,000 and 6,000, a part-time counselor with a 24-hour hotline may be ideal. If your employee roster is considerably smaller than that, you may wish to join with other companies of about the same size and create a consortium with one counselor among you. Or you may wish to contract with an EAP serving several other companies. Another option is to arrange for a broad-based community-service agency accustomed to dealing with a variety of adjustment problems to do assessments and referrals. On the humblest level, a program may be simply a hotline and a detailed booklet available to employees at any time, but especially at performance reviews, listing and describing the spectrum of resources available in the community.

If your advisory committee decides that a full- or part-time in-house program is warranted, it will be time to choose the program's referral and assessment (A/R) agency and hire a program coordinator. Your advisory committee will need to know the criteria for choosing an A/R agency and exactly what services it will be expected to perform.

Criteria for Assessment and Referral Agency

Competence

The agency that is right for the job will understand the needs of both management and employees. Its personnel will have broad experience in social service with particular expertise in workplace impairment and chemical addiction, including polydrug abuse. It will recognize that the therapeutic and treatment needs of women in some ways differ from those of men. Agency employees' will have the skills to assess, counsel and motivate employees to seek help as well as familiarity with and willingness to refer employees to community resources. Employees may be occupational program consultants, certified drug and/or alcoholism counselors, licensed clinical social workers, or the like.

Location

The agency should have a pleasant physical plant centrally located to minimize employee travel time, ample parking, preferably free.

Time

Flexible operating hours to complement employee needs, so as to avoid the need for scheduling far in advance, are necessary.

Ability to Perform Necessary Tasks

* assessment of employee's primary problem
* motivational counseling to convince employees of the need for care and the effectiveness of care
* referral to community agencies
* monitoring and coordinating client care
* employee follow-up
* sharing the program evaluation task with the program coordinator

Another important task of the advisory committee is setting a timeline for hiring a coordinator, choosing an A/R agency, writing the final policy and procedure document, supervisory training, employee notification, and program review. It is impossible to make a general statement about how long it will take to establish an EAP at your worksite. If you live in a region where such programs are commonplace, where program consultants are available and where social service agencies are experienced at working with employers, it may be possible to have a program in operation within three months. If, however, your program is complicated and your company large or if you are located away from metropolitan regions, you may need as long as a year to get the elements of your program in place. A word of caution. Once the advisory committee agrees to the size and scope of your EAP and a coordinator is hired, there is an impulse to move quickly. Haste can be disastrous for your program if it means over-looking important details and failing to cement the vital personnel and community linkages.

Management of a trucking company in the Northwest was advised to implement an EAP when one of its drivers was involved in a drunk driving incident. The program was developed too quickly and without sufficient input from rank-and-file employees. Those at the highest levels of management had never driven trucks themselves. In fact, as it turned out, they didn't even know any truck drivers well enough to sit down and have a conversation with them. They did not realize that most of their employees lived by a code that said psychologists and counselors were for women and sissies. In design-ing the company EAP, no one on the advisory board considered how difficult it would be to get the drivers to seek help in the first place. Ultimately, the advisory board was reconstructed to include many lower-level employees, and the program itself was redesigned with a much greater emphasis on employee education.

HIRING A COORDINATOR

For economic reasons, the advisory committee may decide that rather than hire a full-time coordinator, it will appoint someone from the committee or elsewhere in the company to work full-time until the program is established and thereafter continue on a part-time basis. Occasionally a company tries to combine coordinator and assessment and referral. For this job description you will need to find someone equally at home as an administrator and as a counselor, which will be extremely difficult to do. Full- or part-time, the qualifications and job description for the coordinator are the same.

Qualifications

- committed to the theory and practice of EAPs
- an ability to plan and organize
- good interpersonal skills
- free of negative associations, acceptable to management, employees, unions

Job Description

- draw up contracts with assessment and referral agency
- disperse funds

- do advocacy for the program
- educate
- train supervisors to do job performance based interventions and referrals
- train key employees to act as unofficial referral agents
- keep records of utilization
- coordinate publicity
- evaluate the program

Although many experts can agree that a failure to enlist and maintain the support of management is a chief cause of EAP failure, there is a second—and, we think, equally important—reason: lack of supervisory cooperation. Earlier in this book we discussed the important role of supervisors. We described their problems with denial and the kind of training that can prepare them for their tasks as performance evaluators and referral agents. Whoever you hire to act as program coordinator, he or she must be respected by the supervisory employees, must feel comfortable talking to them, and must be concerned for the problems they face implementing the company's EAP.

IMPLEMENTING AND EVALUATING AN EAP

Having completed the headnoted tasks, you, your committee and your coordinator are finally ready to implement the program. This is done in several phases:

1. Policy Statement
2. Procedural Statement
3. Employee Orientation
4. Supervisory Training
5. Publicity
6. Evaluation

POLICY STATEMENT

A strong, clearly written policy statement encourages supervisors to act with confidence and objectivity when dealing with impaired employees. Earlier in the book we described how to go about developing, writing, and publicizing a company drug and alcohol policy. We believe every company must have such a policy regardless of whether it has an EAP. But when we speak of policy in this chapter, we are referring to the second, procedural section of that drug and alcohol policy.

A broadbrush EAP policy describes the management's attitude toward personal/

emotional problems in general and their effect on job performance without singling out specific problems for attention. The policy outlines management's responsibilities, as well as those of supervisors and other employees. Finally, it clearly states who is eligible for the program and the costs. In this document, employees at all levels are assured that utilizing the EAP will not threaten their job security, nor will it be held against them at promotion or bonus time. A central tenet of every successfully working EAP, one that is repeatedly stated in every document, is the confidentiality of its services.

PROCEDURAL STATEMENT

A procedural document must accompany the policy statement. In this it is plainly stated how supervisors may refer employees and how employees may refer themselves to the EAP. This procedural document is important for several reasons. First, it assures the fairness and uniformity of supervisory referral. Second, it lets employees "know where they are." When a man is called in to an informal job performance evaluation as was described earlier in the book, he knows that if he does not improve his performance within a set time, he will be formally called on the carpet. He also knows what he can do to help himself at this point. In the procedural statement it is made clear that there will be no second informal warning. In the same way, an employee who has signed an improved performance contract and failed to live up to its terms will know that he faces disciplinary action. A third importance of the procedural document is that it encourages employees to use the EAP when a situation first becomes a problem instead of waiting for it to threaten their position in the company. Here is a sample statement based on the procedures described in the book. Here also is a flow chart illustrating the procedural statement. A similar chart and a written explanation of the procedure should be made available to your employees.

SAMPLE PROCEDURAL STATEMENT

INFORMAL PERFORMANCE EVALUATION

1. Review the problem with the employee. Make sure he understands what level of job performance is expected and the specific ways in which his performance is seen as unsatisfactory: absenteeism, tardiness, poor workmanship, complaints from coworkers, etc.

2. Make sure the employee is familiar with the company EAP and remind him that if anything is troubling him, the EAP is designed to help.

3. Write a short report of the informal evaluation and attach to documentation.

4. Continue to document job performance.

FORMAL PERFORMANCE EVALUATION

1. Offer to include a union representative in the meeting; document this offer.

2. Review the problem with the employee and make sure he understands that this review serves as an official warning that his work is unsatisfactory in given ways. Cite specific documentation of impaired performance including dates, times and relevant details.

3. Make sure the employee is familiar with the company EAP and remind him that if anything is troubling him, the EAP is designed to help. Present him with written material about the EAP.

4. Employee agrees to and signs Improved Performance Agreement.

5. Date for follow-up review is set.

6. Continue to document job performance.

IMPROVED PERFORMANCE REVIEW

1. Offer to include a union representative in the meeting; document this offer.

2. Review the earlier agreement with the employee

3. Document the employee's continued impaired performance.

4. Strongly recommend that the employee avail himself of the services of the EAP.

5. Make sure the employee understands that this review is the last verbal warning that his job is in jeopardy due to impaired performance.

LETTER OF REPRIMAND

1. Specify the ways in which the employee has failed to improve his job performance satisfactorily and according to the terms of the improved performance agreement.

2. Refer to the previous two performance reviews.

3. Refer to the repeated reminders to the employee that an EAP exists to assist him.

4. Warn the employee that the next step will be suspension, demotion or termination.

5. Copies to the employee's personnel file, manager, personnel officer and labor representative.

IMPLEMENT APPROPRIATE SANCTIONS ACCORDING TO ESTABLISHED COMPANY POLICY.

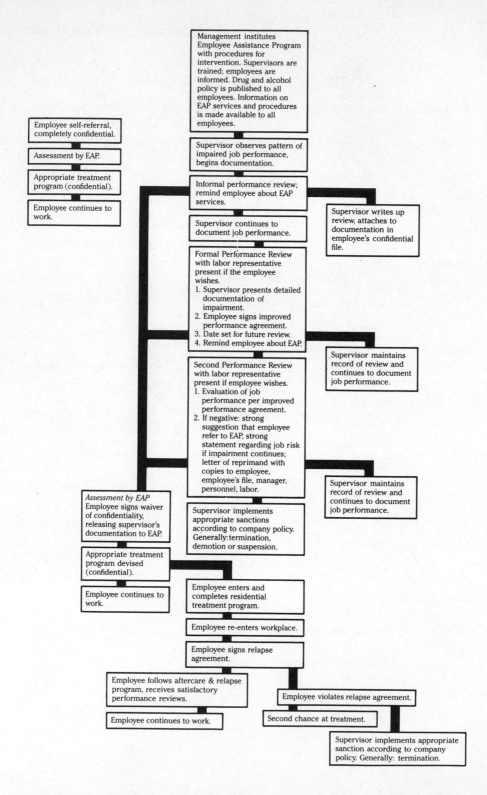

EMPLOYEE ORIENTATION

The purpose of orientation is to educate employees about EAP policy, procedures and services.

Although it will not be financially practical to spend a lot of time on this phase, it is important that an organized effort be made to inform all employees of what the EAP is, how it works and for whom it is intended. Obviously, it is no good having a program if employees fail to use it. You may choose to do orientation in a series of informal discussions at lunch or during the half hour before the end of the workday. It may be most effective to combine orientation with written handouts, posters and pay envelope enclosures. Perhaps all of the above worked in combination with a thoroughly oriented team of key employees ready to talk about the program and answer all questions informally will be the scheme that works best for you.

However you choose to do it, the important thing is to inform employees of information under these subject headings.

- substance of the policy and procedure documents
- labor and management endorsement of program
- services offered
- confidentiality
- nonpunative nature of the program
- how to self-refer

SUPERVISORY TRAINING

As we discussed in an earlier chapter, the success of this training is crucial to the success of your program. Rather than repeat the material from that chapter, we will list the important points here to refresh your memory. A good supervisory training will include the following:

- explanation and discussion of policy and procedure statement
- role of supervisors
- motivation to make referrals
- drug and alcohol education
- characteristics of the impaired workplace
- impaired job performance patterns
- importance of early identification of impaired job performance
- explanation, maintenance and use of referral instruments
- conducting job performance reviews
- problems the supervisor may encounter
- discussion of confidentiality, nonpunitive nature of program
- sources of help and assistance for supervisors

PUBLICITY

Not surprisingly, there is a direct correlation between the successful implementation of an EAP and the amount and quality of publicity that goes with it. You can inaugurate your program with posters, handouts, buttons, pay-envelope enclosures, information booths and a visit from Santa Claus himself, but in a few short weeks the majority of employees will have forgotten all about the company EAP. To promote program use you will have to give employees the same information several times a year, including the following:

- brief restatement of EAP policy and procedures
- outline of services
- eligibility
- where services are offered
- when services are offered
- confidentiality
- anonymity (if provided for)
- hotline (if available)
- cost

To make the most effective use of funds budgeted for publicity, your program coordinator should be aware of seasonal-interest trends that affect program utilization.

Summertime is considered by some to be the slow period for EAPs; nevertheless, problems arise at this season that your coordinator can bear in mind and offer specific programs—lunchtime discussions, recreational activities, etc.—to counteract. For single mothers who must work, children are apt to be a worry. For those on a tight budget, planning for a vacation can mean resentment, anger and frustrated desires, which may lead to increased chemical use. Summer is partytime in most parts of the country. This means your employees will probably be using more drugs and alcohol.

In the autumn children return to school. School behavior, truancy and homework add to the tensions of the household. Marriages may experience added stress. At this time of year, an EAP we know sends home in pay envelopes a tip sheet of how working parents can become involved in their children's education. As the weather becomes gloomy and the days shorten, some of your employees will suffer from depression.

Christmas is a time of year associated with depression, chemical abuse, expense and family reunions—any one of which is enough to lower the morale of an employee and create job performance problems. Your coordinator may decide that this is a good time to remind employees of the season crisis intervention hotline the EAP operates from November through January.

Spring, a hopeful time of budding life and longer, warmer days, is also a season when many people suffer bouts of depression as they confront the discrepancy between their seasonal expectations and their more mundane reality. To remind employees about the counseling services of the EAP at this time of year, we know a coordinator who held a drawing for opening day baseball tickets. Another replaced all the old EAP posters in employee lounges with new ones that were brightly seasonal. Yet another included as an Easter message in the company newsletter, a first person narrative by an employee who had used the EAP and was happy with the results.

Finally, in all publicity, be aware of the image your EAP is broadcasting to employees. Are you paternalistic? A "big daddy" offering to fix everything for his children? Or are you so caring that the sacharine message is apt to make employees gag? Your image carries a strong message that can either draw people to the EAP or effectively keep them away. One of the most successful EAPs we know combines caring with a prevention theme. Every piece of publicity that leaves that EAP office strikes a note of restrained caring combined with a conviction that employees are intelligent adults who would rather be well than sick, prefer to succeed rather than fail. The EAP motto is "Prevention: First, Fast and Smart."

EVALUATION

Back when you were developing your EAP and enlisting the support of your colleagues you probably promised something like this: "If our EAP doesn't work, if the employees don't make use of the services and job performance doesn't improve, then we'll disband the whole program." Twelve to eighteen months later, it is time to find out if you will have to keep that promise. Although it is perfectly legitimate to solicit input from the personnel office, the A.R. agency and even the Chairman of the Board if you wish, employees and supervisors are the two groups able to tell you the most about how your EAP is working.

Employees

You will want to learn three things from this group. First, out of the total employee population you will want to know how many used the program, for what purpose, under what motivation and with what result. For those who did not use the service, you will want to know why. No problems? Forgot the service was available? Fears for job security? Lack of confidentiality?

Second, it is helpful to provide a representative group of employees with a survey to determine employees' awareness of the programs offered by the EAP. You may discover some employees are not getting the publicity message. A company operating near the Arizona/Mexico border discovered that the two thirds of its employees who were Mexican-Americans were uninformed about the EAP. The coordinator had been hired from out of the region. He assumed that because these Mexican-Americans spoke English, they would read it just as easily. In fact, although many could read English, it was difficult for them, and they threw away pay-envelope enclosures that were not written in Spanish. Subsequent information sheets about the EAP were written in both languages and program utilization increased.

Third, from the population of employees who actually used the program, you will want specific utilization information. For this you will devise your own questionnaires and survey forms. The following format is a workable sample.

```
NO NAME
Sex _____
Age _____
Marital Status _____
Years with the company _____
How did you enter the program?
        supervisor referral _____
        suggested by a friend _____
        self-referral _____
        other
What kind of help did you get?
        marriage counseling _____
        whole family counseling _____
        counseling for children _____
        drug/alcohol treatment _____
        financial counseling _____
        career counseling _____
        eating disorder counseling _____
        stress management _____
        other _____

How long were you in counseling or treatment? _____
Do you see a change in those problems which brought you to the
Employee Assistance Program originally?
_____Improved _____No Change _____Worsened




Would you use the services of the Employee Assistance Program
again? _____

What services would you like to see offered in the future?
_____
```

Supervisors

Supervisors know if EAP services helped impaired employees to improve their job performance. If they did not, chances are your supervisor doubts the worth of the whole enterprise and will be glad to tell you exactly how he or she feels. Somewhere on the survey form, allow supervisors the opportunity to express their opinion for or against the program and solicit their suggestions on how to make it better.

The following survey is an example of the kind of instrument developed to evaluate the effectiveness of the program from the supervisors' point of view. Supervisors should fill out one such form for each referred employee. And in the interests of employee relations, don't give the forms out on Thursday and expect them back by Friday. One of the complaints some supervisors have about referring employees for impaired work performance is that all the documentation takes too long. It's the kind of paperwork they hate. To avoid playing into this negative bias, give them plenty of time to fill out these surveys.

COMPARISON OF WORKPLACE PERFORMANCE PATTERNS
BEFORE AND AFTER EAP REFERRAL

Cause of Referral	Before EAP	After EAP	Change (+ or -)
Late to Work			
Left Work Early			
Absenteeism			
Missing from Desk (line, office, etc.)			
Accidents			
Short Term Disability			
Medical Leave			
Sick Days			
Other_____			

Complaints
When you referred the employee to the program, what was the basic
problem? _____

How would you rate his overall job performance at that time?
(completely unsatisfactory) 1 2 3 4 5 6 7 8 9 10 (excellent)

Have you observed any improvement since the employee entered the
program? _____

Have there been any slips in job performance since the employee
entered the program? _____

How would you rate his overall job performance today?
(completely unsatisfactory) 1 2 3 4 5 6 7 8 9 10 (excellent)

You will also want your program coordinator to evaluate the effectiveness of the training sessions provided for supervisors. This can be done through the use of another survey. We recommend that this one by anonymous so as to encourage candor on the part of the supervisors who may feel that the EAP is management's "baby."

```
          SUPERVISORY EVALUATION OF EAP TRAINING

An effective EAP needs the full support of all supervisors.   To
help us design the most effective EAP training, we would like
your comments and reactions to the following questions about your
last training session.

     Please rate the following training segments according to
     how helpful you found them.

                              not at all helpful          very helpful
Need for the Program.................1  2   3   4   5   6   7   8   9   10
Overview of the Program.............1  2   3   4   5   6   7   8   9   10
Role of the Supervisor..............1  2   3   4   5   6   7   8   9   10
Benefits to the Supervisor..........1  2   3   4   5   6   7   8   9   10

Drug and Alcohol Education..........1  2   3   4   5   6   7   8   9   10
                              not at all helpful          very helpful
Characteristics of an
Impaired workplace..................1  2   3   4   5   6   7   8   9   10
Identifying patterns of
Job Impairment......................1  2   3   4   5   6   7   8   9   10
Importance of early
Identification......................1  2   3   4   5   6   7   8   9   10

Explanation,Maintenance
and Use of Referral
Instruments.........................1  2   3   4   5   6   7   8   9   10
Job Performance Review..............1  2   3   4   5   6   7   8   9   10

Role Playing........................1  2   3   4   5   6   7   8   9   10

Overall, did you find the training helpful?    Yes_____  No_____
Did you understand everything presented?       Yes_____  No_____
If you answered "no", please explain_____
Do you think the training will help you
to be a more effective supervisor?             Yes_____  No_____

Comments:
```

SUMMARY

The three parts of this chapter have described what an EAP is and how it can help your employees and you by improving job performance. We have taken you step-by-step through each stage of developing, implementing and evaluating your EAP. In the end, if yours is a midsized company and the program is working, you can expect a utilization rate of between 5 and 15 percent with 15 percent being extraordinarily good. Smaller companies where an EAP's reputation for confidentiality and success can spread quickly may do much better. Duane E. Rogers provides services for one company with 64 employees of which 23 percent utilize the program. And if your program is successful, supervisors will tell you that patterns of impaired job perforamnce have decreased and company morale is high.

If an employee-assistance program is a service you want to provide for your employees, you are now in a position to take the appropriate steps to contract for one or to design your own. If, on the other hand, an EAP seems a too ambitious scheme for your company, the procedures discussed in the chapters "Documentation" and "Intervention" will still enable you to identify impaired employees and use job leverage to get them the help they need.

13

PRIMARY
PREVENTION

Drug abuse is not a contagious disease, but it does spread among workers. Chances are that if you have one employee who has a drug-abuse problem, you will soon have others. Cocaine users often become pushers to support their own expensive habit. Marijuana abusers commonly "score" a few ounces to sell to friends. Although these sellers in three-piece suits or running shoes may not fit the stereotypical image we have of the sinister drug peddler, their presence in your workplace is a serious problem.

Until now, this book has been about preventing problems in the workplace caused by drug and alcohol abuse—what we call secondary prevention. We've said little about primary prevention: creating a workplace environment that is hostile to drug and alcohol abuse and where drug traffickers cannot gain a foothold. This chapter's placement at the end of the book is no indication of the importance of preventive measures, however. Quite the opposite, for the truth is that unless we as a nation want to expend our time and fortune fighting chemical abuse for the rest of our history, we have to focus as much attention on primary prevention as we do on secondary.

To discourage the abuse of drugs and alcohol in the workplace, we recommend five preventive measures.

HAVE A STRONG COMPANY POLICY REGARDING THE USE AND ABUSE OF DRUGS AND ALCOHOL

This policy will accomplish two things. It *informs* the employee of management's attitude toward the use and abuse of drugs and alcohol and it *protects* management legally by stating that attitude with complete clarity so that no employee can claim ignorance of the rules. The policy must forbid drug use and discourage the inappropriate use of alcoholic beverages. Failure to mention alcohol specifically sends a double message to employees. In effect, it announces, "We don't want you drinking on the job because it may inconvenience us in management, but we don't really think alcohol abuse is a problem, and to prove it, we're going to set up a bar in the executive dining room and let our executives expense their three-martini lunches."

Compare that attitude with the liquor policy of one of the world's largest manufacturing companies. It states unequivocally that alcoholic beverages are not to be served as part of any business meeting held by the company to conduct its internal affairs. That includes expensive lunches and dinners. The policy also cautions management about its responsibility in determining when the use of so-called "light" alcoholic beverages such as wine and beer is appropriate. Alcohol, it stipulates, is never to be served at functions where children are present.

An inclusive policy document is not easy to write, and we recommend that to avoid conflicts of interpretation in the future you confer with an attorney early in the writing process. Your company lawyer may not be the person for the job since this is a rapidly changing and unpredictable area in which even experts can disagree.

MINIMIZE THE OPPORTUNITIES FOR ON-THE-JOB USE AND DISTRIBUTION OF CHEMICALS

Management of a company producing parts for airplanes was surprised to learn that during the workday, drugs were being sold through the chain-link fence behind some warehouses in an area of the plant unused for several years. When questioned, security guards admitted they never bothered to patrol that area because "nothing was going on back there."

It is good to remember that drug-related activities can go on anywhere. To minimize the opportunity for drugs to enter the workplace, employers are wise to review security measures regularly. Eliminate isolated areas where small groups can congregate in privacy. But do not overlook what goes on in public places. Drug business is often transacted in high-traffic areas like the cafeteria and restrooms, lounges and locker rooms. See that your security guards cover the areas assigned to them, and encourage both supervisors and managers to move around the plant as much as possible, maintaining high visibility.

Most security programs are designed to keep employees from taking things off the premises illegally. What is generally overlooked is the contraband being brought in. Make sure your security personnel realize that preventing the sale and use of drugs on company grounds is a top priority with you. It is good prevention to scrutinize every vendor, every delivery truck, every visitor that comes through the front gates. Drug sellers are often those people who move fairly freely about the workplace: delivery persons, vehicle operators, sales representatives, mail deliverers.

A defense contractor employing many thousands of men and women was chagrined to learn that for more than two years, drugs had been sold every noontime right in the company parking lot. A lunch vendor had been dealing in sandwiches, sodas, candy, cocaine, marijuana and assorted pills, right under the tower housing security offices.

Part of preventing the problem is knowing where drugs are most likely to *be* a problem. Because of the stressful or repetitive work they do and the hours when they do it, some of your employees are particularly vulnerable. A quick analysis of company records can tell you which work areas and on which shifts employees are most frequently absent or accident prone, which suffer from a proportionately greater number of physical problems. In those areas and shifts, you are likely to find drugs being used and possibly sold. For example, medical experts tell us that 80 percent of night-shift employees report problems with insomnia, fatigue, digestive disorders and chronic low-energy levels. Not surprisingly, studies hav discovered that the use of intoxicants and marijuana are four times as likely to occur among night workers.

Although they are not suitable for all workplaces, in some companies trained dogs are an effective way to clean up the worksite and deter drug and alcohol use. Four-footed detectives have been used on offshore oil platforms owned by Mobil, Exxon and Penzoil to sniff out marijuana, cocaine, alcohol and numerous other substances. At the Rockwell International plant in Palmdale, California, dogs were used to sniff employee cars in the parking lot.

The Alpha Academy of Dog Training in Atlanta will furnish German shepherds, golden retrievers and even spaniels trained to sniff out drugs. Larry Katz, the owner and trainer at Centurion Kennels in El Cajun, California reports that in testing situations, his dogs are 95 percent successful.

From an employer's point of view, dogs have two advantages. Because of their size and agility, they can investigate difficult-to-reach areas where drugs may be concealed. And most people do not object to their presence in the workplace as they might to a security guard or a police officer. Just the sight of man's best friend padding about the worksite serves as a not-too-threatening reminder that your company has an aggressive policy against drugs and alcohol.

In some companies, searching lockers, workstations and even the employees themselves is regarded as good prevention. One such company is Crowley Maritime Corporation, which operates ships in all our coastal waters. A few years ago drugs aboard ship were a major problem for Crowley and threatened the company's long-standing reputation for reliability. When Crowley management got serious about its problem, it wanted to avoid alienating employees with the appearance of a witch hunt. It took pains to enlist the cooperation of all levels of the workforce by actively soliciting opinions and questions about the company drug and alcohol policy. In compliance with this policy, Crowley uses several procedures, including inspections of workstations and living quarters. The first inspection is with prior notice—eliminating claims that the searches are arbitrary or that employees' rights to privacy are being violated. Subsequent searches are carried out when there is *cause* and without warning. Under supervision and with a peer or labor representative as witness, an employee may be asked to perform a body search on himself.

Crowley fires only those found in possession of sufficiently large quantities of a controlled substance to make the intention to sell apparent. Treatment is recommended for those who show signs of chemical dependency. Possession of any amount requires that the employee take a 12- to 15-hour drug and alcohol education course. Crowley has been able to prevent problems by making the company policy known to all employees and by demonstrating a strong managerial commitment to a drug-free workplace.

As to the legality of searches, the employer has the advantage. Citizens are protected from unwarranted police searches, but there is no such protection from employer searches, particularly when they can be shown to be in the best interest of the company. However, if a union organization is involved, almost any disciplinary action stemming from a search is liable to be appealed. In such cases, arbitrators are more and more likely to take a compromise position between the rights of the involved parties. The extent of their inclination toward management often depends on the company's ability to convince them that drugs and alcohol are a problem and that searches are a responsible solution. Arbitrators also weigh fairness in their decision. There cannot be one policy for the rank and file and another for management. Crowley Maritime's policy is very clear about the fact that *all* cabins, lockers and personnel are subject to search—from the captain down to the least senior deckhand.

Preemployment drug screening is an increasingly routine preventive measure. In 1985, about 2 million screens were performed with enlightening, often surprising, results. For example, management at Alcoa Aluminum in Vancouver, Washington had no idea of the size of the drug problem until half its job applicants tested positive for controlled substances. In New York, a large company used preemployment urinalysis and screened out 25 percent of job applicants. A followup study of employees found that a quarter of them were users who had either "slipped through the screen" or developed substance-abuse problems after coming to work. This last explanation may be closer to the truth. In studies conducted among young employees, many report that they experienced their first intense peer pressure to use drugs not in high school, as is commonly supposed, but on the job, from coworkers.

General Electric offers applicants who fail their first drug screen a second chance six months later. The Sacramento Municipal Utility District policy reads, "Persons who test positive may apply for a second screening within five days of receiving their results."

One of the clear strengths of preemployment screening is the fact that it has not been seriously challenged in the courts. Furthermore, organized labor appears willing to accept this form of testing although most believe the information gained from a screen should be used as only part of a total fitness-for-work picture. Other factors should be a proven ability to do the job, references, test scores etc. Finally, while screening will not eliminate the problem of drugs, it will keep many of the hardcore offenders off your worksite.

MAKE HELP AVAILABLE TO ALL EMPLOYEES EXPERIENCING PROBLEMS AFFECTING JOB PERFORMANCE

Duane E. Rogers of Personal Assistance Services, a San Diego based EAP, believes that the strongest preventive measure an employer can take is providing help resources for troubled employees. He does not believe it is necessary to do much more than remind employees frequently that by calling a given number or visiting a particular office they can get help for whatever problem complicates their lives and threatens their livelihood. Like many EAP providers, Rogers believes that emphasizing specific problems like alcoholism or drug addiction only encourages employee denial. "Just let them know where they can get help," he told us. "Then let us help them figure out what their real problem is."

MAKE THE WORKPLACE ENVIRONMENT AS PLEASANT AS POSSIBLE

Let's face it, some places are pretty unpleasant to work in. We once knew two men who worked every day in temperatures well over 100 degrees, and they told us overtime was virtually mandatory if they wanted to keep their jobs. Both had serious alcoholism problems, and it was hard not to sympathize with them when they said, "anyone would drink under those conditions."

It has long been acknowledged that workers in stressful or repetitive jobs have a high level of drug use, and in some environments they do little to conceal it. In the plant where these two men worked, employees can be seen rolling marijuana joints as they pass through the gates at the end of their shifts. They don't even wait to get to their cars. The former medical director for a southern California aerospace firm employing thousands to work on government contracts estimates that during his tenure almost a quarter of the workers on the assembly line there were high on alcohol, drugs or both. The director of a successful employee-assistance program in the Southwest believes almost 50 percent of employees in heavy industrial settings have drug and alcohol problems.

Why the frequency of abuse in these jobs? The explanations given are many, and all are probably correct to one degree or another. We have been told that day after day of stultifying and mindlessly repetitive work increases the attractiveness of escape by means of a drug high. Work with dangerous materials or in risky environments seems to have a similar effect. The Nuclear Regulatory Commission has reported a nationwide trend toward increasing arrests and terminations for trafficking among nuclear-power-plant employees. In 1983, the *Los Angeles Times* reported that the use of drugs was widespread among those who built and maintained the reactors at Southern California Edison's San Onofre Nuclear Power Plant.

No doubt there will always be dangerous and/or boring jobs. The question then becomes, how can employers minimize the problems associated with this kind of work? Some companies provide stress-reduction classes for employees as well as exercise breaks and wellness incentives. Workers are rotated in and out of noisy, hot, repetitive, exhausting positions on a regular basis. Flextime is made available to break the monotony of the day's work. Employers are discovering that it pays in the long run to give workers more say in their company's decision-making process.

EDUCATE EMPLOYEES ABOUT THE AFFECTS OF DRUGS AND ALCOHOL

Countless surveys and research projects have uncovered one dominant fact about the use of drugs and alcohol: most people are ignorant of what constitutes abuse and few know the effects abuse has on abusers, their families, friends, coemployees and their work. Recently, we had one of the common misunderstandings about alcohol literally brought home to us in a children's newspaper.

An article on alcohol pointed out that most people think a glass of beer or wine contains less alcohol than a mixed drink—say a martini. How many times do we hear someone say, "I'll just have a glass of wine." As if a glass of wine were a minor-league form of alcohol not really worth mentioning. True, the per-ounce percentage of alcohol is lower in wine (about 12 percent) and beer (about 5 percent) than in liquor (40-50 percent), but wine, beer and liquor are normally served in different-sized glasses—five-ounce glasses for wine, 12-ounce glasses for beer, 1 1/2-ounce glasses for 80-proof liquor. It works out that each drink has about the same amount of alcohol—the only difference is the concentration.

When people know more about drugs and alcohol, our society will become less tolerant of abuse. Instead of ignoring or excusing a person who routinely drinks three glasses of beer in the hour after work and criticizing the person who has three martinis in the same time period, both will be regarded as part of the same problem. This shift may already be occurring. In many urban environments it is seen as healthy, smart and sophisticated to drink soda water "with a twist." According to a Harris Poll conducted for *Business Week* magazine, 45 percent of those questioned reported drinking less today than they did five years ago and 57 percent favor a ban on beer and wine ads on radio and television. Gradually, the glamorous mystique that surrounds drinking and drug use is disappearing; with a continuing emphasis on drug and alcohol education, the line between use and abuse will be more boldly drawn, less easily crossed.

An EAP oriented toward prevention as well as intervention and treatment can do many things to educate employees and their families about drug and alcohol abuse. We know of one that included cards in employees' pay envelopes on which were printed the famous 20 questions used by Alcoholics Anonymous to help people recognize the disease. "We had more calls about alcoholism the next month than in the six months preceding," the EAP director said. "You wouldn't believe how many people didn't know blackouts weren't normal." At a company picnic another EAP had no trouble giving away colorful posters depicting a popular rock hero exhorting students not to drink or take drugs. The posters had been donated by a national coalition against drug and alcohol abuse and cost the EAP nothing. The opportunities for education are virtually unlimited if a strong commitment exists. Brochures, information cards, newsletters, discussion groups, seminars, movies, informal conversation groups—these are just a few of the means by which employees can learn the legal, physical, psychological and symptomatic consequences of drug and alcohol abuse and be reminded of your support for the company drug and alcohol policy and program.

Most of us think of peer pressure operating only among children and teenagers when actually it is a powerful force for behavior modification at any age. Perhaps the best example of how it can work among adults is demonstrated by this nation's growing disaffection for cigarettes. A woman who had recently moved from an industrial city in the Midwest to a town on the coast of California remarked to us that she was experiencing a strong pressure to stop smoking cigarettes. At dinner parties she felt self-conscious when she was the only person who wanted a cigarette with her coffee.

At meetings she was made to sit alone by the door or window. She knew people who did not even own an ashtray.

As this woman will attest, peer pressure is a powerful force, one you can harness if you educate your employees about drugs and alcohol. A researcher told us that between 70 and 80 percent of employees want a clean and safe work environment. For the most part they know who their stoned, hungover, drunk and doped up coemployees are, but they rarely say anything to them or exert any pressure for them to change. They are unlikely to become involved because labor and mangement so often appear tolerant of the situation. If the company has no program to assist troubled employees, then the 70 to 80 percent are even more likely to tolerate their drug- and alcohol-impaired coworkers in silence. As they see it, there really isn't any way they can be of help so they might as well keep quiet. They certainly don't want to risk getting someone into the kind of trouble that can result in loss of a job.

But silence is the weapon of denial, and it is precisely this denial that has allowed drug and alcohol abuse to reach crisis proportion in the workplace. The crisis did not occur overnight, despite the sudden media emphasis given the subject. It has been growing for a long time, but few have had the courage to deal with it. Nor will the crisis evaporate overnight.

As long as people remain ignorant of the problem and its solutions—or worse, educated with half-truths and prejuduces—as long as management and employees tolerate the impaired workers in their midst, drug and alcohol abuse will continue to waste this country's time and money and human resources. The crisis will be diminished not by parents or teachers or clergymen, not by the president or members of Congress, not by drug enforcement officers or policemen, but by businesspeople willing to take the time and accept the challenge.